Theater Made Military Knives of WWII

Dedication

This book is dedicated to all of the men and women of WWII who sacrificed to keep freedom alive and win the war for all of us. To all of the people that made Theater Knives. To the collectors that will study, enjoy, and protect the most interesting and historical knives of the last century.

Information Wanted

Anyone with information about any knife in this book or any other Theater Knife PLEASE contact us. For a personal response please include a self addressed stamped envelope.

Bill and Debbie Wright
325 Shady Dr.
New Albany, IN 47150

Theater Made Military Knives of WWII

Bill & Debbie Wright

Schiffer Military History
Atglen, PA

Acknowledgments

Special THANKS and credit is given to the following people that have inspired me, added to my knowledge, or helped in the writing of this book. Debbie Wright, the co-author, my BEST FRIEND and WIFE has always helped and supported me. Without her help this book would not have been possible. Roger Ballard, Howard Cole, Bill Stone, Mark Zalesky, John Gibson, Ernie Modlin, David Petty, Bill Claussen, Ted Dazialo, Mike Silvey, Tom Clinton, A.L. Hunt, Larry Thomas, Paul Basch, Larry Schaffter, George Torres, Mike Wright, Dennis Stapp, Barbie Adams, Frank Binder, Daniel Bishop, Duane Blackburn, Joe Martin, Roger Gelbuda, Bob Blanchette, Mike Hasket, Jim Goodman, Jim Sargent, Art Green, and Ian Robertson have also made this book possible.

Book Design by Ian Robertson.

Library of Congress Control Number: 2001089807

Printed in China.
ISBN: 0-7643-1390-8

We are interested in hearing from authors with book ideas on related topics.

Published by Schiffer Publishing Ltd.
4880 Lower Valley Road
Atglen, PA 19310
Phone: (610) 593-1777
FAX: (610) 593-2002
E-mail: Schifferbk@aol.com.
Visit our web site at: www.schifferbooks.com
Please write for a free catalog.
This book may be purchased from the publisher.
Please include $3.95 postage.
Try your bookstore first.

In Europe, Schiffer books are distributed by:
Bushwood Books
6 Marksbury Avenue
Kew Gardens
Surrey TW9 4JF
England
Phone: 44 (0) 20 8392-8585
FAX: 44 (0) 20 8392-9876
E-mail: Bushwd@aol.com.
Free postage in the UK. Europe: air mail at cost.
Try your bookstore first.

Contents

	Introduction	6
Chapter 1:	Double Edge, Dagger, and Spear Point Knives	8
Chapter 2:	Knuckle Knives	48
Chapter 3:	Bowie Knives	82
Chapter 4:	Identified Knife Makers	110
Chapter 5:	Personally Identified, and Presentation Knives	156
Chapter 6:	Sword Knives	184
Chapter 7:	Bayonet Knives	192
Chapter 8:	Modified, Factory and Issue, Knives	204
Chapter 9:	Sheaths	220
Chapter 10:	Other Styles and Patterns	228
Chapter 11:	Philippine Victory Knives	258

Introduction

The first question often asked is, "What is a 'Theater Knife?'" Is it a knife used in a theatrical play or on stage? Most people who collect military items or who have been in military service quickly know the answer to the question. The word "Theater" refers to an area or region of military operations, such as the Pacific Theater or European Theater. I conclude the term Theater Knife refers to special handmade knives, made in or used in the various theaters of WWII. In the past these knives have had several different names: shipboard knife; soldier made; secondary knife; radar knife; handmade fighting knife; or workshop knife. All of these names would describe a WWII Theater Knife.

America was drawn into WWII almost overnight after the surprise attack on Pearl Harbor on December 7, 1941. The U.S. had to convert peacetime production of goods to production of war materials immediately. We had to make everything from tanks, planes, and ships to rifles and pistols to equip our service men heading to war. It seems that commercially made knives were very scarce at that time, both to the government and to the soldiers enlisting in the armed forces. One of the basic tools for survival in day to day military life is a good knife. Whether it is for use in everyday living or as a defensive or offensive weapon, a good knife was essential for every member of our fighting force.

Everyone was asked to contribute whatever they could to the war effort. Many of the knife makers well known to us today contributed greatly to this effort. Some of these people include Scagel, Randall, John Ek, Warther, Murphy, Nichols, and Howard Cole. However, the largest contributors of knives for the war effort were the many thousands of individuals whose names are long forgotten. They often included the soldiers themselves, or their fathers, uncles, or neighbors. Many knives were made in large commercial machine shops and factories. Workers employed there would make knives during their breaks and lunch times, and also before and after work. They used scrap or discarded materials to make the knives. Other knives were made by individuals in backyard workshops. They made knives out of whatever materials they could find. Many of these privately made knives were given, rather than sold, to members of our armed forces that were headed to the front lines. It also has been learned that a large number of high quality knives were made aboard ship. On the long voyages across the ocean U.S. Naval ships were equipped with well-stocked machine shops and machinists capable of making quality knives.

Early in 1943 a man by the name of Frank Martinelli of San Francisco formed a committee called "Save a Life with a Knife." With the help of Major General Barney Giles, Forth Air Force Commander, Martinelli actively advertised by using radio, newspapers, posters, magazines, and word of mouth to send knives to him. Every type of knife was asked for, including hunting knives, stilettos, machetes, toad stickers, daggers, dirks, Bowie knives, and clasp knives. People were asked to make and donate these types of knives. The only requirement was that the blade be at least 4" long. The first month of the "Save a Life with a Knife" campaign produced 7,500 knives, which were immediately flown to the Southwest Pacific Theater and given to our soldiers and marines. I am sure that many campaigns like this one were started all over the United States, providing hundreds of thousands of knives to our servicemen in all theaters of WWII.

Another source for knives was the people in every branch of military service; Army, Navy, Air Force, and Marines, as well as the Seabees. These Theater Made Knives were made in every shape and description using materials at hand. The every day combat soldier made many of these knives in the field. They used old files, leaf springs, and steel from wherever they could find it. Handles were made from electric box insulating material (Micarta), aluminum, wood, Bakelite, brass, copper, leather, and Plexiglass. One of the best sources for all materials necessary to make a knife was found in shot down aircraft. Good quality steel was used in many parts of the aircraft, as well as the Plexiglass from the windshields. The propellers and other parts of the airplanes were made from aluminum. This aluminum could be easily cut, hammered, and cast into guards, pommels, and handles. Other materials, such as brass, copper, and lead were also used in the parts that were commonly used in the manufacture of aircraft. Leather from harnesses, seats, and machine gun belts could make sheaths, and could be cut into round discs for handle spacer material. In fact, the downed aircraft was a virtual supermarket to the custom knife maker of WWII.

One WWII veteran told me that he was stationed on a sub tender off a small island in the South Pacific. He said they would go weeks at a time without anything to do, so he made knives. He traded or sold them to soldiers and sailors in passing ships and submarines for cigarettes, candy, and other manufactured goods from the States. Other soldiers have told me that their time was spent doing the following: 20% going to the fighting; 20% fighting; and 60% with nothing to do. Some soldiers altered their issued knives and bayonets by removing the old handle and replacing it with handle spacers made from Plexiglass, aluminum, brass, or red, white, blue, and black materials. Some of these knives would include MK1, MK2, and MK3 fighting knives, as well as the Cattaraugus 225Q and Pal RH37 knives. Some of the blade shapes would be altered. In some cases the back edge of the blade would be sharpened to make a double edge fighting knife. These knives I would call GI Altered, or Theater Altered. The knives that were made from start to finish I would call handmade.

One of the most interesting accessories to go along with these knives is the sheath. Many times Theater Knives may be of low or medium quality, but the sheaths are of high quality. Why that is I am not sure. Often times the sheaths were made of heavy leather with carved or embossed designs. Other times the sheaths will have the owner's name, rank, and serial number. Some sheaths have all of the above, plus a pictorial story of the owner.

One knife I have has a hand carved sheath with a picture of a sailor on the front, along with a palm tree. On the back is the sailor's name and service number. The knife that goes in the sheath is made from a Japanese bayonet, with an aluminum guard and pommel and Plexiglass handle spacers.

The center of the handle is wood with an aluminum square containing a photo of his wife or girlfriend encased in Plexiglass. This knife and sheath really tells the story of a sailor in WWII who was on an island in the Pacific Ocean. He captured a Japanese bayonet, and likely used parts from a downed aircraft to make it into his personal fighting knife. Knives and sheaths like this one are very historical and sought after by collectors.

Collectors have long overlooked these Theater Knives because they did not understand the quality and history in front of them. However, many collectors are now realizing that these knives have great quality and are a valuable piece of American history. At this time Theater Knives are still available at almost every flea market, gun show, and knife show, but are quickly being bought up by collectors. The price of Theater Knives is still reasonable, and you can still find quality examples. Prices for average examples are $35.00 to $125.00, while the best knives are bringing $500.00 and more. WWII knives made by well-known makers can be worth from $500.00 to $5,000.00 or more.

Some of the things that make Theater Knives valuable are size, quality of workmanship, sheath, and personal information. This information can be about the knife, sheath, owner, or maker. Knuckle knives are knives that have holes in the handles to put your fingers into, or have a D guard or knuckle bow. Knuckle knives have been popular for many years and are very hard to find. They range in price from $100.00 to $750.00 for unknown or unmarked examples. Quality examples of knuckle knives made by known makers, such as Howard Cole, Taylor Huff, and Eugene Stone will bring $2,500.00 to $5,000.00 or more. Many Civil War swords were still held in arsenals at the beginning of WWII. They were cut down, and one sword could make 3 fighting knives. Sword knives range in price from $50.00 to $500.00 or more. Many quality fighting knives were made from bayonets. Some of these bayonets were used as early as the Civil War, while some were made from WWII issue bayonets. Bayonet fighting knives are worth usually between $25.00 to $125.00 depending on the quality of workmanship. Some quality bayonet Theater Knives, with the proper sheath, can be worth up to $500.00 or more. As with all collectibles, condition effects the price and quality speaks for itself.

The collecting of Theater Knives is one of the fastest growing areas of knife collecting today. Theater Knives are not only sought after by knife collectors, but also military collectors and collectors of American History.

Theater Knives are much akin to the Bowies, daggers, and dirks of the Civil War time period. They were used by similar men for similar purposes, and were often made for the same reasons by people much like those who did so 80 years before. One difference is many of the men that made, used, and carried them are still alive. They can personally tell us of their own experiences of the war. When acquiring a Theater Knife, always get as much information as possible about the knife and the person that used it. This historical information will add great value to the knife. Whether or not these Theater Knives will attain the same value levels achieved that knives made during the Civil War time period remains to be seen. However, they are rapidly catching up, and in some cases surpassing the value of Civil War knives. Theater Knives represent a vitally important event in our history and the men that shaped it, because they used Military Theater Knives of WWII.

A Word about Pricing

The prices given in this book are given as Collectors value. Collectors value represents the approximate value of the knife pictured. This value is for the exact knife with or without sheath, as pictured, in the same condition as shown in this book. Most Theater Knives are different. Another Theater Knife similar to, but not exactly the same as, the knife pictured may be worth more or less. This book is only a guide. The authors and publishers of this book, Military Theater Knives of WWII, do not in any way guarantee the price of any item shown in this book. The prices given are prices based on the same or similar knives that have been sold, or that are being offered for sale. This price reflects the current market conditions at the time of the writing of this book. As market conditions change, so do the price of the knives. Because of the increased interest in Theater Knives, we are expecting prices to increase soon by 25% or more, especially for the higher priced quality knives. However, we do not make any promises, guarantees, or predictions as to what the market conditions will be or the value of Theater Knives in the future. Prices also differ in different areas of the country. This means that the price of a knife being offered for sale in California might be more or less than the same knife being offered for sale in Indiana. Ultimately, the price and value of a knife is between the buyer and the seller.

Fakes, Counterfeits, Reproductions

The rising price of any collectible increases the likelihood of fakes, counterfeits, and reproductions. In this case we are talking about Theater Knives. It must be profitable for a counterfeiter to make a Theater Knife. There are custom knife makers out there today that can make a Theater knife. Because of the time involved in making a knife of this type it is usually not profitable. The knives with the greatest value will likely be counterfeited most often. It is important that a person who collects Theater Knives be knowledgeable of the type of materials that were used to make knives during WWII. Some of these materials were not readily available after 1950. Knives made for the Korean and Vietnam Wars may be of a similar type of construction, but will likely be made with different materials. Most Theater Knives are one of a kind items. A knowledgeable collector must also know the proper color and the proper pattern of rust. Acid or other kinds of aging materials can make a new knife look old. An old sheath is hard to counterfeit. If an old sheath fits the knife properly and has the proper wear pattern on it, this can often help the collector decide if the knife is new or old. Restoring, on the other hand, is a different matter. Lightly cleaning, replacing broken parts using the same kind of old materials, or repairing broken tips of a blade is acceptable and not considered counterfeit. If an old knife is buffed hard, or "Cleaned to Mint," it is sometimes difficult to tell if the knife is new or old, and therefore reduces the knife's value. Knives are usually worth more to collectors if they are left alone and sold "As Found."

1

Double Edge, Dagger, & Spear Point Knives

This chapter will show knives that have blades on which the point will be in the center of the blade. A double edge knife is a knife that has both sides of the blade sharpened. Daggers are double edge knives, usually with narrower blades under 6" in length. A spear point knife can be either double edge, or can have only 1 cutting edge. The 2 double edge knives pictured above are of excellent quality. The top knife has a 7 1/4" blade and is 12 7/8" in overall length. It has a round handle that was made using black and red Micarta and thick aluminum spacers. The cross guard and pommel have been cast of aluminum. The blade of the lower knife measures 7 7/8", and the overall length is 12 3/4". The handle on this knife is somewhat smaller, and is flat on both sides. The handle is constructed using the same type of materials as the top knife. The price includes the high quality sheath that is pictured with each knife. Collectors value $500.00 each. (Wright Collection)

The quality double edge knife on the top is the knife that convinced me to start collecting "Military Theater Knives of WWII." This knife has a 7 1/4" blade that is 5/16" thick. It has a brass hand guard and a bronze skull crusher pommel. The handle is made using Micarta and brass handle spacers. The sheath is hand tooled, and has a belt slit large enough for a web pistol belt. A couple of weeks later I was able to purchase the knife at the bottom of this picture. This knife has a 7 5/8" blade that is precision ground and still razor sharp. The handle has Micarta and Bakelite spacers. The sheath is of the best quality. The next weekend I was lucky enough to find the center knife in an antique mall. This was another super WWII fighting knife and sheath. This knife has a 7 1/2" blade, and is also razor sharp. After examining the quality of these knives I quickly realized that WWII Theater Knives were wonderful and historic collectibles that have gone unnoticed. Today I have over 1,200 WWII Theater Knives in my collection. Collectors value (top) $500.00, (center) $400.00, (bottom) $650.00. My Personal Collection, Bill Wright

This knife has an 8 1/2" double edge blade that is 1 9/16" wide. The overall length of the knife is 13 1/2". It has a stainless steel cross guard and an aluminum pommel. The handle is made up of 43 colorful spacers. They include copper, red, brass, leather, black, and aluminum materials. The heavy-duty leather sheath is sewn completely around and has 11 steel rivets. This knife and hand made sheath are above average quality in fit and finish. Collectors value $350.00. (Wright Collection)

This WWII fighting knife was likely made from a British Bolo Machete. The double edge blade is 11 7/8" long and is engraved "To Hank U.S.N. 410-81-92, From Zyggie, Aug. 18, 1944." Collectors value $375.00. (Wright Collection)

The same unknown maker made both of the quality WWII hand made knives pictured above. The only clue to the maker is both sheaths are marked CARLBOM'S – MINNEAPOLIS – SINCE 1890. Both knives have a thick heavy double edge blade 5 3/4" long. These knives are heavy for their size. One of the sheaths has been carved and decorated with a skull and crossbones and a scorpion. Also, the initials VLL are carved into the front of the sheath. This carving is professionally done and is a work of art. The other sheath is of the same high quality, but not hand carved. These knives are hand made because, while looking the same, they are in fact different. Collectors value (with carved sheath) $500.00, (with plain sheath) $400.00. (Wright Collection)

This WWII double edge knife has a very sturdy blade. The 7 1/2" blade is made of 3/8" thick steel. This knife has a stainless cross guard and an aluminum pommel. The handle was made to fit a large hand and has red, aluminum, and brass spacers. The inside of the sheath has a copper liner. This sheath was made to hang low on the belt and to be strapped to the leg. Both knife and sheath are of excellent quality. Collectors value $500.00. (Wright Collection)

This high quality dagger has a 7 1/2" blade. The blade is almost 1/4" thick, precision ground, and very sharp. It has a stainless cross guard. The handle is made of 5 stainless steel spacers, red and brown Micarta spacers, and brown Micarta pommel. The high quality sheath has the front embossed. Collectors value $350.00. (Wright Collection)

A very nice group of double edge hand made fighting knives. Blade lengths are from 7 3/4" to 8 3/8". Collectors value (top picture, top to bottom) $175.00, $300.00, $250.00 (bottom picture, top to bottom) $175.00, $300.00, $125.00, $100.00. (Ballard Collection)

The dagger pictured above is well made and very sturdy. The 6 3/4" blade is more than 3 /16" thick. The thick brass cross guard is turned downward to help protect the hand. The heavy-duty aluminum pommel tops the Micarta and aluminum spacer handle. The sheath, which is oversized, is the original sheath for this knife. Collectors value $275.00. (Wright Collection)

This large Theater Knife has an aluminum guard and pommel. The double edge blade is 9" long and just under 1 1/2" wide. The Plexiglass spacer handle has finger grooves in it to give a better grip. The sheath is made of heavy leather, laced around the outside, riveted together, and marked on the back W-2503. This is the first letter of the owner's last name and the last 4 digits of his serial number. This knife is of average quality. Collectors value $275.00. (Wright Collection)

This well made knife has a 7 3/8" spear point blade and has a sharpened false edge. The aluminum handle was cast on to the blade. This aluminum casting is of high quality and has no flaws. The sheath is very well made and is riveted and sewn. The design of a flower is embossed into the front. I have seen two more knives like this one. Collectors value $275.00. (Wright Collection)

Two nice Theater Knives are pictured above. The top knife has a 7 3/8" spear point blade with a sharpened false edge. It has a brass cross guard and pommel. The main body of the handle is Birdseye Maple. The lower knife has a 7 7/8" double edge blade. The handle was made using different colors of Bakelite spacers. Both knives are above average quality and have nice leather sheaths. Collectors value (top) $250.00 (lower) $400.00. (Wright Collection)

The double edge knife pictured here has a 7 11/16" blade and is 12 1/8" overall. It has a brass cross guard and pommel. The handle is made of brown fiber. The blade is marked "S.A. McKINNON MELBOURNE AUSTRALIA." This knife was the personal side arm of 1st Sargent S.A. McKinnon. He was in charge of the U.S. Guards at the trial of Lt Gen. Nikotsro Tijima and Lt. Gen. Masaharu Homma, Manila, 1945. The Collectors value is hard to evaluate because of the history involved with this knife. The knife on its own merit has a value of $300.00. The history value could easily double that value. (Ballard Collection)

Bottom Right: These two daggers are small but very useful in times of war. The top knife has a 4 7/8" blade. It is heavy and fills the hand when held. The high quality sheath has a carved design in the front. The lower knife has a 5" blade that is made from a file and is lightweight and sleek. The sheath, which has a belt slit, could easily be concealed in a boot. Collectors value $225.00 each. (Wright Collection)

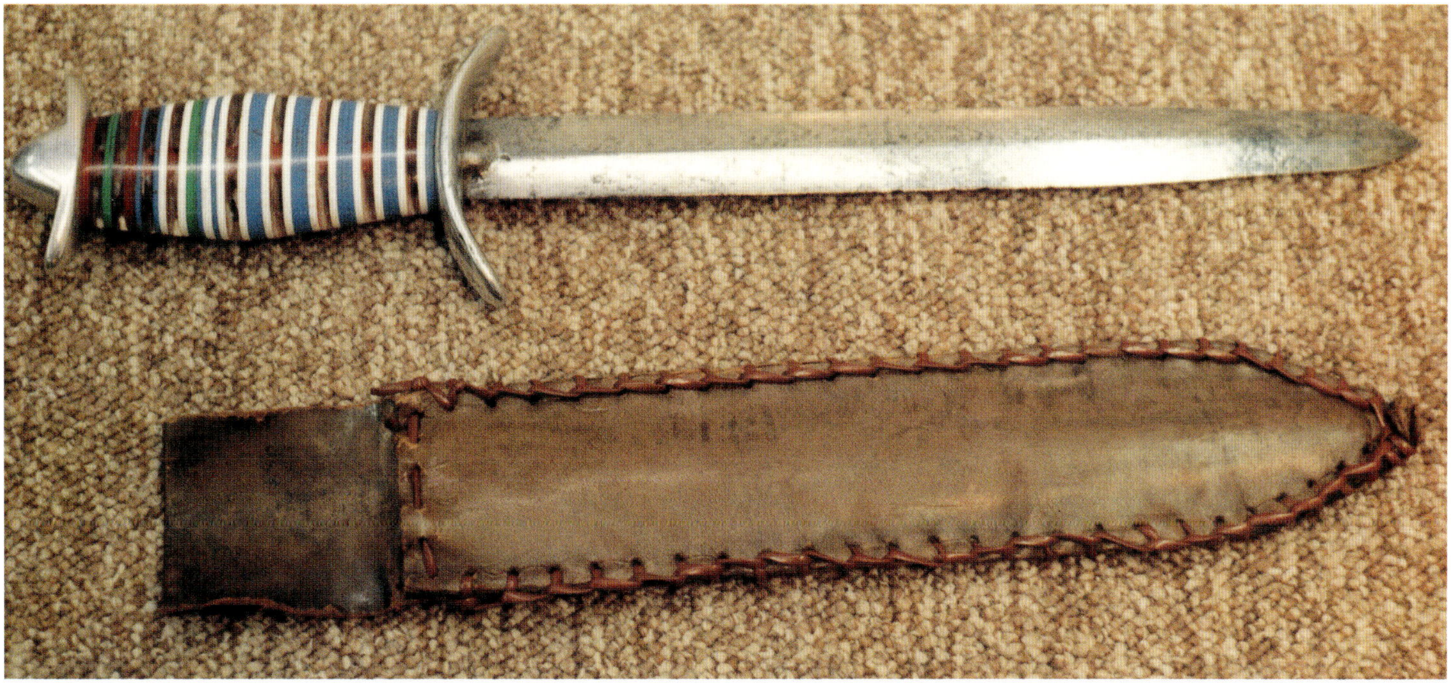

This is a whopper of a WWII Theater Knife. The blade is hand forged from a file and is almost a foot long. The teeth of the file remain on both edges of the blade. The large curved cross guard and the hat shaped pommel are both made of aluminum. The handle is made of red, white, blue, green, and clear Lucite spacers. The overall length is 17 1/4". Collectors value $500.00. (Wright Collection)

Seeing double? The same unknown knife maker made both of these quality knives aboard ship during WWII. The 6 7/8" blades are ice pick shaped. The blades are made from 1/4" stock and are expertly ground and finished. These knives came without sheaths. These fine hand made sheaths were made for me by Stan Koshoski of Euclid, OH. Collectors value $375.00 each. (Wright Collection)

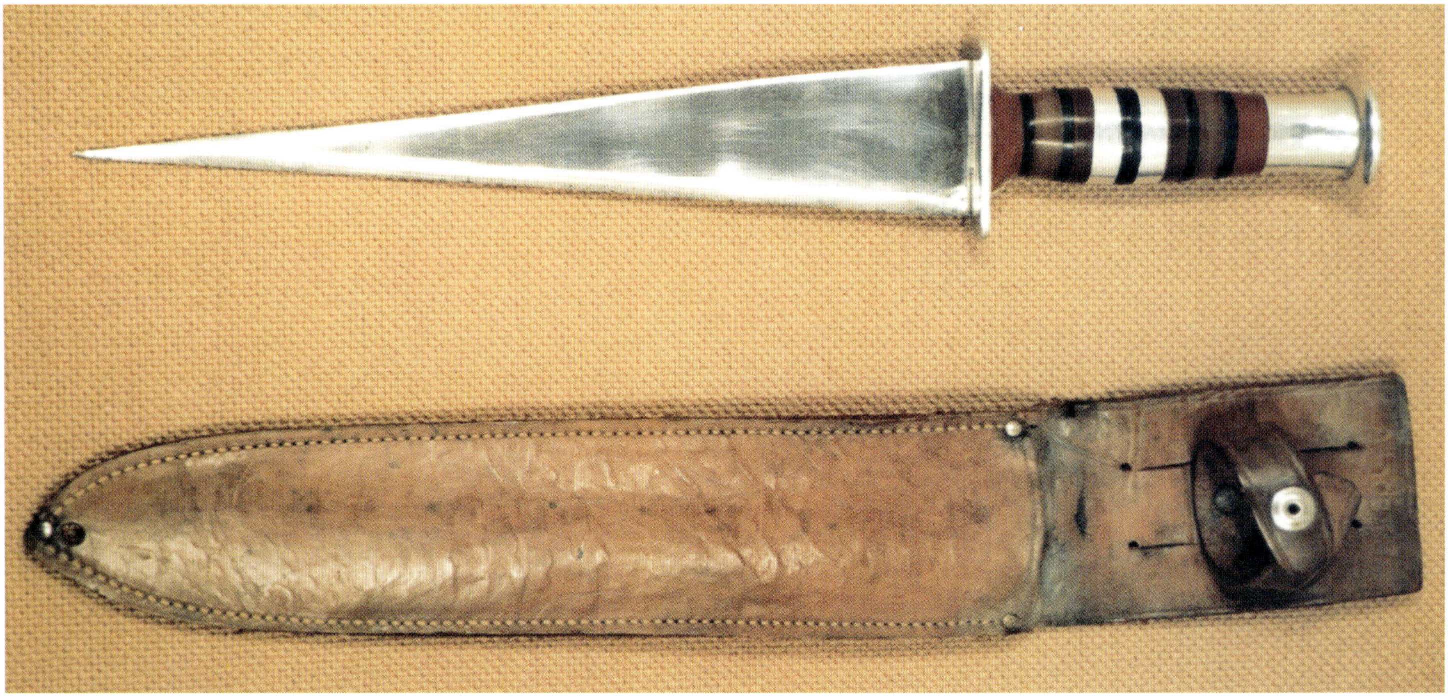

When most people think of an "Arkansas Toothpick," this is the kind of knife they think of. The term "Arkansas Toothpick" was popular in the late 1830s and was originally a clip point Bowie Knife. The double edge blade measures 9 3/4" and is 1 3/4" wide at the bottom close to the aluminum cross guard. This quality knife came in a generic sheath numbered 2500SKS. Collectors value $400.00. (Wright Collection)

This high quality Theater Knife has an 8 3/4" double edge Kris shaped blade. This type of blade is very hard to make, which explains why Theater Knives with Kris blades are rare. This knife shows great skill and artistic ability. The thick S shaped brass cross guard is braised to the blade. This is done to make the cross guard more sturdy, and to help prevent water from getting into the tang of the knife. If the tang rusts it could break or swell the handle and break the handle spacers. The handle is made of Micarta and aluminum spacers. Collectors value $750.00. (Wright Collection)

This heavy-duty WWII fighting knife has an 8 1/4" blade that is 1 3/4" wide and is 5/16" thick. It has a thick copper cross guard and large brass pommel. Most of the handle is made from leather spacers. The quality heavy-duty sheath is made to fit on a web pistol belt. Both knife and sheath are quality items. Collectors value $700.00. (Wright Collection)

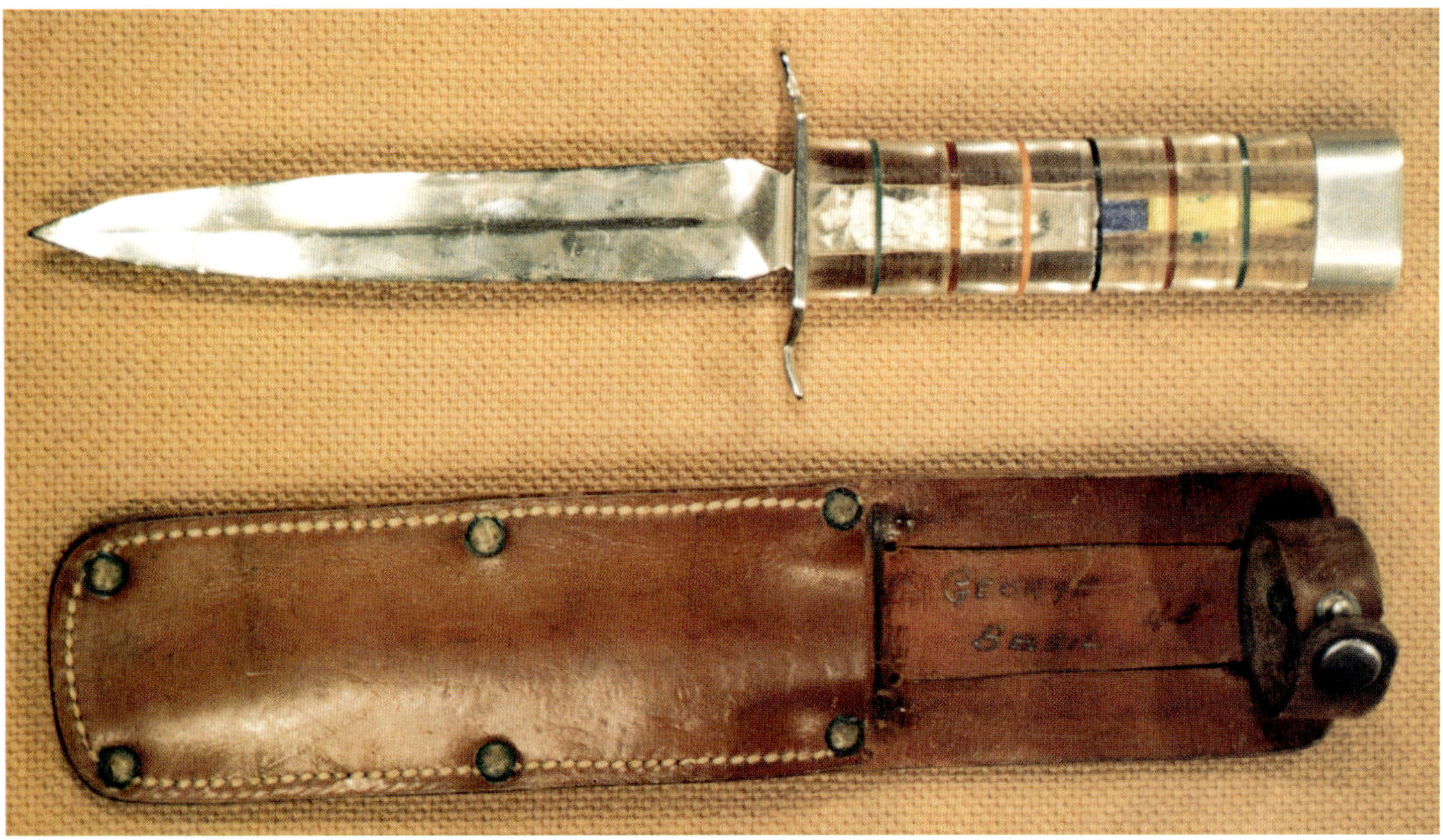

The sheath for this knife is marked "George Basil, 43." The double edge blade measures 6 1/8" and is nickel-plated to help keep the blade from rusting. There is a lady's picture on the tang of the blade under the thick Plexiglass spacers. Thin colored foil is wrapped around the tang to make the handle colorful. Collectors value $250.00. (Wright Collection)

An impressive display of WWII Theater Knives is pictured here. All of the knives on this page are of excellent quality and have colorful handles. The blade lengths of these double edge knives vary from 6 3/4" to 9". Collectors value (top picture, top to bottom) $300.00, $300.00, $250.00, $300.00 (bottom picture, left to right) $275.00, $275.00, $300.00, $250.00, $275.00, $200.00, $275.00, $250.00, $200.00. These prices include an original sheath of a similar quality to their respective knife. (Ballard Collection)

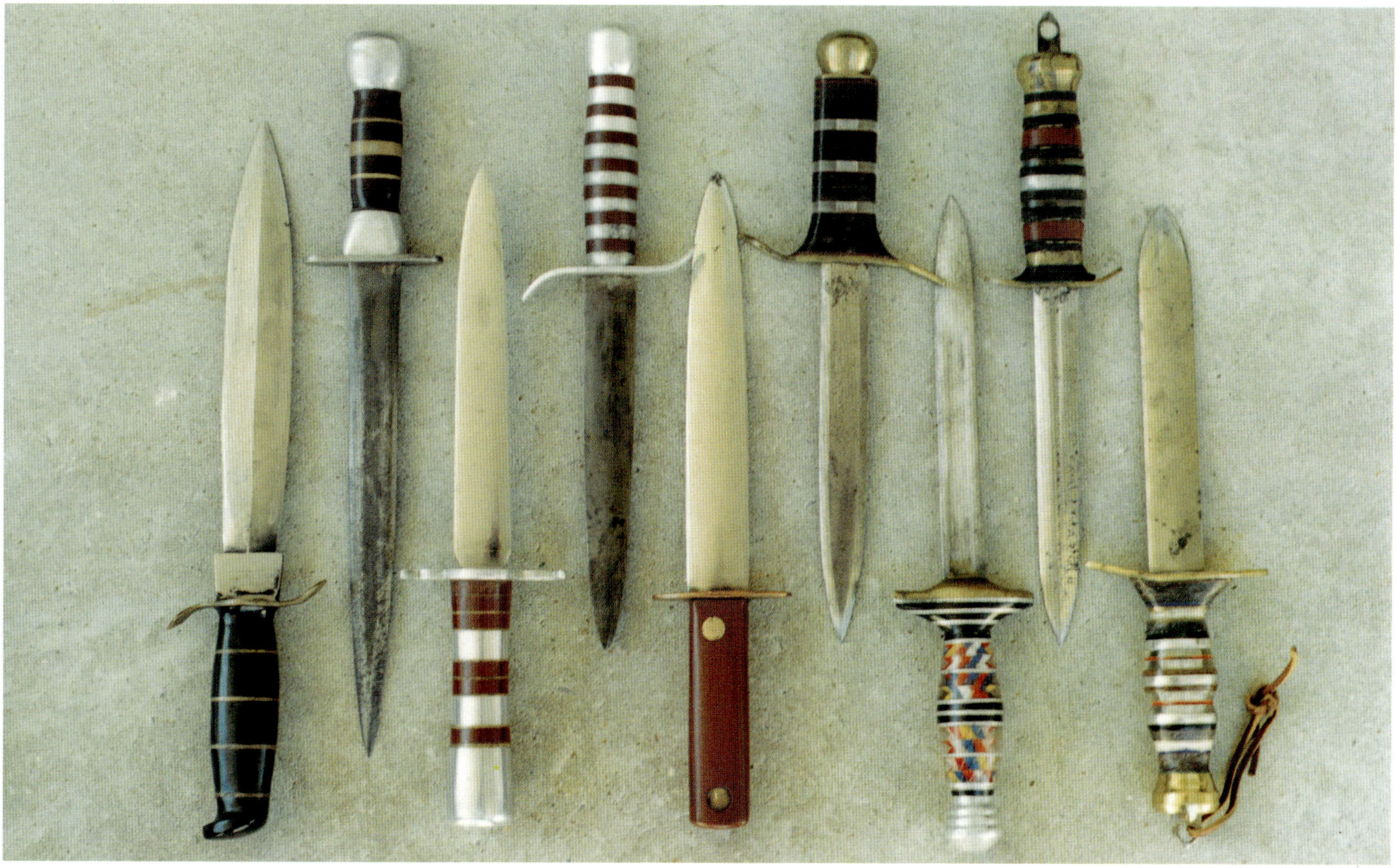

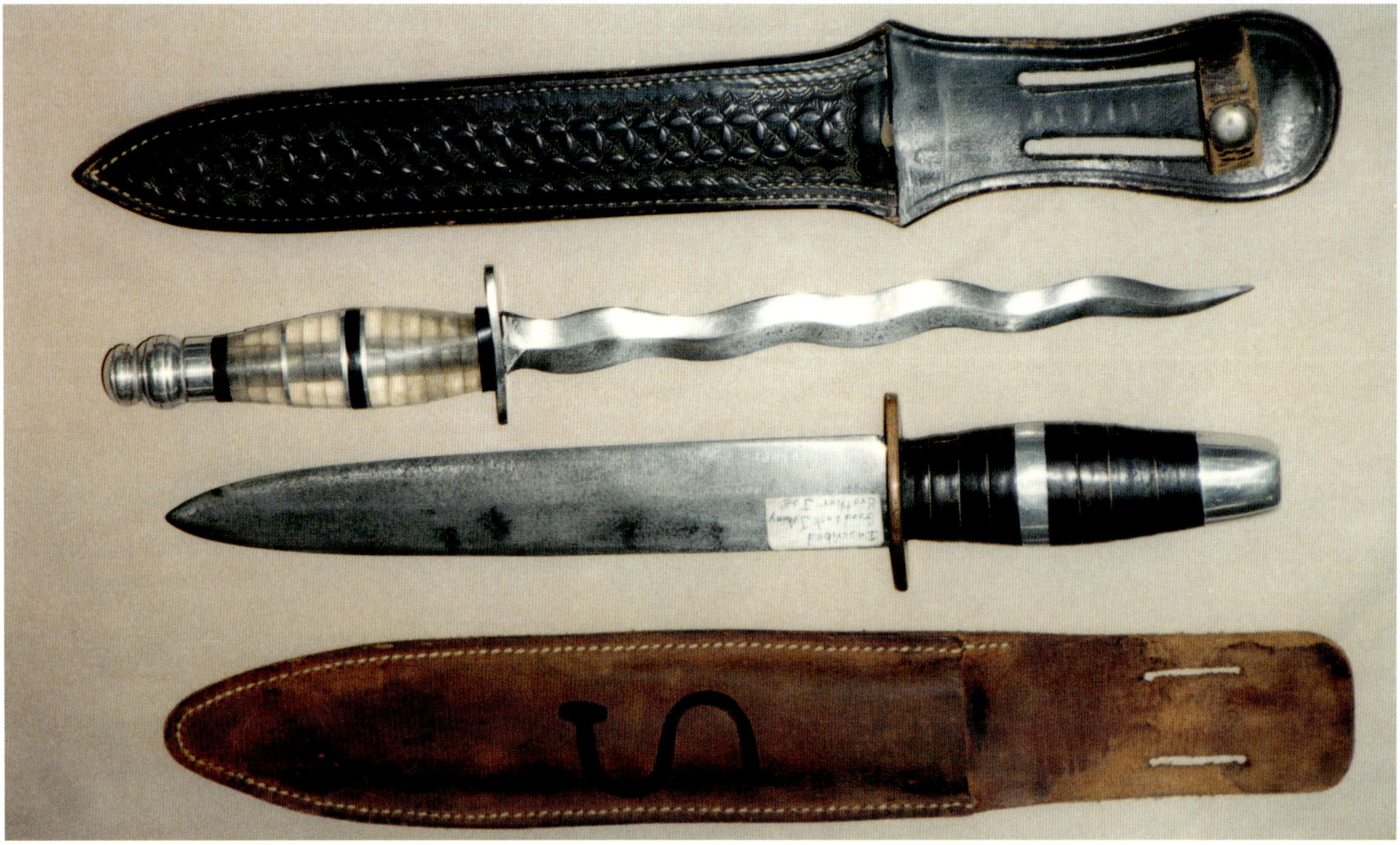

The knife on the top has the rare Kris shaped blade. The blade is 9 5/8" long, and the overall length is 14 7/8". The front of the heavy-duty sheath is hand tooled. This is a high quality knife and sheath. The bottom knife has a 9 3/4" double edge blade that is 1 1/2" wide. The blade is engraved "Good Luck Johnny-Brother Joe." Collectors value (top) $600.00 (bottom) $400.00. (Wright Collection)

The Theater Knife pictured above has a 9 1/8" double edge blade and is 13 7/8" overall. It has a 3/16" thick brass guard and heavy-duty pommel. The handle is made of thick black, and aluminum spacers. The hand made sheath has two rivets at the top, one at the bottom, and is stitched all around. Both knife and sheath are of excellent quality in both fit and finish. Collectors value $375.00. (Wright Collection)

The blade of this double edge knife is 6 3/4" long and has a total length of 11 3/16". This quality knife has a brass cross guard and pommel. The handle is made from different colors of Bakelite. Multi-color Bakelite handle knives are rare. The heavy leather sheath is bound with wide leather lacing. Collectors value $300.00. (Wright Collection)

The 7 1/16" blade, cross guard, and pommel of this WWII Theater Knife are made of aluminum, which is very unusual. The handle was made using leather spacers. Collectors value $175.00. (Wright Collection)

Left: These are two very fine and desirable WWII Theater Knives. The knife on the right has a wavy Kris shaped blade. This style of blade is very hard to make. This knife is exceptionally well made and has a heavy 9" blade. It has a brass cross guard that is braised to the blade and a large round pommel. The handle is constructed of stacked leather, aluminum, brass, and Plexiglass washers. The sheath is made from a cut down Medical Corpsmen sheath. The knife on the left is a very massive knife, yet when held in the hand it is not heavy or cumbersome. The double edge blade is 8 1/2" long and 2 1/4" wide. It has a copper cross guard and pommel with a ring in the end for a lanyard. The handle, which is a one piece aluminum casting with grooves cut into it, is filled with some kind of plastic. The original heavy leather sheath has a web pistol belt hanger attached. Collectors value $1,000.00 each. (Ballard Collection)

Right: This well made dagger could have been made aboard ship or in one of the theaters of action in WWII. It has a 7 7/8" double edge blade and is 12 3/8" total length. It has a heavy aluminum guard and pommel. The handle is stacked leather with red, black, and aluminum spacers. The leather sheath is covered with thin hand hammered aluminum and held together with aluminum rivets. This is the right thickness for the aluminum used on the body of an aircraft. The keeper strap looks like it is from a USN MK2 knife. This knife and sheath is well above average quality fit and finish. Collectors value $375.00. (Wright Collection)

This is an interesting and unusual group of Theater Knives. There are two knives with Kris style blades, a double edge dagger with an unusually long cross guard, and a fine knife with a Bowie clip blade. The Bowie Knife (second from right) is pictured in Cole's Book 4, P. 145. The blade lengths vary from 7 1/2" to 9 1/2". Collectors value $500.00 each. (Ballard Collection)

The larger knife above is shaped similar to a Russian Kindjal. The 9" hand forged blade is well finished and in mint condition. The oval brass cross guard is braised to the blade. The red Micarta handle slabs are 3/8" thick and are held on by two large domed copper pins. The leather covered wooden sheath is well made. The smaller knife has a triangular shaped blade, possibly made from a file. It is well finished and very sharp. These knives came together and were made by the same maker. Collectors value (large) $250.00 (small) $125.00. (Wright Collection)

This is an outstanding example of a WWII Theater Knife. The 8 1/2" blade is hollow ground on each side of the center ridge. The double edge blade is 1 15/16" wide at the bottom and is 7/16" thick. It has a brass cross guard and pommel. The handle was made using red and black Micarta and aluminum and brass spacers. The sheath for this knife is high quality. It is double stitched and has large rivets to keep the stitching from being cut. This is similar to the sheaths made for the Taylor Huff knuckle knives. Collectors value $1,000.00. (Wright Collection)

The age of this knife is hard to determine. Is it WWII or Civil War? WWII stag (or deer horn) handle knives are rare, but they do exist. The tang of the knife extends through the pommel and is hammered over. This is similar to a type of construction of Civil War knives. The 10 1/8" double edge blade is hand forged. The brass cross guard is soldered to the blade. The cross guard being soldered and the type of sheath are the biggest clues to the knife being of WWII vintage. Civil War knives did not have their cross guards soldered. It is very common for WWII knives to have their cross guards soldered or braised. Collectors value $350.00. (Wright Collection)

This knife has always been a puzzle to me. Is it WWI or WWII? The sheath is made of hammered copper, which is likely a large shell casing. This is typical of WWI Trench Art. The 11 1/2" double edge blade is marked "POW:BF." The wooden handle, which appears to be walnut, is spiral wrapped with a twisted brass wire. This is similar to wrappings on sword handles. I have never seen a WWI Trench Art Knife of this size, quality, or type of construction. Collectors value $750.00. (Wright Collection)

The 8 7/16" blade of this double edge fighter has been bright blued. The one-piece aluminum handle has been turned in a lathe and knurled to give a better grip. Both top and bottom of the aluminum cross guard have been decorated with punch marks. The sheath is riveted top and bottom and sewn with heavy leather lacing. The sheath is inscribed "BILL FROM DAD." Collectors value $450.00. (Wright Collection)

The blade of this 7" double edge fighter was made from a file. It has an aluminum cross guard and pommel. Leather and brass spacer materials were used to make the handle. This knife is of average quality with a little rougher fit and finish. The well-made sheath has a nice embossed design on the front, and it is bound around the outside with leather lacing. Collectors value $125.00. (Wright Collection)

This high quality knife has an 8 3/4" double edge blade that is 1/4' thick, precision ground, and has a blood groove in each side. The knife has a steel cross guard and an aluminum pommel. The handle was constructed using three thin O.D. green spacers between each aluminum spacer. The heavy-duty leather sheath is held together with eyelet type rivets that surround the outside of the sheath. Collectors value $650.00 (Wright Collection)

This super WWII Theater Knife has an 8 3/8" double edge blade and is 13 3/8" in overall length. It has a copper cross guard and a brass pommel. The handle is made from red Micarta and aluminum spacers. I am unsure of what the sheath markings are. The markings are "US" and crossed cannon barrels. The letters "CAC" is likely the owner's initials. The marking "S5783" is on the back of the sheath. This marking is the first letter of the owner's last name and the last 4 numbers of his serial number. This one letter and four number marking is known as a laundry mark, and was commonly used to mark a serviceman's personal effects. This is one of my favorite WWII Theater Knives. I like it so well that I used a likeness of it on my business card. Collectors value $500.00. (My Collection, Bill Wright)

This fine WWII fighting knife has an 8 3/4" double edge blade. This knife has a brass guard and long skull crusher aluminum pommel that is heart shaped. The handle is made of Bakelite spacers. There are red, white, and blue rhinestones set into the handle. The fine leather sheath is marked "MADE IN THE PHILIPPINES," and "I.C. BAUTISTA'S HARNESS SHOP '44'." This sheath has a belt type keeper strap. Collectors value $800.00. (Wright Collection)

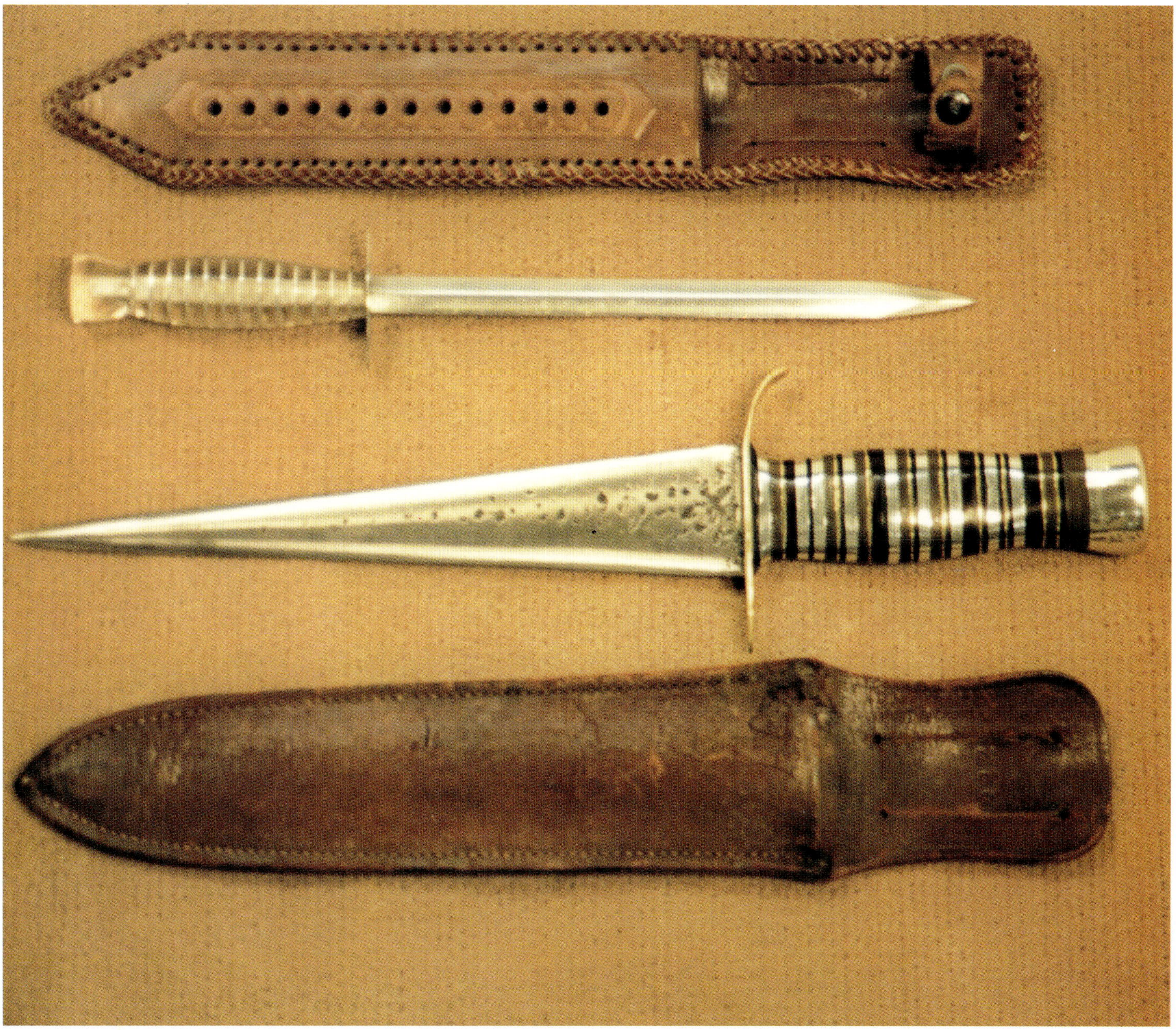

The top knife in this photograph has a thin 7 1/8" stiletto blade. It has a stainless steel guard. The handle and pommel are made of Plexiglass, and the handle has thin aluminum spacers between each Plexiglass spacer. The leather sheath was made with great skill and is of a high quality. It is hand bound around the outer edge with thin leather lacing. Both knife and sheath are of top quality. The bottom knife has an 8 1/2" dagger blade and is 13" in overall length. It has a brass cross guard that is bent downward in the front to help protect the fingers. The handle has 41 individually cut spacers. They are made from aluminum, brass, black, green, and maroon colored Micarta. The sheath is generic and has the number "228" stamped on it. I believe many knives were made here at home during the war and donated to the war effort. They were donated without sheaths. The government contracted a number of different sheaths to be made so they would fit the many different kinds of knives that had been donated. This explains why so many sheaths have shown up with the same number and have different knives in them. Collectors value $250.00 each. (Wright Collection)

This nice WWII fighting knife has an 8 1/16" double edge blade that is 1/4" thick. The total length is 12 3/4". The blade is convex ground and has a blood groove in each side. There is a brass cross guard and pommel. The materials used for the handle consist of red and brown Micarta, brass, and aluminum. Collectors value $350.00. (Wright Collection)

This grouping of quality double edge Theater Knives has colorful handles. The blade lengths vary from 5 15/16" to 7 15/16". Collectors value (left to right) $135.00, $150.00, $125.00, $225.00, $225.00. (Wright Collection)

The red handled knife pictured above has a 9 1/4" double edge blade and has an overall length of 14 3/4". This knife was made and used by Maurice Pressler, who carried this knife during the Battle of the Bulge. The knife below it, with the leather handle, has an Italian coin on the bottom. This knife belonged to a friend of Maurice Pressler who did not make it back from the battle. Collectors value (red handle knife) $375.00 (leather handle knife) $150.00. (Wright Collection)

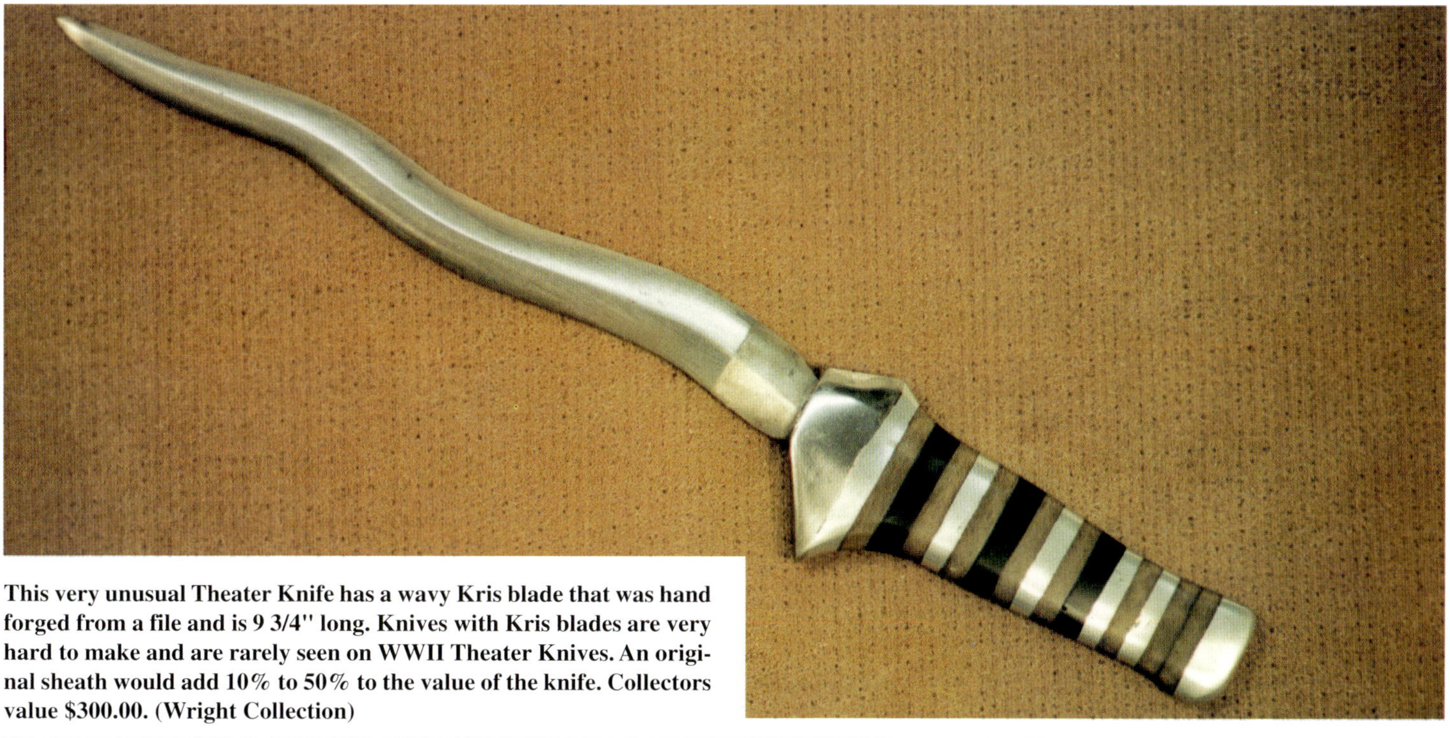

This very unusual Theater Knife has a wavy Kris blade that was hand forged from a file and is 9 3/4" long. Knives with Kris blades are very hard to make and are rarely seen on WWII Theater Knives. An original sheath would add 10% to 50% to the value of the knife. Collectors value $300.00. (Wright Collection)

The 10 3/4" hollow ground blade on this knife started out as a 1/4" thick file. It has a brass cross guard. The thick red Micarta handle slabs are held on with five large brass pins. The tang of the file is brazed into a brass plate and has aluminum spacer plates between the brass and the handle slabs. The heavy-duty leather sheath is plain, but well made. Collectors value $375.00. (Wright Collection)

The knife pictured above has a 9 1/8" hollow ground blade. The blade is made of 1/4" stock and has two blood grooves on each side. This knife has a stainless steel cross guard and an aluminum pommel. The handle is made of brown, green, and white Micarta spacers with a brass ferrule and center spacer. Also included is a heavy-duty leather sheath dated "1943." Collectors value $375.00. (Wright Collection)

This very interesting knife was found in an antique mall in Louisville, KY. The knife somewhat resembles a British Fairbairn-Sykes Knife. It was found mounted on the arrowhead shaped oak plaque displayed above. This may mean that the knife belonged to a member of the 1st Special Service Force. The 1st Special Service Force was a specially trained unit made up of Canadian and American soldiers that carried out some of the most secretive and dangerous missions of WWII. There was a movie made about them entitled "The Devil's Brigade." Mounted on this plaque are 2 brass medallions that could have possibly been worn on a hat. Both have a Royal Crown on top of them. One medallion is marked "ROYAL ARMY ORDNANCE CORPS." The other medallion has the letters "R, E, M, E," equally spaced around it. This high quality knife has a 6 1/2" double edge blade that has an engine turned finish. The knife has a brass S shaped cross guard that was specially made for it. The leather handle has a red spacer at top and bottom. I wish I knew more history about this important knife. Collectors value $475.00. (Wright Collection)

A group of quality double edge WWII fighting knives is pictured above. The knife on the left has a 7 5/8" blade made from a British bayonet. The cross guard and pommel are made of bronze. The cross guard is marked "LOUIS SHEPARD." The sheath for this knife is a British bayonet scabbard. The top knife has a 7 1/4" blade that is 1 5/8" wide. The center knife was made from a British Brunswick Bayonet, marked "ENFIELD 1848." This knife has a 9 1/16" blade that is 5/16" thick. The bottom knife has an 8 1/4" blade and is 13 1/4" overall. Collectors value (left) $375.00 (top to bottom) $300.00, $600.00, $375.00. (Wright Collection)

This is a super WWII Theater Knife. The 8 1/4" hand forged blade is very well finished and still sharp. It has a stainless steel cross guard and a heavy aluminum pommel. The large handle is 5 3/4" long and made of thick colorful Micarta spacers. The colors are in a pattern of black, brown, and red. The outstanding heavy-duty sheath is marked "Alfred Cornish, Omaha, NE." Alfred Cornish made high quality sheaths for individuals who may have made only one knife, as well as famous knife makers, such as Frank Richtig of Clarkson, NE, and Floyd Nichols of David City, NE. Collectors value $1,500.00 (Wright Collection)

An interesting group of WWII Theater Knives is pictured above. The knife to the left is marked "LANGBEN, NEW YORK." This very sturdy knife is made from one solid piece of 5/16" steel. The top knife is believed to have been made at the San Antonio Iron Works from a Patton Saber. "D. HEYE" of San Antonio, TX, made the sheath. Another knife and sheath are known similar to this one. The second knife has a 9" blade that is 1/4" thick. The third knife down has a hand forged blade that is 10" long, 2" wide, and 1/4" thick. The bottom knife has a 7 1/4" blade that was made from a file. Collectors value (left) $700.00 (top to bottom) $350.00, $225.00, $275.00, $150.00. (Wright Collection)

This high quality WWII fighting knife has a 7 1/2" double edge blade. The total length of the knife is 12 1/2". The handle has dark red and black Bakelite spacers, along with aluminum and brass. The cross guard and pommel are made of brass. The sheath is outstandingly embossed with a floral design. Collectors value $700.00. (Wright Collection)

This heavy-duty knife has a single edge 8 1/4" blade and is 13 3/8" in overall length. The brass cross guard is cast directly on to the blade, making it very strong. The handle spacers are made of Micarta, copper, and aluminum. The copper and aluminum spacers are raised above the Micarta. This gives the handle a better grip. The leather sheath is covered with aluminum that is pierced with the owner's initials "PAK." The thin aluminum could have come from the skin of an aircraft. Collectors value $650.00. (Wright Collection)

This group of hand made double edge daggers has blade lengths from 6" to 7 1/2". They vary in quality from very good to excellent. The collector's value given is for the knives only. A sheath matching the quality of each knife would add from 10% to 50% to the value listed. Collectors value from top to bottom $40.00, $175.00, $85.00, $60.00, $100.00, $45.00. (Wright Collection)

Two outstanding heavy bladed WWII fighting knives are pictured above. Both knives have double edge blades. The knife on the right has an 8 1/8" blade that is 1 7/8" wide and 1/4" thick. This knife has a stainless steel cross guard and an aluminum pommel. The knife on the left is even heavier. The blade on this knife is 8 1/2" long, 1 5/8" wide, and 1/2" thick. The sheath for this knife is marked "Will Tekaat, Cairns, Australia." Both knives are high quality. Collectors value (left) $500.00 (right) $650.00. (Wright Collection)

This outstanding Theater Knife has a 9" double edge blade and an overall length of 13 3/8". The quality of both the knife and embossed sheath is A+. The handle is made using thick clear Plexiglass, with red and black Micarta spacers. Collectors value $750.00. (Wright Collection)

This double edge WWII fighting knife has a 9" blade and is 14 7/16" in overall length. The blade has a long thin blood groove in each side. The cast aluminum handle is sculptured to fit your hand and has a large skull crusher pommel. The hand made leather sheath is plain, but very well made. This knife is well above average quality in design, fit, and finish. Collectors value $500.00. (Wright Collection)

The above knife and sheath were likely made overseas using many different pieces and parts. The double edge blade is 8" long and brazed securely to the S shaped cross guard. The handle is made of aluminum and leather spacers. The unusual brass skull crusher pommel is made of two different pieces. The hand carved wooden sheath was made to be worn on a web pistol belt. Collector value $375.00. (Wright Collection)

The 8 5/8" blade of this knife has a sharpened back edge. An unknown Seabee must have made this knife, because there is a Seabee emblem mounted in the pommel. The pommel is decorated with green and red stones. There is a 14K gold ladies ring soldered close to the brass cross guard. The sheath is hand decorated with designs and a seahorse. Collectors value $450.00. (Wright Collection)

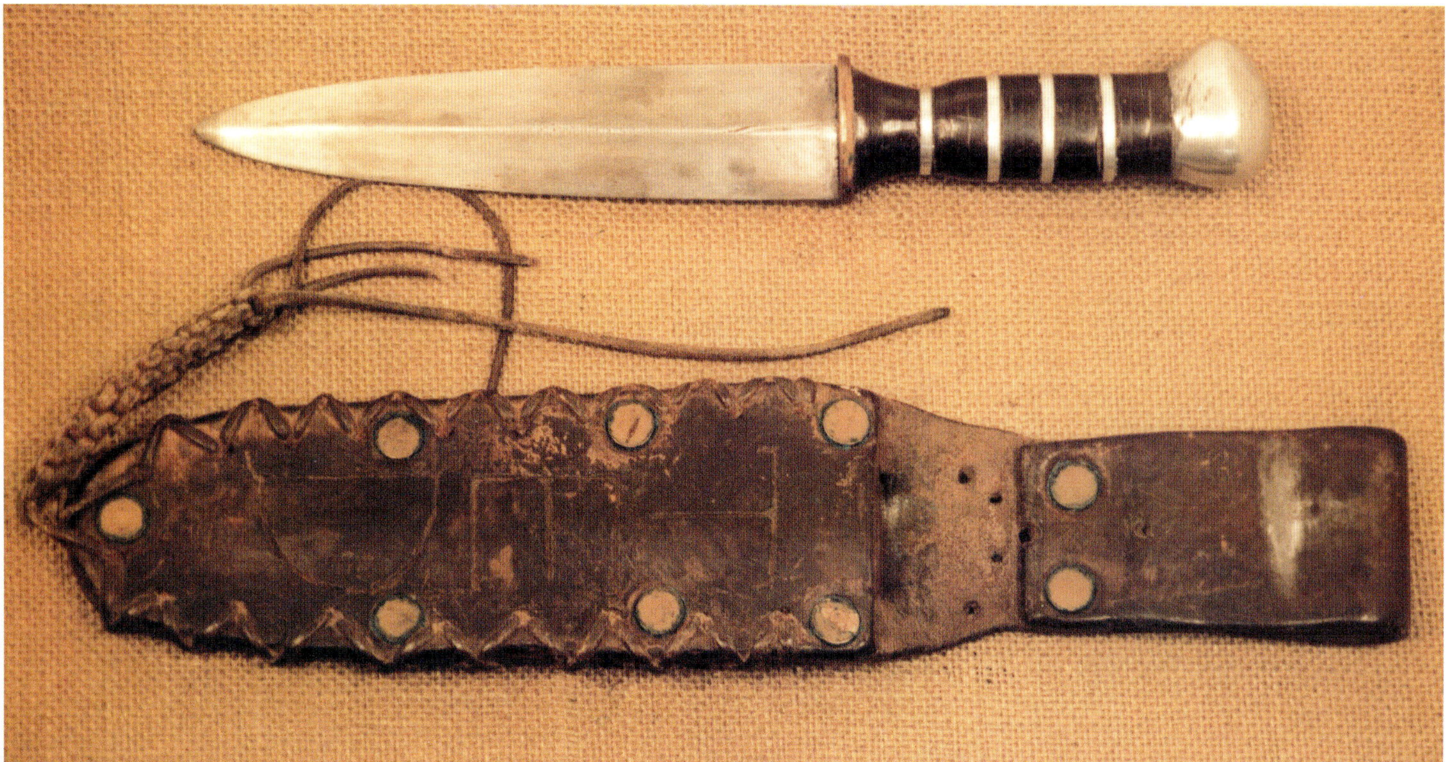

The 7" blade of this well made heavy-duty fighting knife is hand forged. There is a brass hand guard and a large aluminum pommel. The handle is made using leather and aluminum spacers. The heavy-duty leather sheath is marked "TED." Who is TED? The only thing known is that TED owned this knife and sheath. Collectors value $275.00. (Wright Collection)

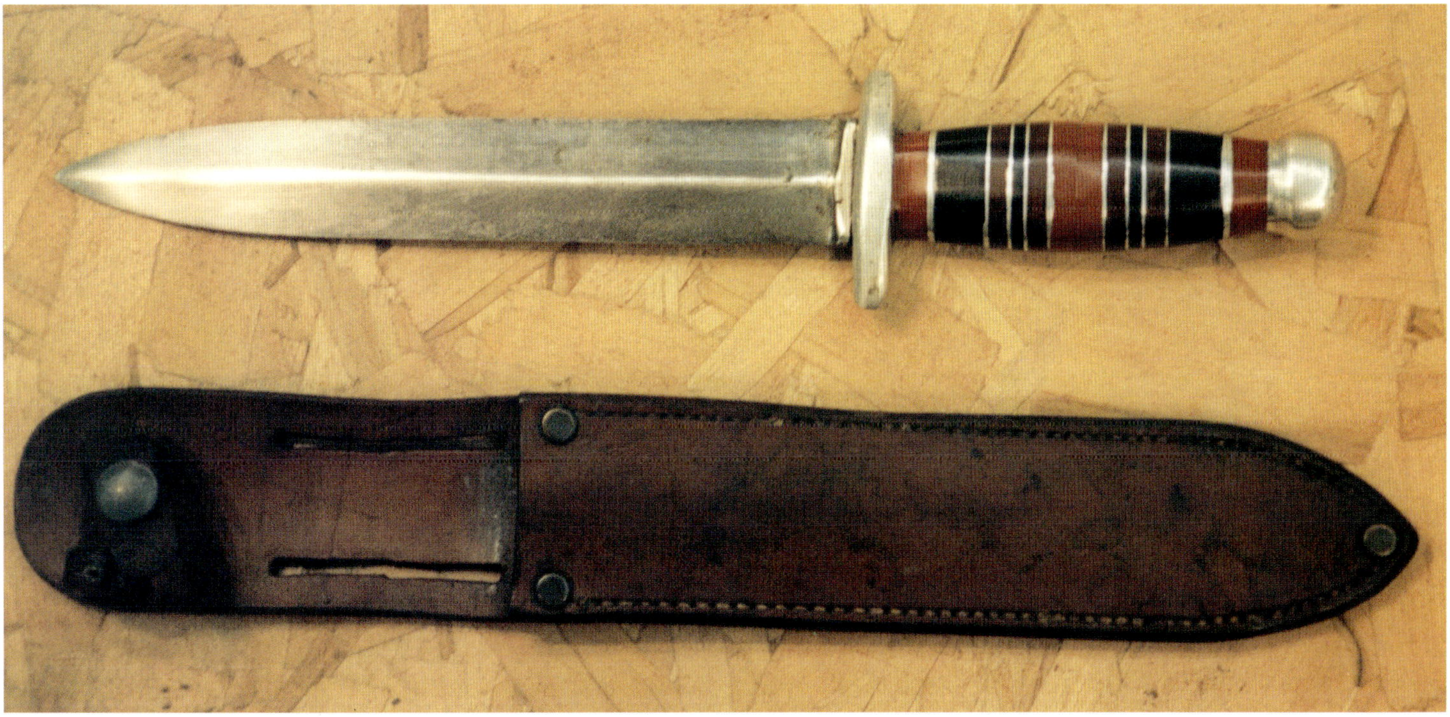

The double edge knife pictured above shows excellent quality in fit and finish. The 8" blade is 1 5/16" wide and was made from 3/16" stock. This knife has an aluminum cross guard and pommel. The handle is very colorful, being made from red, brown, and aluminum spacers. The leather sheath is stitched and riveted. Knife sheaths are riveted at the top to help keep the knife from cutting the stitching when taking the knife in and out of the sheath. Collectors value $350.00. (Wright Collection)

Pictured above is a well made 7 7/8" double edge Theater Knife. The blade is 1 1/2" wide and 3/16" thick. The long cross guard is turned downward to help protect the user's hand. The round handle is made of aluminum and brown Micarta spacers. The leather sheath is well made. Collectors value $275.00. (Wright Collection)

2

Knuckle Knives

A knuckle knife is a knife that has holes in the handle to put your fingers through. These knives can also have a knuckle bow, which is sometimes called a D guard, instead of the finger holes. The purpose of all of this is to protect the hand, give a better grip, and make the knife a more fearsome weapon.

The above pictured double edge knuckle knife has a 9" blade and is 14 1/2" overall. The one piece brass handle was cast directly onto the blade, which makes the knife very substantial. This knife is of medium quality and comes with a heavy-duty hand made sheath. Collectors value for knife and sheath $450.00. (Wright Collection)

The above pictured knuckle knife has a 9 1/2" blade that is 1/4" thick. The double edge blade was expertly ground from a Kearney & Foot file. The knuckle guard and skull crusher pommel is made from heavy steel and marked EBER EMERSON. The handle has 2 red Bakelite spacers, along with 6 aluminum spacers and assorted colors of Micarta. This heavy well made knuckle knife shows excellent quality and workmanship. Collectors value $875.00. (Wright Collection)

This is a very unique and dangerous weapon. This knife was almost as harmful to the user as the person it was to be used on. The knife has an 8 1/2" double edge blade in the usual place, and a 3 1/2" double edge blade attached to the back of the handle. The knuckle points have been sharpened to make the knife more fearsome. The entire knife was made out of 1 piece of 1/4" steel. The handles are made of bone. The sheath is hand sewn and has a brass web pistol belt hanger on the back. This knife was made and used by Sargent Nolan P. Rasnick, USMC. As pictured above, the knife came with a souvenir war club inscribed "Samoa 1942," and a diary with Rasnick's initials on the outside cover. This diary gives a detailed description of this Marine's every day life for 2 years during WWII. In this diary he describes making this knife, as well as other knives which he sold for a profit or traded for items he needed. Collectors value (knife, war club, and diary) $875.00. (Wright Collection)

Above, Left: This group of hand made WWII knuckle knives shows many different designs and ideas of how to make a Theater Knife. Blade lengths are from 5 1/2" to 8 7/8". Collectors values (from left to right) $250.00, $300.00, $500.00, $275.00, $300.00, $300.00, $325.00. These values include a sheath of comparable quality to each knife. (Ballard Collection)

Below, Left: This group of WWII hand made knuckle knives have various blade lengths. They measure from 6 7/8" to 8 7/8". They are all of excellent quality and have their original sheaths. A knuckle knife similar to one on the bottom was offered for sale in a 1944 catalog of Thomas Woroniecki of New York City. The knife above the Woroniecki knife appears similar, but it is not the same. Collectors value (top to bottom) $300.00, $350.00, $500.00, $800.00. (Ballard Collection)

The two knuckle knives pictured above were hand made. P.D. HENRY of Birmingham, AL, made the knife on the top. He was in the scrap metal business in Birmingham during WWII. This knife has a 9 1/2" double edge blade and a cast aluminum handle. The knife on the bottom has a 9 1/8" double edge blade and is 14 5/8" in overall length. It also has a cast aluminum handle. The sheath is marked "Stelzig Saddlery Co. Houston, TX." There are several known examples of each of the above two knives. Both knives have their original quality leather sheaths. Collectors value Henry Knife (top) $600.00, Stelzig knife (bottom) $650.00. (Ballard Collection)

Three well-made knuckle knives are pictured here. The blade lengths are (top) 8 7/8", (center) 8", and (bottom) 7 1/2". Collectors value (top to bottom) $300.00, $350.00, $500.00. (Ballard Collection)

The knife pictured above is known as the 1st Ranger Battalion Knuckle Knife made in Australia. These knives were a "Private Purchase" item and were not issued to any one group. The picture above shows an original knife and sheath. There have been many reproductions made of this knife. The way I can tell a repro from an original is the brass will slightly flow from the cross guard on to the blade. Also, the knuckle bow will have file marks inside, and in the bottom of the teeth on the knuckle guard. Some clever fakers have tried to put file marks on the repros, but they have not been able to fake the brass spilling on to the blade. Collectors value $500.00. (Wright Collection)

The two knives pictured (right) have thick heavy knuckle guards. The top knife was made using an M2 blade and has the number "55654" stamped into the front of the guard. The sheath is ink stamped in several places, "R.A. VAN ACKER." The lower knife has a hand made blade and a 3/8' thick knuckle bow. The handle is wrapped with heavy string. Collectors value $375.00 each. (Wright Collection)

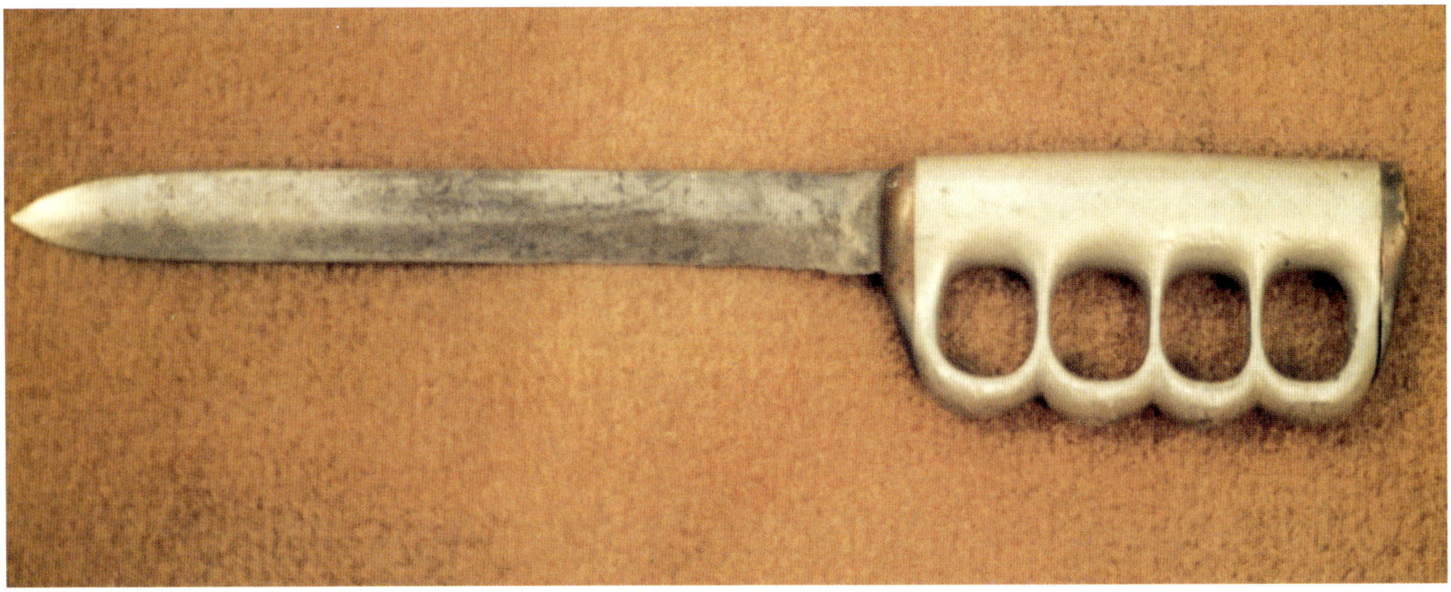

This cast aluminum handle knuckle knife has a 9" double edge blade. A piece of copper was cast on to the blade and pinned to the aluminum knuckle handle. There is a similar copper piece screwed on to the bottom of the handle keeping everything tight. Collectors value $275.00. (Wright Collection)

The knuckle knife pictured above was made from an M1 Garand bayonet. It was ground down to the size of an M4 bayonet and has a US M8 scabbard. The barrel latch has been removed and the lug slot filled. Brass knuckles have been brazed on to the top. When the knife is held in the hand the cutting edge of the blade is pointed upward. Collectors value $175.00. (Wright Collection)

This knuckle knife appears to be Theater Made. The blade is made from a Japanese bayonet. The pommel is made from a Japanese mortar detonator. The 1/8" thick brass knuckle bow has a single row of teeth that are bent, alternating one to the left and one to the right. The knuckle bow is pinned to the aluminum cross guard with a copper pin. The handle is made using 39 separate spacers of several different kinds of spacer material. The sheath looks similar to the sheaths used on the San Antonio Iron Works Patton Saber Knives. Collectors value $500.00. (Wright Collection)

The top knife pictured here was made using a "KA-BAR MK2" blade. This "KA-BAR" marked blade likely had a "USMC" marking on the back, which has been removed. One reason for the marking being removed is the handle is marked USN. The owner was likely in the Navy and did not want the blade to be marked "USMC." The handle for this knife was likely made aboard ship because of the quality of the casting. This knife has its original sheath. The lower knuckle knife has a 7" blade that is hand forged from 1/4" stock. The maker of this knife used a handle pattern from a WWI trench knife. The aluminum handle was cast directly on to the blade. The sheath is nicely made and held together with heavy leather lacing. Collectors value (top) $450.00 (lower) $325.00. (Wright Collection)

The two knuckle knives pictured on this page were made using bayonet blades. The top knife reportedly was made in Australia. It has a 9" blade and is 13 1/4" overall. The bottom knife has a 7 7/8" blade and has a skull crusher pommel. Both of these knives are made with the sharp edge of the blade pointing upward when gripped in the hand. Collectors value $400.00 each. (Ballard Collection)

The blade of this knife appears to have been made out of a sword blade. The blade is 6 7/16" long. This knife has a brass cross guard, cast aluminum knuckle guard, and pommel. The main body of the handle is made of wood. The leather sheath is hand stitched. There is a V notch cut out of the back of the sheath to let the cross guard set in and let the knife set flat. Collectors value $400.00. (Wright Collection)

This WWII fighting knife was made out of a mid-1850s German sword. The blade was shortened to 10" and the back of the point sharpened 3". The hand made leather sheath is nicely bound around the outer edge with thin leather lacing. Aluminum rivets were used to keep the top of the sheath lacing from being cut. Collectors value $300.00. (Wright Collection)

Left: Two wonderful Theater Knives made by the same unknown maker are pictured above. Both knives are similar in shape and design. The knuckle knife has a 7 1/8" blade, while the dagger has a 7 1/2" blade. Both knives have high quality leather sheaths with the same design embossed into the outer edge. Collectors value (knuckle knife) $750.00 (dagger) $500.00. (Ballard Collection)

The same unknown maker made the above two knuckle knives. The knife on the right and the sheath to the left belonged to Frank M. Barber, Technician 4th Grade, First Special Service Force. The knives have a 9" clip point blade that was double hollow ground out of a file. The knuckle bow is similar in design to the 1917 trench knives and has a double skull crusher pommel. The wooden handle has finger grooves for a better grip. The sheaths are steel and are gas welded. An interesting note: both knives have left hand sheaths. There is a small hole in the bottom of the sheaths for water to drain. Collectors value (Frank Barber knife) $1,500.00 (other) $1,000.00. (Wright Collection)

Harland F. Smith made the top knuckle knife in this picture. He made it while on board the USS Corregidor. The knife was made using a 1917 trench knife blade. The handle was made of the aluminum from a propeller of a damaged U.S. fighter plane. Smith also made the heavy-duty form fitting leather sheath. The knife on the bottom was made using a 1918 LF&C knuckle knife for a pattern. The handle is cast from aluminum, and the finger holes were opened up. Collectors value (top knife) $500.00, (bottom knife) $300.00. (Ballard Collection)

The handle of this knuckle knife is made of steel and is 5/8" thick. The knife has an 8 5/16" double edge blade that was made from 1/4" stock. Collectors value $500.00. (Wright Collection)

These two knuckle knives were made from standard issue knives. The top knife was made from an M3 knife, and the lower knife was made from an M2 knife. Collectors value $375.00 each. (Wright Collection)

The top knife in this picture was made from a German Puma Bayonet. The original sheath was shortened to fit the reground blade. The bottom knife is totally hand made. It has an M2 sheath. Collectors value $400.00 each. (Wright Collection)

The above picture shows three hand made knuckle knives of average quality. They are certainly a fierce and sturdy side arm that the owners were glad to have. The blade lengths are from 6 1/4" to 11 3/4". Collectors value (top to bottom) $300.00, $175.00, $200.00. (Ballard Collection)

Right: This knuckle knife has a 9 3/4" double edge blade and has a total length of 14 3/8". This is a professionally made knuckle knife. I know of two more knives like this, all of which were made by the same unknown maker. One of these knives is shorter than the other two. This knife is marked "CHUBBE- 1943." The blade and the knuckle guard are made in separate pieces. The knuckles are slotted and the blade inserted, then all is brazed together. Three copper pins hold the red Micarta handle slabs to the blade. The heavy leather sheath is hand stitched with heavy white string. Collectors value $650.00. (Wright Collection)

Below, Left: The Kephart Knife Works of Des Moines, IA (for more information about Kephart see chapter 4), made the top knife in this picture. It is marked KEPHART on the handle. It has a 7 1/2" double edge blade. The center knife has a 7 1/4" blade. The bottom knife is made from one piece of steel and has a 9 1/2" blade. Collectors value (top to bottom) $875.00, $225.00, $350.00. (Ballard Collection)

Pictured above are two cast aluminum handle knuckle knives. The bottom knife was made using a Western Cutlery Co. blade and has a horse head pommel. The top knife has an 8 1/8" double edge blade. Collectors value (top) $250.00, (bottom) $350.00. (Ballard Collection)

The double edge blade of this WWII knuckle knife is 10 3/4" long and 3/8" thick. The copper knuckle guard has six .30 cal. Carbine bullets set into it. The handle was made using thick leather and two red spacers. The extra heavy-duty leather sheath has 23 decorated steel rivets holding it together. Collectors value $600.00. (Wright Collection)

Is this a Civil War D guard Bowie, or a WWII knuckle knife? The answer is on the back of the sheath. Carved into the back of this sheath is "Cpl. Thomas Ponte, Co. A Fld. Tng. Bn., O. R. T. C., Camp Picket, Virginia, Feb-9-44." The knife has a 9 1/4" double edge blade. The brass D guard is brazed into the back of the blade. The handles are wood. Collectors value $500.00. (Wright Collection)

Pictured (Below, Left) are two WWII knuckle knives. The top knife has a 7 7/8" blade and has a bottle opener built into it. The bottom knife is totally hand made. Whoever made this knife must have used a 1918 LF&C trench knife as a pattern. The leather sheath of this knife is marked "TO MEL FROM BOB." Collectors value (top) $200.00, (bottom) $250.00. (Ballard Collection)

The top knife pictured here was made by "BUD" Fhaver in Oklahoma City during WWII. The 8" double edge blade is 1 3/4" wide. The handle is brass that has been silver plated. The lower knuckle knife was made using an MK3 blade. The handle is cast in brass. The blade has been leaded into the handle and held in place with two bolts. Collectors value (top) $375.00, (bottom) $300.00. (Ballard Collection)

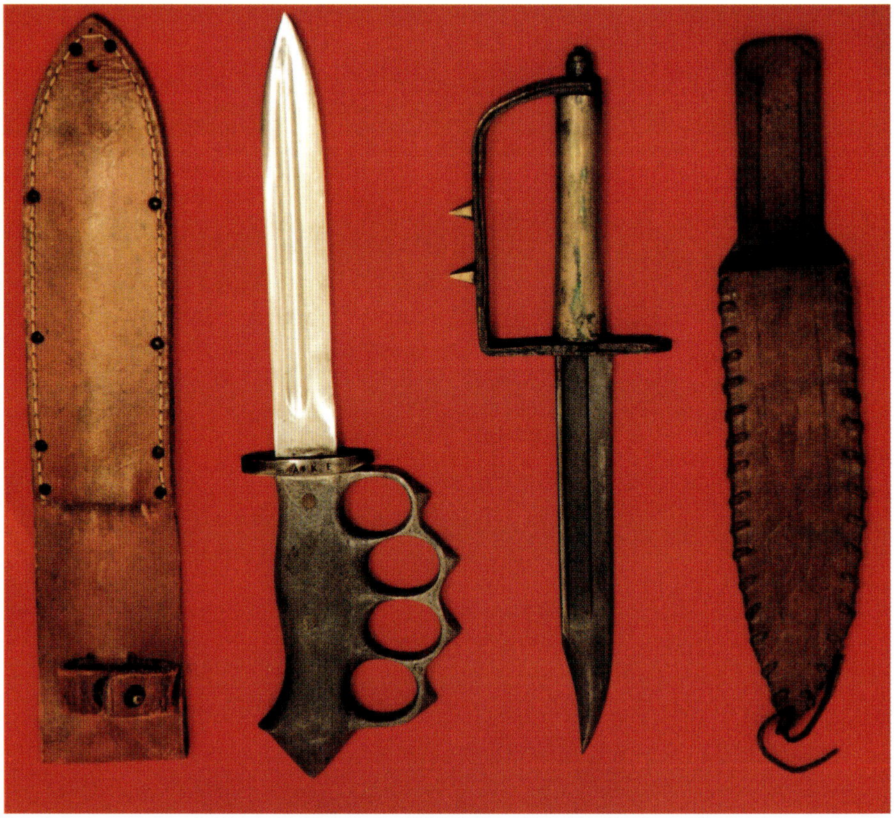

The knife on the right was made out of a WWII British MK4 bayonet. The knuckle bow is made out of a sheet of copper, folded to make it thicker. The handle is made from a brass tube. The knife on the left was made from an M1 Garand bayonet. The cast aluminum handle is very well done. The owner's initials, "AKE," are marked on the cross guard. Collectors value (right) $275.00 (left) $500.00. (Wright Collection)

This knuckle knife was made out of a WWI bayonet. It was reported to me that the unknown owner of this bayonet brought it home after the war. When WWII came around he expertly converted it into a knuckle knife to take with him when he went back to war. This knuckle knife has a 6 3/4" double edge blade. The sheath is marked "Brauer Bros. Inc., St. Louis, Moose Brand Sporting Goods." The only clue to the owner's identity is the serial number stamped on the cross guard. Collectors value $675.00. (Wright Collection)

This hand made WWII knuckle knife has a 7 7/8" double edge blade. The knuckle bow was made from 3/16" steel and has 6 large steel points set into it. The brass pommel is marked "B.F. Grim," which is likely the owner's name. The hand made sheath is large enough to protect the owner's leg from the sharp points on the knuckle bow. Collectors value $575.00. (Wright Collection)

The knuckle knife on the right has a 7" double edge blade, a stainless steel knuckle bow, and an aluminum pommel. The sheath is decorated with a skull and crossbones, 4-leaf clover, horseshoe, and 5-point star. The knife on the left has a 6 1/4" blade made from a 1/4" thick file. This knife has a quality sheath with the front embossed with floral design. Collectors value $375.00 each. (Wright Collection)

Both knuckle knives pictured (Below) have cast aluminum handles. The knife on the right has a 7 1/4" clip point blade that is flat on the back and saber ground on the front. The knife on the left has an 8 3/8" double edge blade that is 1/4" thick. This knife was carried by A.F. McMilan, 4th Squadron, Army Air Force, Lemoore Flying School, Class of 1943. Collectors value $500.00 each. (Wright Collection)

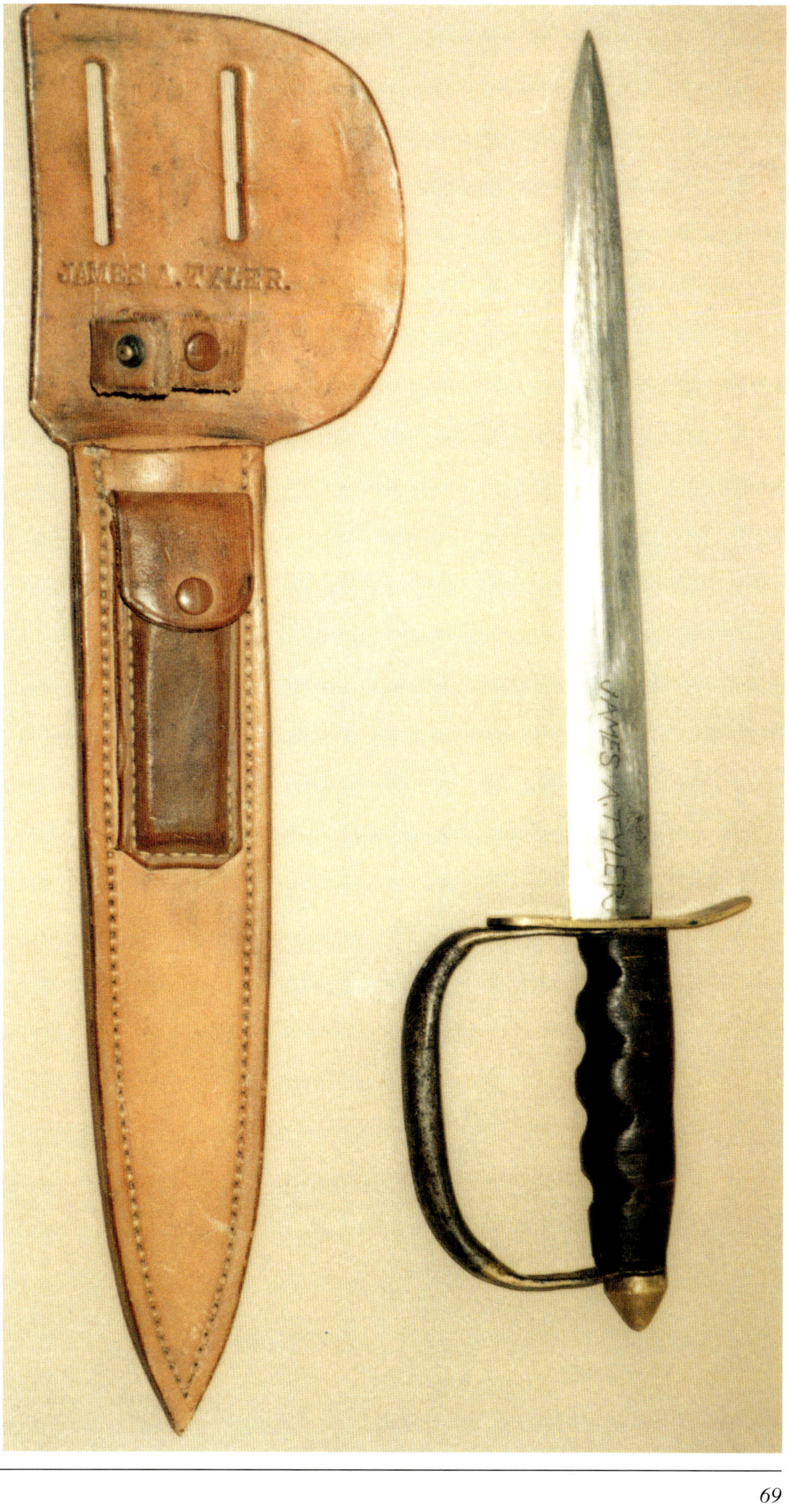

This knuckle knife was made for JAMES A. TYLER at the Nansimona Ordnance Depot near Norfolk, VA. The knife has a 9 7/8" blade that was made from a file. The handle was made using leather spacers. The knuckle bow is made from a thin wall pipe. "James A. Tyler" had his name on the blade, knuckle bow, and sheath. The high quality leather sheath has a stone pouch on the front, which still has the original sharpening stone inside. Collectors value $575.00. (Wright Collection)

Percy R. Huff of Berlin, NY, made the bottom knuckle knife in the picture above. As far as I know he was not related to Taylor Huff, who made knuckle knives in Fort Knox, KY. This knife has an 8 5/8" blade and is 13 5/8" in overall length. It has a brass cross guard, knuckles, and pommel cap. The handle is made of wood, which is likely walnut. There are other known knuckle knives by Percy Huff with spikes attached to each knuckle hole. The top knife in this picture is a double edge knife that was made by an unknown maker. Collectors value (Huff knife) $800.00 (double edge knife) $250.00. (Ballard Collection)

The knuckle knife in the picture above has an 8 1/4" double edge blade. The knuckle bow has a double row of teeth. The handle is constructed of dark brown and red Micarta spacers. The dagger has a 7 3/4" blade and is of unusually good quality. Collectors value (knuckle knife) $400.00 (dagger) $300.00. (Ballard Collection)

These two hand made knuckle knives were designed after the 1918 LF&C trench knife. The top has an 8 1/8" blade and has a solid cast brass handle. The lower knife has a 7 7/8" clip point blade that has a sharpened false edge on top. The name "Lloyd V. Phelps" is engraved on the back. Collectors value $425.00 each. (Wright Collection)

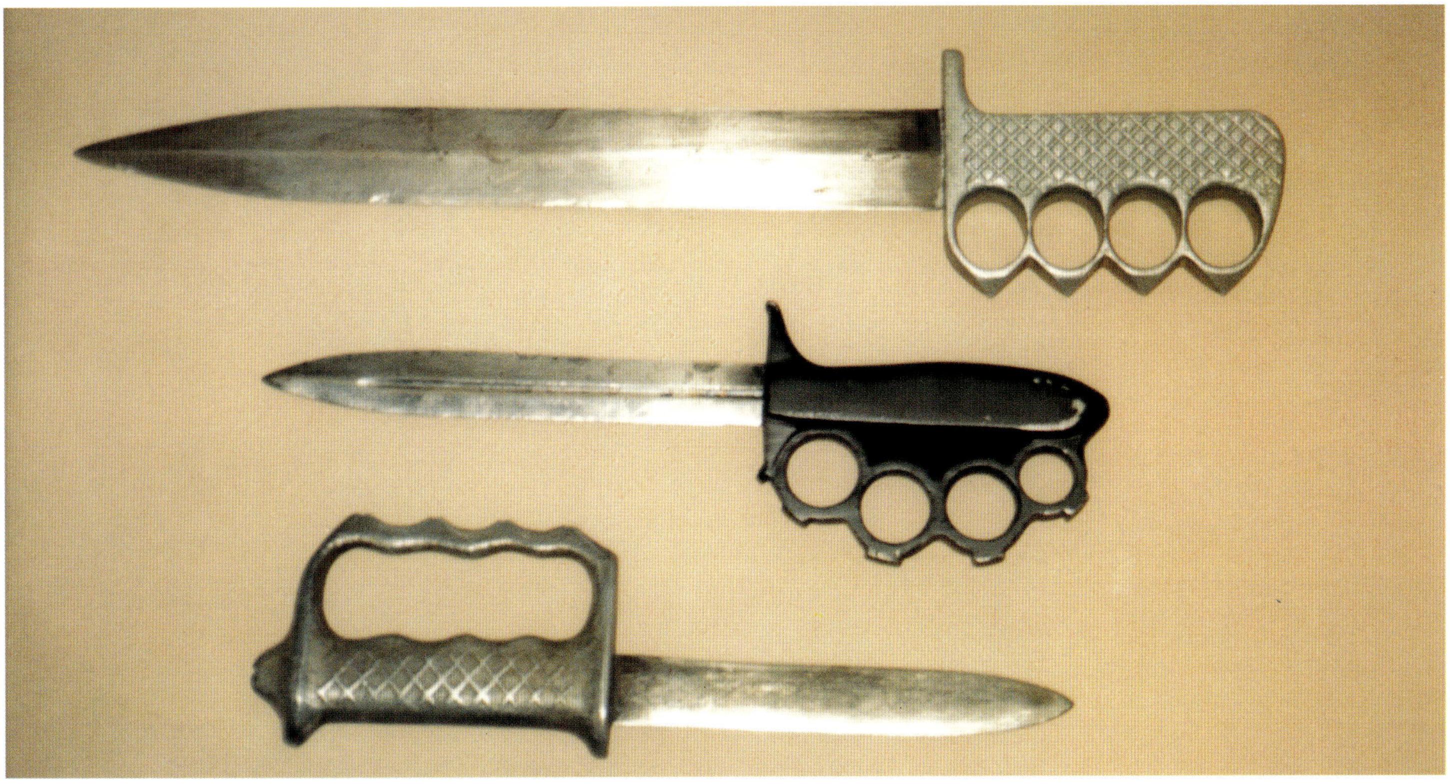

The top knuckle knife has a 12" double edge blade and a cast aluminum handle. The center knife has a 6 7/8" blade with the sharpened edge up. The lower knife was made in Australia, and is one of the most common patterns of WWII knuckle knives seen today. Collectors value (top to bottom) $500.00, $300.00, $200.00. (Wright Collection)

The above pictured knuckle knife has a 12 1/4" double edge blade. The cast aluminum handle is sculptured to fit your hand, thus providing a very secure grip. There are several other known knives with a similar handle, but they have different types of blades. Mike Silvey pictures two of these on page 173 of his book, "Knives of the United States Military WWII." Collectors value (as pictured above) $500.00. (Wright Collection)

The knife on the right has a 7" hand forged double edge blade. The brass knuckle bow has two rows of seven points in each row. This knife was carried and used by "C.R. Bowlsby." The knife on the left has a 7" clip point blade. The cutting edge of the blade is pointing upward when held in the hand. Both knives still have their original quality sheaths. Collectors value (left) $325.00 (right) $450.00. (Wright Collection)

It was reported to me that this hand made WWII knuckle knife was made by a member of the 82nd Airborne Division while in Belgium in 1944. The 9 1/2" blade is hand forged. A wooden handle pattern was used to make the mold that the handle was cast in. You can still see the wood grain pattern in the handle. Some of these knuckle knives were made with a Damascus steel blade hand forged out of old shotgun barrels. The leather sheath has a belt buckle keeper strap, attachment for hooking to a web pistol belt, and a leg tie down at the bottom of the sheath. Collectors value $575.00. (Wright Collection)

This WWII knuckle knife was made using a WWI LF&C knuckle knife for a pattern. The handle is marked "TRADES SCHOOL HUNTING-TON, WVA." The top of the handle is marked "27 CLIFF N. BAUGH." This is a heavy, above average knife that has a well-made sheath to match. There are several known knives like this one. Collectors value $500.00. (Wright Collection)

This unusual knuckle knife is made totally of steel. It has an 8 1/8" blade and has a total length of 13". The double edge blade is only sharpened half way down each side. The round handle is finely knurled to give a better grip. The letters "OSS" are stamped individually, one at a time, into the blade and the bottom of the guard. These letters are likely the owner's initials. The sheath is well made, being both stitched and riveted. Collectors value $400.00 as pictured. (Wright Collection)

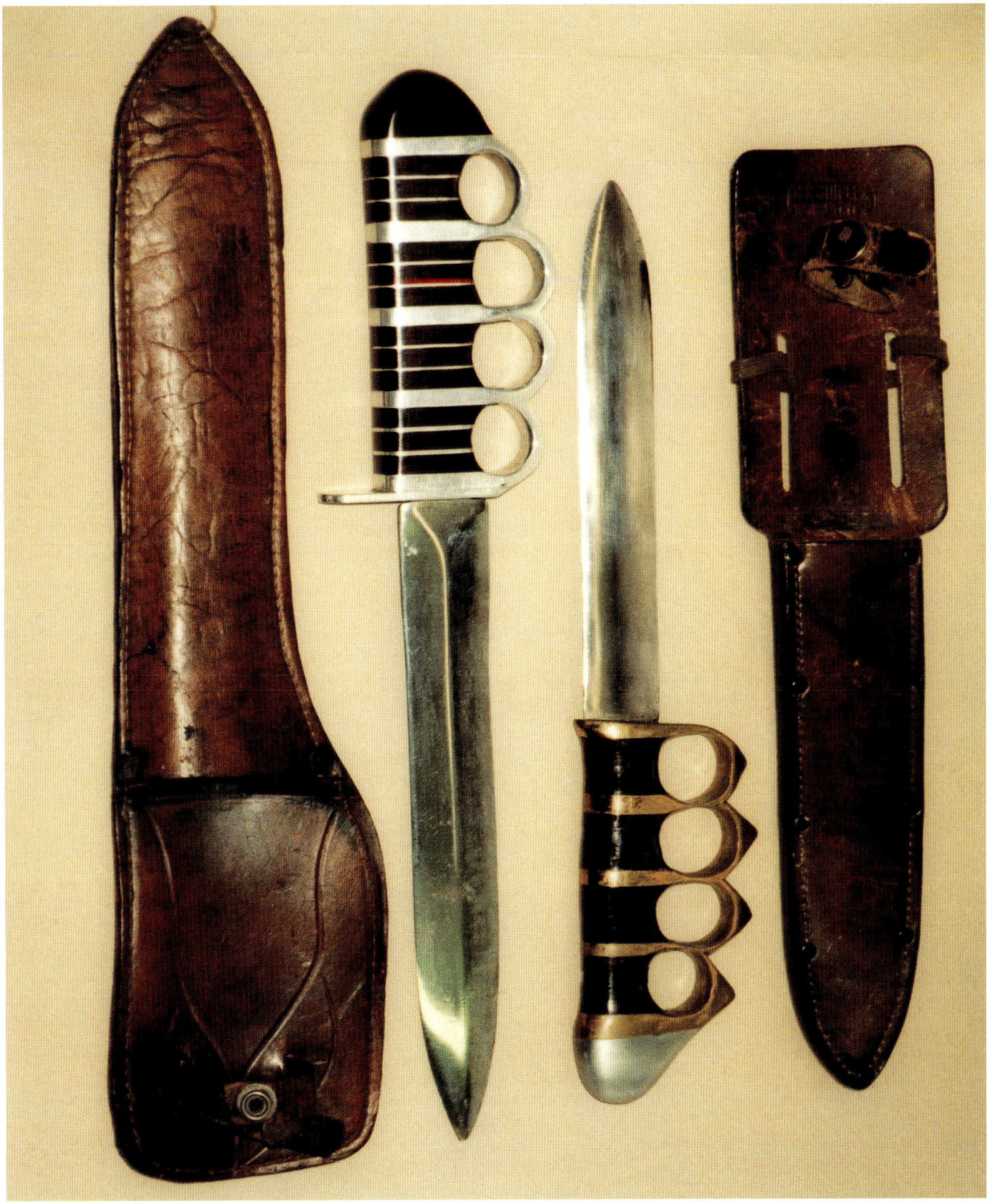

These two high quality knuckle knives are very similar in design. I do not think the same maker made both knives. The knife on the right has a 7 3/8" blade and is 12 5/8" overall. The knuckle guard is made of brass and the pommel is aluminum. The handle spacers are made from Micarta. The sheath is marked "C.R. Shipley, Kansas City." There are two knives like this one pictured on page 216 and one on the back cover of Silvey's book, "Knives of the United States Military of WWII." The knife on the left has an 8 3/4" blade and is 14 1/2" overall. The knuckle guard is made of aluminum. The pommel and handle spacers are made of Micarta. The high quality sheath has a cut in the back for a leg tie down. Collectors value (left) $875.00 (right) $2,000.00. (Wright Collection)

Above: The top knife has a 6 1/2" hand made blade. The deer horn handle has been filled with lead. The knuckle guard is 1/2" thick. The 8 1/8" blade of the bottom knuckle knife appears to have been made out of a Springfield bayonet. The back edge of the blade has been sharpened. The walnut handles have been checkered. The quality sheath has a web pistol belt hanger on the back. Collectors value $450.00 each. (Wright Collection)

Right: The top knife has a 6 7/8" double edge blade. This knife has a cast handle of unknown metal. It is too heavy to be aluminum. There are other known knuckle knives with a similar handle design. The lower knife is marked "Mexico." This knife has a 5/16" thick steel knuckle guard that has been welded to the tang of the blade. Collectors value (top) $375.00 (lower) $300.00. (Wright Collection)

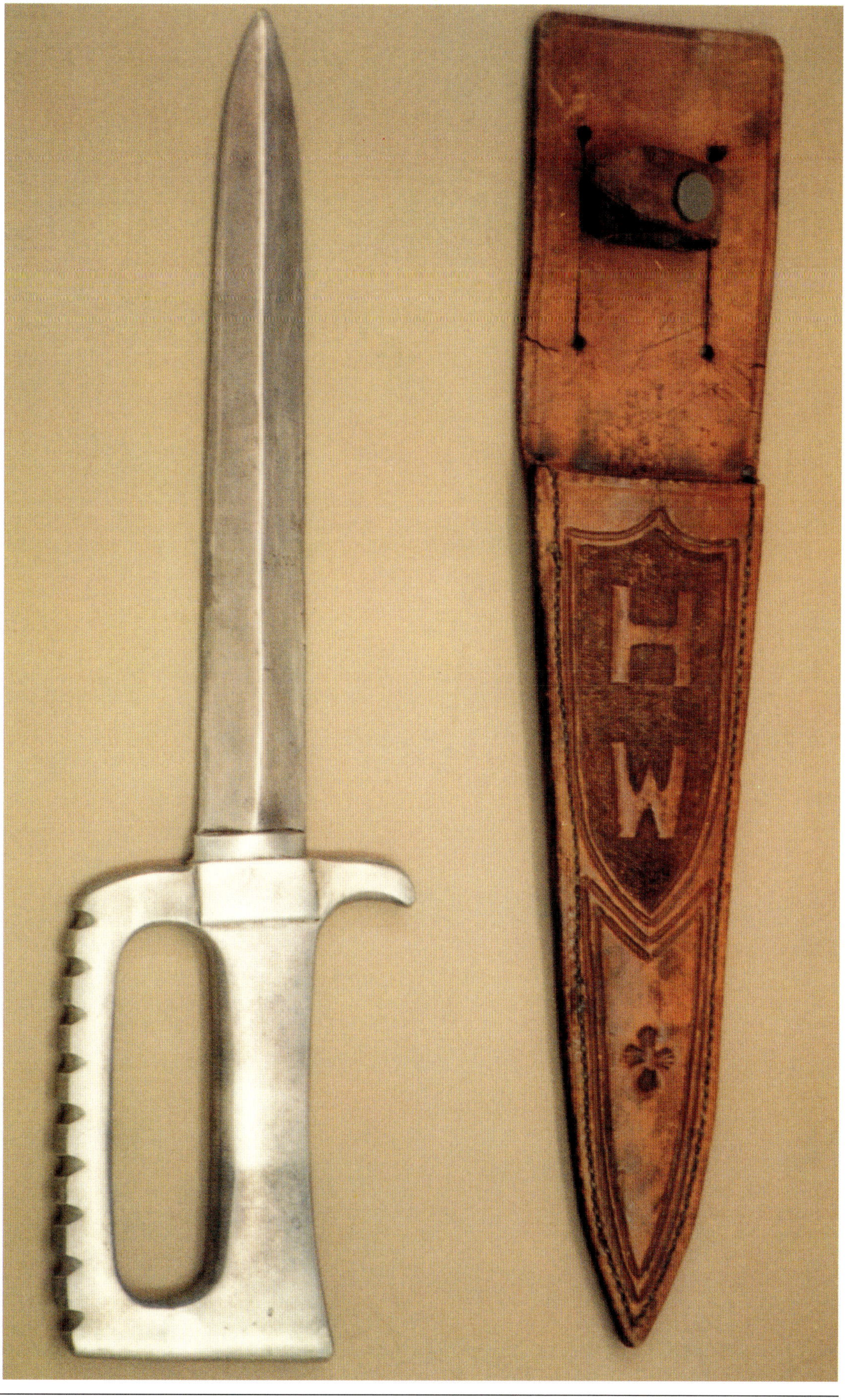

This WWII hand made knuckle knife has a high quality cast aluminum handle. The double edge blade is 8 5/16" long and 1 1/8" wide. The high quality sheath is tooled and embossed with the initials "HW." Collectors value $700.00. (Wright Collection)

The same unknown maker made both of these knives. The handles of both knives were made using the same mold. Both knives have a 12" double edge blade. The blade of the top knife is 1 1/2" wide and 3/16" thick, and the blade of the lower knife is 1/2" wide and 1/16" thick. The sheath for the lower knife is marked "F. Muller, Denver." Collectors value (top) $500.00 (lower, with sheath) $650.00. (Wright Collection)

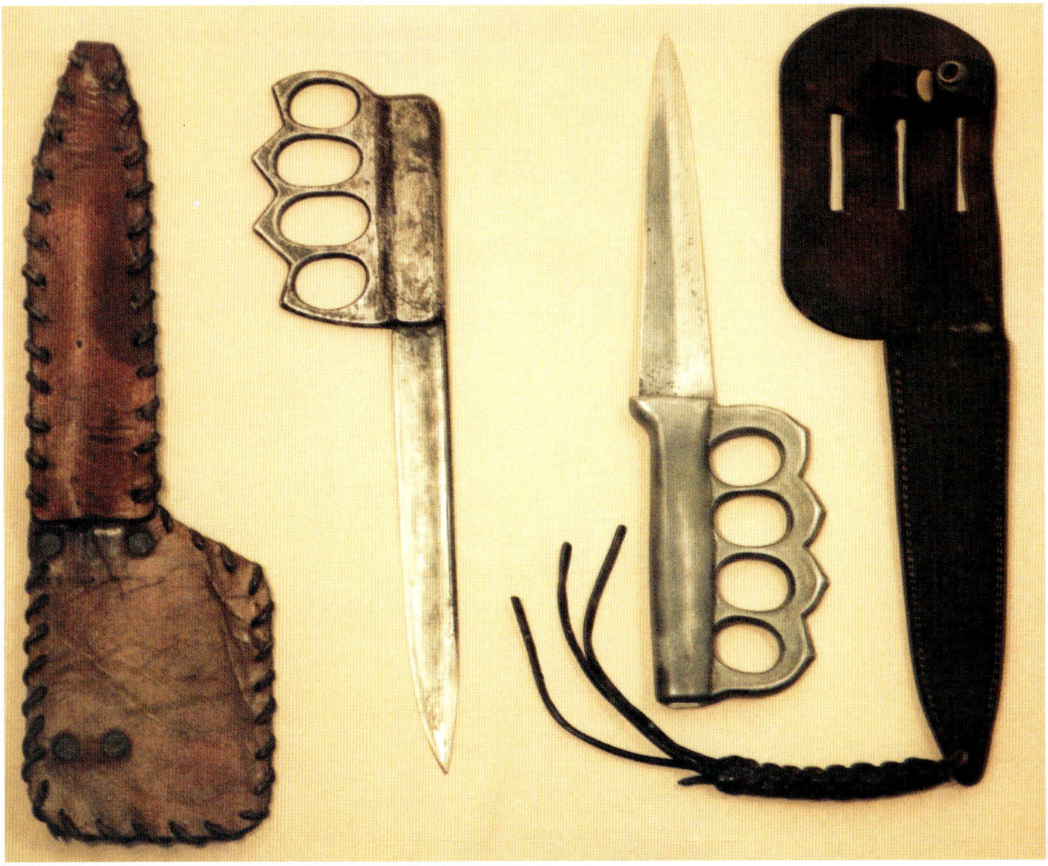

The knife on the left is made totally of steel and is heavy and thick. The 7 3/4" blade has a sharpened back edge. It has been reported to me that other knives like this one were used by the "Eagle Squadron." This Squadron was made up of American flyers that flew for the British early in WWII. The knife on the right has a 6 3/4" double edge blade and a cast aluminum handle. There are other known knives like both knives pictured above. Collectors value (left) $500.00 (right) $400.00. (Wright Collection)

Smiths in New Zealand made the brass handle knife to the left. This knife has a 6 9/16" double edge blade. It has a steel cross guard that is round in the back and square in the front. The knuckle knife to the right has a 6" blade that is 1 1/2" wide. The cast aluminum handle has the letters "USMC" stamped into it. Collectors value (Smiths knife) $700.00 (right) $400.00. (Wright Collection)

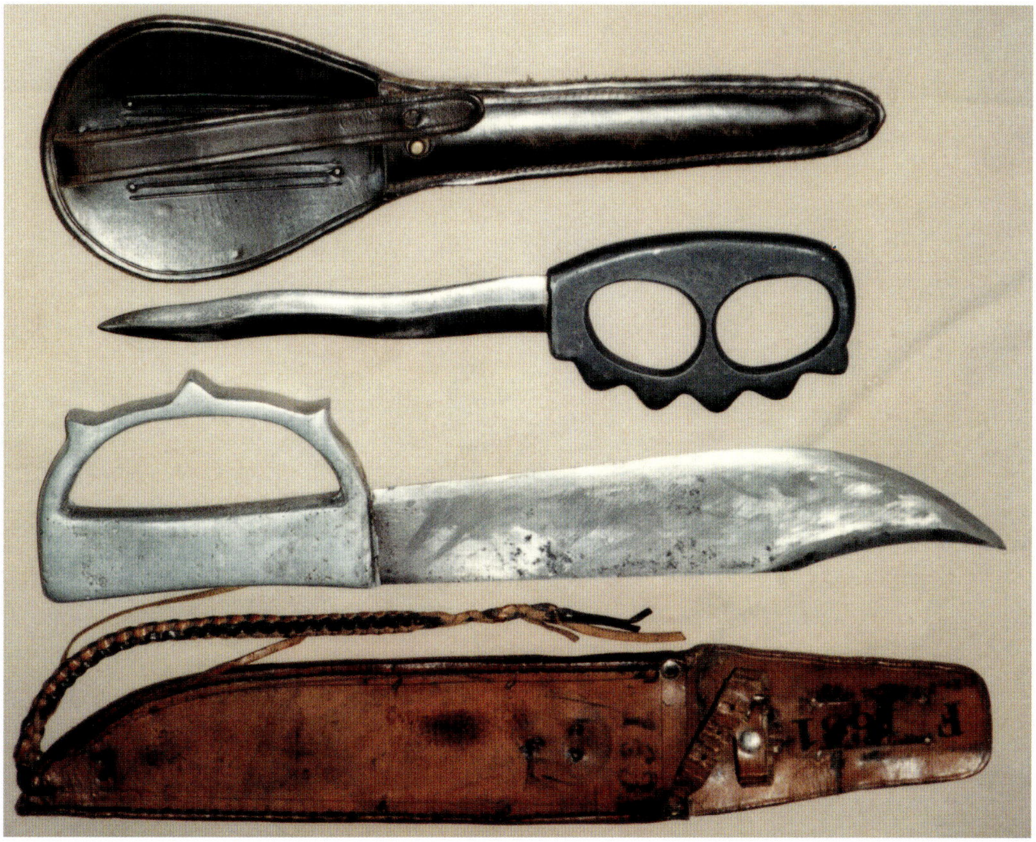

The top knuckle knife in the above picture came with three other knives that were all OSS knives. I was told that these four knives belonged to a U.S. serviceman, and that he got these knives during WWII in Australia and used them. No other information was available. The lower knife is one of several different designs of "Ranger" knives made in Australia. Collectors value (top) $1,000.00 (lower) $600.00. (Wright Collection)

This knuckle knife has an 8 3/8" double edge blade. The cast aluminum handle is 7/8" thick and has four nails cast into the knuckle bow. The hand made heavy-duty leather sheath is made large enough to protect the user's leg from being hurt by the nails. The handle has a lanyard hole in the end. This knife is of average quality. Collectors value $400.00. (Wright Collection)

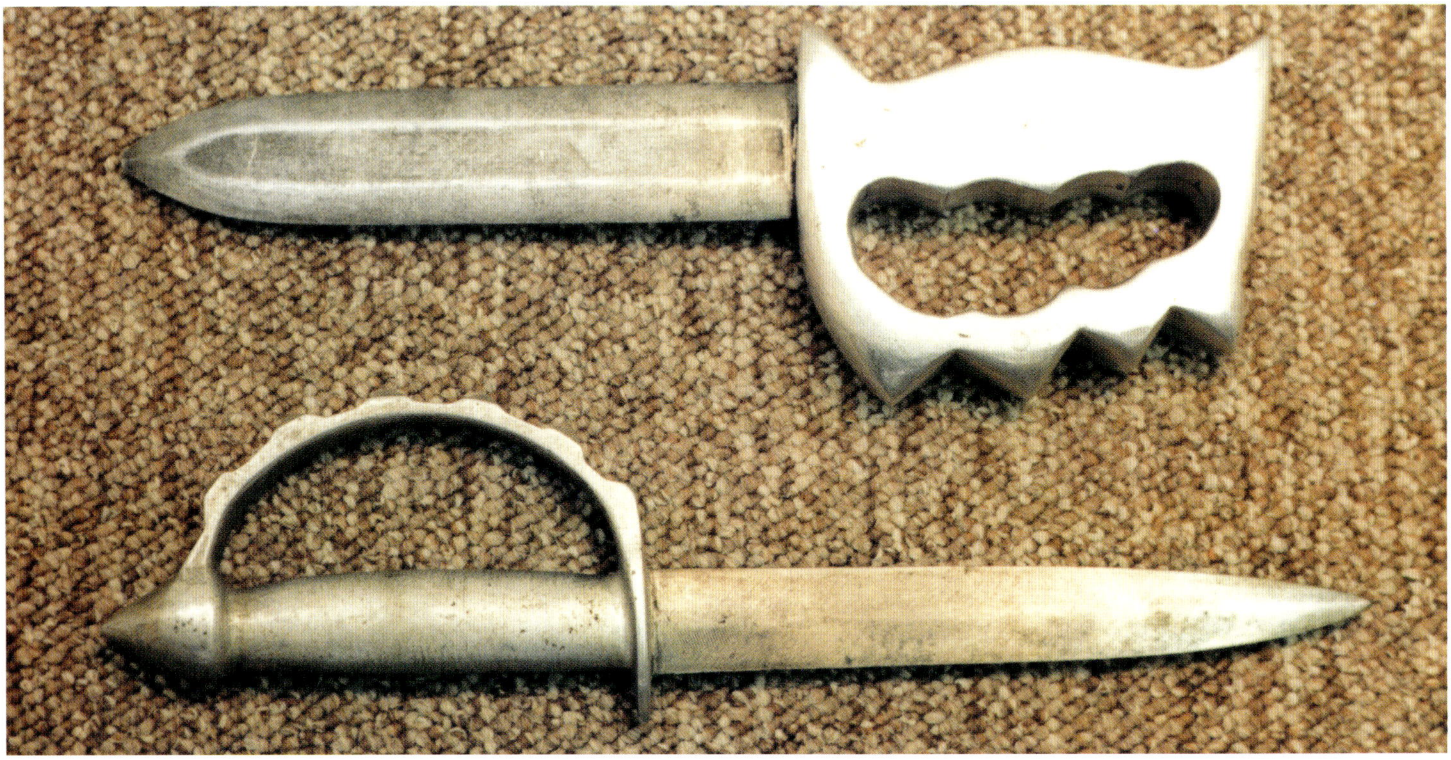

Both of the above-pictured WWII knuckle knives have aluminum handles. The top knife has a 6 5/8" double edge blade. The handles are made in two halves of 1/2" thick aluminum plates. These plates are riveted together with aluminum rivets. The bottom knife has a 6 7/8'' blade hand forged from a file. The sheath for this knife is marked "TO DAD FROM BUD." Collectors value (top) $325.00 (bottom) $350.00. (Wright Collection)

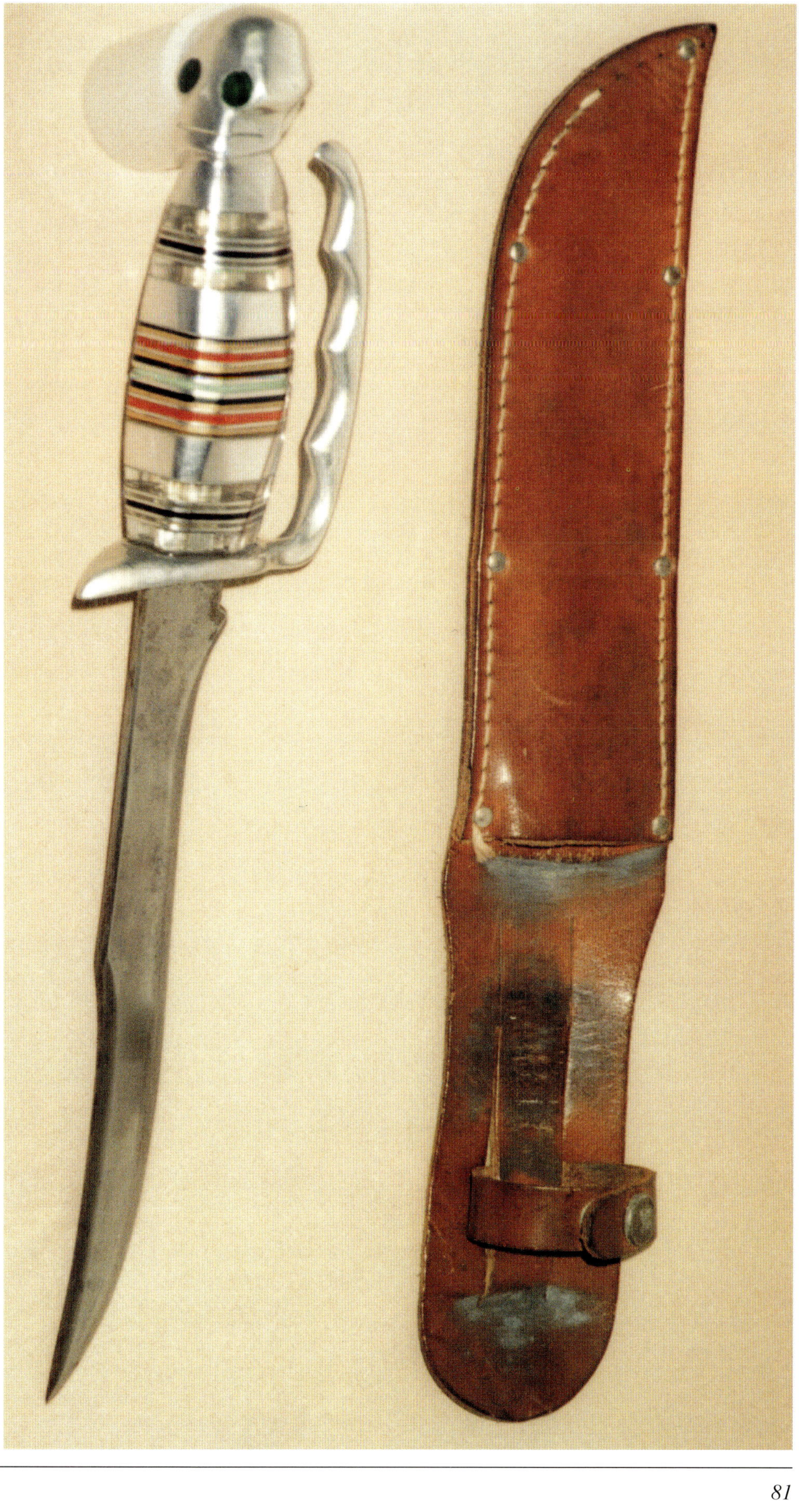

This high quality WWII knuckle knife has a skull pommel. The unusual shaped 7 7/8" blade is 1/8" thick. The handle spacer materials are Plexiglass, Bakelite, brass, and aluminum. Collectors value $750.00. (Wright Collection)

3

Bowie Knives

Bowie Knives are knives that were named after James Bowie, who died at the Alamo in 1836. At this time it is not known what the original Bowie Knife looked like. Many collectors of antique Bowie Knives consider them to have a clip point blade, however, the term Bowie Knife has never been defined. The term sharpened false edge will be used throughout this book. Most knowledgeable Bowie knife collectors know that this term is defined as "the back, or top, edge of the blade has been sharpened to make the knife double edge on the clip point."
This Bowie Knife was likely Theater Made on one of the Fiji Islands during WWII. The 6 1/2" clip point blade has a sharpened false edge on the top of the clip of the blade. The cross guard is made of brass and held on with three large copper pins. The wooden handle scales, as well as the pommel, are made out of a medium brown hard wood. The knife is of average quality. The heavy-duty leather pancake sheath has a wooden liner and a copper band at the top. It appears to be bound with a leather bootlace. On the front of the sheath is a very interesting shield type emblem made of tortoise shell that has an aluminum palm tree and the words FIJI. Collectors value $250.00 with sheath. Please note the value of this sheath is 3/4" the value of the combination. (Wright Collection)

This clip point Bowie Knife has an 8 1/4" blade that is 2" wide. It has a sharpened false edge on top of the clip point. There is a large blood groove in the center of the blade. The thick S shaped cross guard is made of stainless steel. Micarta, along with aluminum and white spacers, was used to construct the handle. Collectors value $500.00. (Wright Collection)

The 8 3/4" blade of this clip point Bowie was made from a file. Both blade and cross guard have been chrome plated to help prevent rusting. The crown of a deer horn was used to make the handle. It is not known why, but deer horn handle knives were rare during the WWII time period. The front of the quality leather sheath has been heavily embossed with a floral design. Collectors value $375.00 (Wright Collection)

This picture contains two fine WWII hand made Bowie Knives. The top knife has a blade that is 10" long and 2 3/4" at the widest point. This knife belonged to a veteran from Rinely, PA. The lower knife has a 9 3/16" blade and is 14" overall. The ends of the cross guard are shaped like arrowhead points. Both knives have original sheaths. Collectors value (top) $450.00 (bottom) $325.00. (Ballard Collection)

These two knives are very similar in style and construction. They are made in the style of the famous V-44 Bowie fighting knife. The top knife has a 7 3/8" blade that is 1 3/4" wide. This heavy-duty knife has a thick brass hand guard and a large oval handle. The sheath is bound along the outside edge with leather lacing. The bottom knife is somewhat larger. It has an 8 1/2" blade that is 2" wide. It has a stainless steel hand guard. The aluminum pommel is bird head shaped to help the hand from slipping off the end of the knife. The sheath is plain but well made. Collectors value (top) $300.00 (bottom) $250.00. (Wright Collection)

Below, Left: The knuckle knife pictured is marked on the handle "J.H.L. 1943." It has a 7 1/4" blade and has an aluminum knuckle bow. The handle was made from a 20 mm shell case. The top knife has a 9 3/16" blade and is 15 1/4" overall. The center knife has an upswept blade and is very unusual in design. Collectors value with sheath (top) $275.00 (center) $125.00 (bottom) $400.00. (Ballard Collection)

This knife is of high quality in design, fit, and finish. It was made out of a Kerney & Foot file. The blade is 6 3/8" long, more than 3/16" thick, and has a sharpened false edge. The sheath is of the same quality as the knife. The marking of "I.H. PENNISTON MAKER 1st CAV. SCH. DET. FORT RILEY, KANSAS" is on the keeper strap and the back of the sheath. Collectors value $450.00. (Wright Collection)

Pictured above is a nice 6 7/8" clip point Theater Knife. The red, white, and blue spacers are made out of poker chips. The sheath is outstanding, being a two-piece pancake style that is finely tooled. Collectors value $250.00 (with sheath). (Wright Collection)

All knives on this page have Bowie clip blades. The blades range in length from 5 3/4" to 6 3/4". The first knife to the left in the bottom picture belonged to a sailor. He decorated the sheath of his knife with the name of ten places he was during WWII. Collectors value (top, left to right) $225.00, $300.00, $250.00, $175.00 (lower, left to right) $225.00, $200.00, $150.00, $125.00. (Wright Collection)

Both knives pictured above were made by the same unknown maker. The top knife has a 7 1/4" clip blade. Both knives have the blades brazed into their cast brass handle frames. The Plexiglass handles are applied over colored spacer handle material that has an American Flag on it. Collectors value (top) $250.00 (Wright Collection) (lower) $275.00. (Hunt Collection)

This knife has an 8 1/8" blade that is 1 13/16" wide. This knife is well above average quality in design, fit, and finish. It has an aluminum hand guard with grooves cut into the top to help prevent the thumb from slipping. This knife has a brass pommel. Micarta, as well as Plexiglass spacers were used in the handle. The leather sheath is plain but well made. Collectors value $375.00. (Wright Collection)

This knife has an unusual cross guard. The aluminum cross guard is bent down in the front to help protect the fingers and hand. The 8 3/8" blade is 1/4" thick. The handle materials include Bakelite, copper, and aluminum. The front of the heavy-duty sheath is made from ray skin. Collectors value $375.00. (Wright Collection)

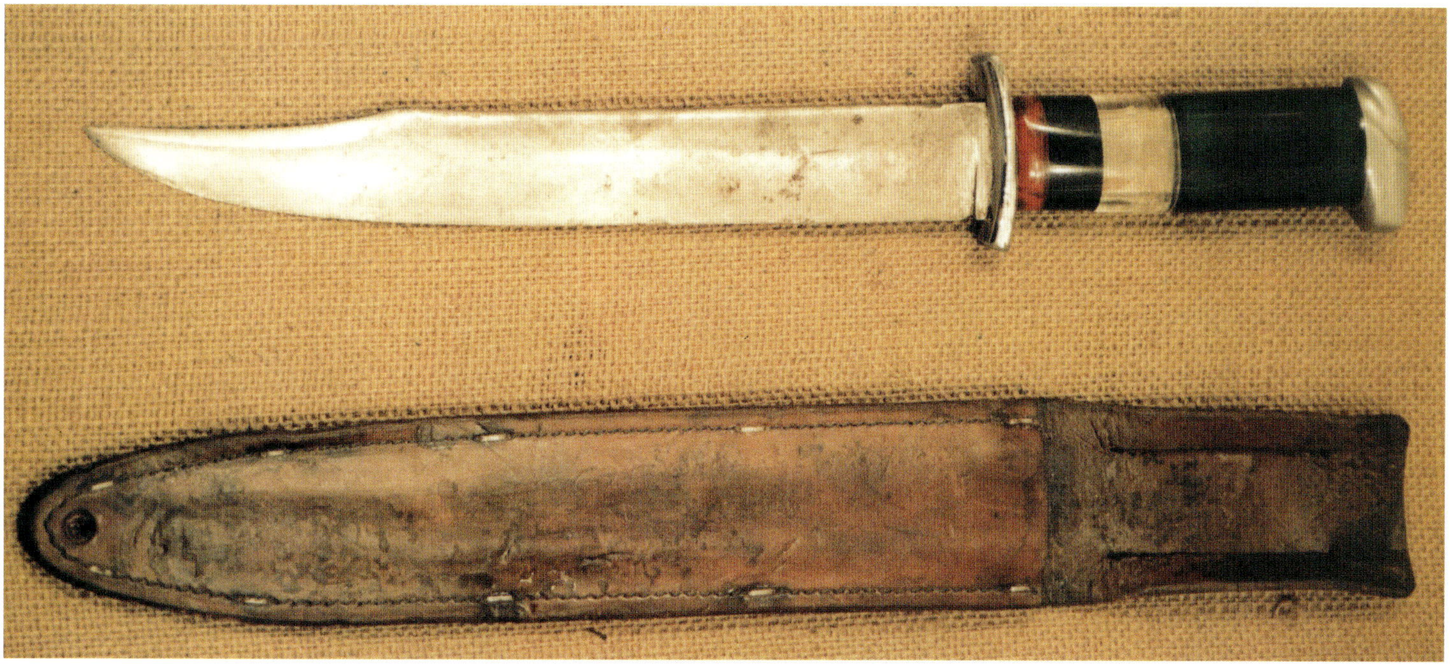

This WWII Bowie Knife has a 9 3/4" clip blade that was made from a file. The handle is made from clear and colored Lucite. The cross guard and pommel are made out of aluminum. Collectors value $275.00. (Wright Collection)

The top Bowie Knife in the picture above has a 9 1/2" blade. It has a large brass tear drop shaped hand guard and aluminum pommel. Red and black Micarta, along with brass were used to make the handle. The lower knife has a 7 3/16" blade, brass cross guard and pommel, and red Micarta handle spacers. Collectors value (top) $275.00 (lower) $250.00. (Wright Collection)

The lower knife in the picture has an 8 3/8" Bowie clip blade that is 3/16" thick. The top knife, while not a Bowie Knife, is unusual and has a 7 3/4" double edge blade that is 3/16" thick. The cross guard is S shaped up and down and back and forth. This well made fighting knife has a quality heavy-duty leather sheath. Collectors value (top) $275.00 (lower) $250.00. (Wright Collection)

This well made Bowie style knife was made from a 1/4" thick file. The blade length is 7 3/8" and has an overall length of 12". It has an aluminum cross guard and pommel. The handle is made using many spacers, consisting of red, black, aluminum, and leather. The sheath is made of two layers of leather sewn together and double stitched. The snap on the keeper strap is marked on the back "UNITED CARR." I am not sure of the history of this company, however, I have seen many WWII Theater Knives with snaps made by this maker. I have not seen sheaths with snaps marked "UNITED CARR" I thought were made later than WWII. To me, this is a clue when trying to date an old unknown knife with its original sheath. Collectors value $400.00. (Wright Collection)

Bowie Knives similar to the ones pictured above were commonly made and used during the Civil War. These knives were made during WWII and fall into the category of Theater Knives. The top knife has an 8" clip point blade with a sharpened false edge. It has a German silver cross guard and pommel. The handles are made out of black Micarta. The lower knife has a 9 1/16" blade and is 14 7/16"in overall length. The design of this knife is similar to Bowie Knives made in the 1830s. It has a dog bone shaped handle. Collectors value (top) $325.00 (lower) $250.00. (Ballard Collection)

Here are four large WWII Theater Bowie knives. All are of excellent quality in design, fit, and finish. The blades have lengths from 7 1/16" to 8 7/16". While the blades are not over 8 1/2" long, these knives are big when actually held in the hand. I believe the same unknown maker made the bottom knives in each picture. They have the same dimensions, and the blades are ground the same way. Collectors value (from top to bottom) $350.00, $500.00, $300.00, $500.00. (Ballard Collection)

This knife has a very similar blade to a Marbles Trailmaker™. In fact, if you hold one on top of the other you cannot tell the difference. The difference is this knife is hand made and has a large blood groove in each side of the blade. It also has a large stainless steel cross guard that is professionally brazed to the blade. The sheath looks similar to the Marbles sheath, except this sheath is wood lined and is made to be attached to a web pistol belt. Collectors value $750.00. (Wright Collection)

This large knife is a bit of a mystery to me. It appears to be of WWII vintage and to be hand made and of very good quality. The blade is 9 3/4" long, 2 1/8" wide, and 1/4" thick. There is a blood groove in one side and a design stamped into both sides. The handle is made from black buffalo horn and leather spacers. I hope someone can identify this knife. Collectors value unknown. (Wright Collection)

An exceptionally well made Theater Knife is pictured above. It has a 7 3/4" Bowie clip blade with a sharpened false edge. The blade is 1 1/4" wide and is 1/8" thick. It has an aluminum cross guard and pommel that extends below the handle to form a better grip. The handle is made using brass, aluminum, and red and black spacers that vary in thickness. The handmade heavy-duty leather sheath is plain, but very well made. Collectors value $300.00. (Wright Collection)

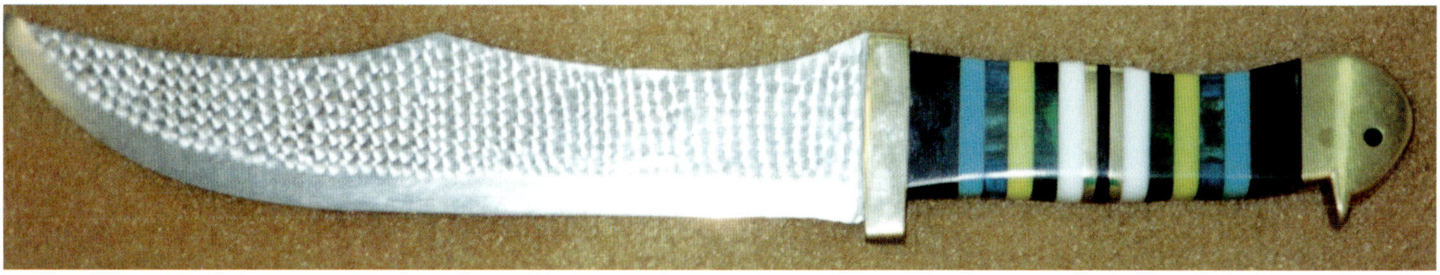

This big clip point Bowie has an 8 1/2" blade that could have been made out of a power hacksaw blade. It has a thick brass hand guard and brass pommel in the shape of a bird's head. The handle is made using different colors of Lucite spacers. The blade has a swirled pattern finish that is known as being "Engine Turned." Collectors value $175.00. (Wright Collection)

Below, Left: The group of Theater Knives pictured here is above average in fit and finish. They were made using many different types of handle materials. Some of the materials include Bakelite, Plexiglass, aluminum, brass, and Micarta. The blade lengths are from 6 1/8" to 7 5/8". Collectors value (from left to right) $200.00, $300.00, $175.00, $250.00, $200.00, $300.00. These prices include sheaths of similar quality to their respective knife. (Ballard Collection)

Above: This smaller clip point knife has a 5 1/4" blade that was likely made from a power hacksaw blade. This knife is very attractive and well made. The handle is very colorful with brown, red, and aluminum spacers. The sheath is of top quality, being bound with thick leather lacing and decorated with a series of lines. Collectors value $125.00. (Wright Collection)

One of the things about collecting or making knives is personal preference, which may help explain why there are thousands of different Theater Knives. One person might really like a knife for many reasons; another person may not like that knife at all. The knife you like might not be a great piece or of high dollar value, but there is just something about it you really like, and like it every time you think about it or look at it. I really like this knife. This knife has a 7 5/8" clip blade that is 1 1/4" wide and 1/16" thick. The large oval handle is made of red and black Micarta spacers. The cross guard is stainless steel, and the pommel is aluminum. The sheath is an issue MK2 sheath. Collectors value $225.00, but it is priceless to me. (My Collection, BILL WRIGHT)

This large Bowie has an upswept 11" blade that is 1 5/8" wide and 3/16" thick. The blade is made of stainless steel and has a large fuller, or blood groove, in each side. The knife has a brass S shaped cross guard and many brass handle spacers. The rest of the handle is made of red, brown, and black Micarta spacers. The total length of the knife is 16 1/4". The outstanding sheath is extremely well made and has a large panel on the front side hand tooled with a leaf pattern. Both knife and sheath are of outstanding quality in both fit and finish. Collectors value $875.00. (Wright Collection)

An unusual double edge clip point Bowie is pictured at right. The blade length is 8 1/2" long and is 1 1/2" wide. The total length measures 13". The blade is sharp all the way down both sides. It has a heavy aluminum cross guard and pommel. The handle is made using brown and red Micarta, and has aluminum spacers. The well made leather sheath has the initials "JB" on the back, and the front is marked "USN, PEARL HARBOR, 1943." Collectors value $475.00. (Wright Collection)

The two WWII Bowie Knives pictured here have clip point blades. The bottom knife has a 7" hand forged blade and is 11 3/4" overall. This knife has a nicely formed nickel silver cross guard. The handle is made of thick red and black Micarta spacers. The pommel is aluminum. The heavy-duty leather sheath has a brass liner and is carved "Made by Daniel H. Martin Feb 13, 1939." The slits in the back of the sheath are wide enough for a web pistol belt. Martin knew the war was coming, and he would need a sturdy knife to take with him into battle. The knife on the top is a high quality Theater Knife. It has an 8" blade and is 13" overall. The hand guard, pommel, and silver colored handle spacers are stainless steel. The quality leather sheath is made pancake style. Collectors value (top) $400.00 (bottom) $425.00. (Wright Collection)

Above is a nice WWII Theater Knife with a 7" clip point blade and a sharpened false edge on top of the blade. This knife has an arrowhead shaped hand guard made of steel. The pommel appears to be made of stone, but it is made of aluminum. I am not sure if it has turned this color naturally or has been treated to give it this appearance. The handle materials include red, brown, and black Micarta with aluminum and 1/4" Plexiglass spacers. The sheath is well made, but plain. Collectors value $150.00. (Wright Collection)

This is a high quality WWII Theater Knife. It has a 7 7/16" clip point blade that is 3/16" thick. There is a well-formed blood groove in each side of the blade. It has a brass cross guard, pommel, and handle spacers. The other handle spacers are made of red and clear Plexiglass. The hand made sheath is decorated with clamshell designs. Collectors value $600.00. (Wright Collection)

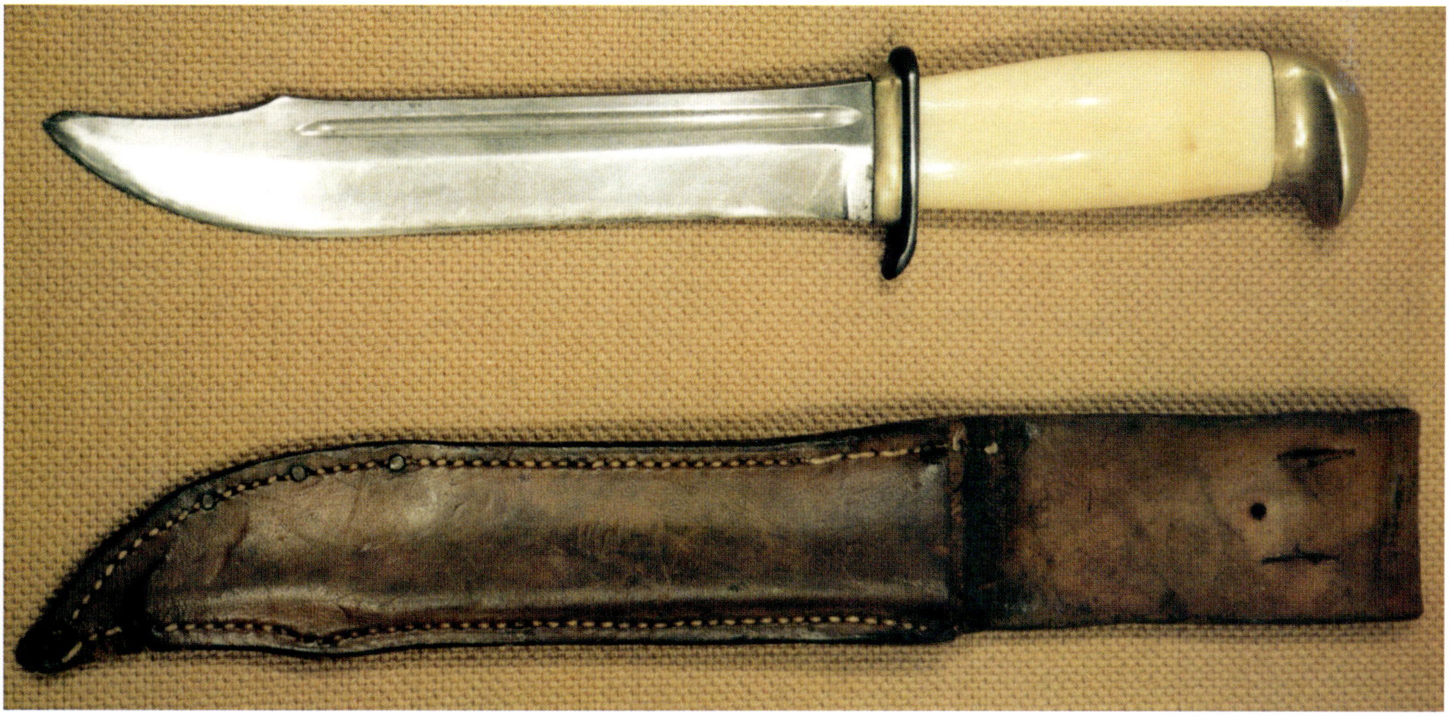

Ivory handle WWII knives are rare. This knife not only has an ivory handle, but it is high quality in design, fit, and finish. It has a 7 1/2" clip point blade that is 1/4" thick. A brass collar is tightly fitted on the blade above the steel hand guard. The sculptured brass pommel is screwed into the end of the knife. The sheath has a large loop so that a web pistol belt will fit through. Collectors value $450.00. (Wright Collection)

The above pictured knife has a 7" clip point blade and is 11 3/4" in total length. This is my first Theater Knife, and is so marked on the tag on the blade. This is a well made knife that has a brass cross guard and pommel, which has a lanyard ring. The handle is made of black Micarta and aluminum spacers. The original sheath is hand stitched with string. Collectors value $175.00. (Wright Collection)

These two WWII Theater Knives have clip point blades. Both knives and sheaths are above average quality. The top knife has a 6 5/8" blade, heavy cross guard, and aluminum pommel, and has a multi-colored Micarta and aluminum spacer handle. The lower knife has an 8 1/4" blade and a heavy brass cross guard and pommel. The center sections of this handle are made of walnut. Collectors value $375.00 each. (Wright Collection)

The knife to the left has a heavy blade that is 7 1/2" long. It has a cast aluminum hand guard and pommel. The handle was made using Plexiglass, aluminum, and red spacers. The knife on the right of this picture has a 7 1/2" blade. The highly polished aluminum cross guard and pommel are well fitted to the handle. There are 3 thick spacers, 2 black, 1 Lucite, and thinner red and aluminum spacers that stand out between the black and Lucite. The well made leather sheath is sewn with a heavy string. A bolt and two nuts were used to make the keeper strap catch. This is a very well made knife and sheath. Collectors value $200.00 each. (Wright Collection)

This Bowie Knife could easily be mistaken for a Civil War knife. It has a 9 15/16" blade and is 14 3/4" overall. The cross guard is soldered to the convex ground blade. The sheath is constructed similar to other sheaths made during the WWII time period. For these reasons I conclude this is a WWII Theater Knife. Collectors value $500.00. (Wright Collection)

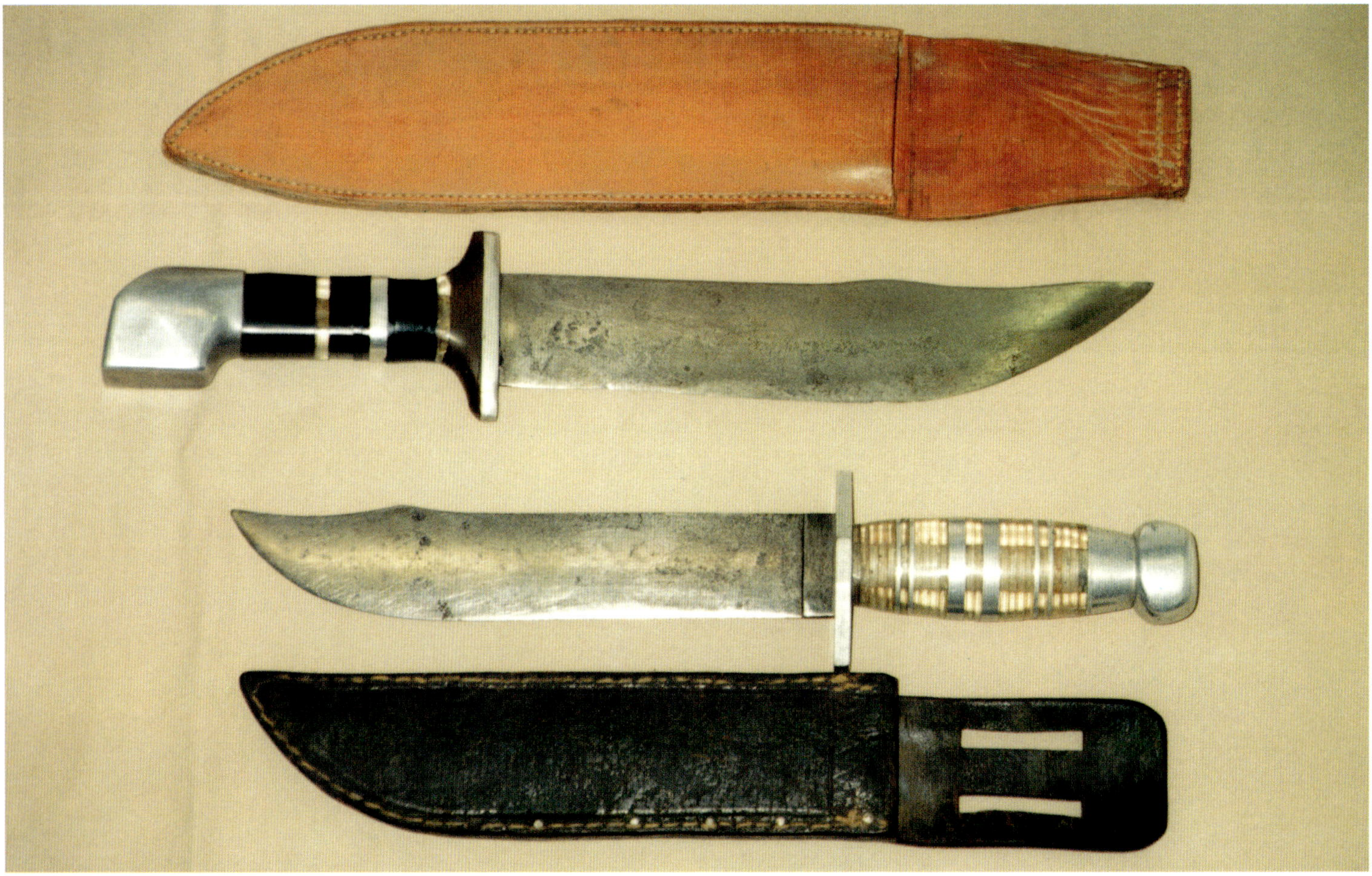

Two large WWII Bowie Knives are pictured above. The top knife has a 9 7/8" blade that is almost 2" wide. This knife has a heavy-duty aluminum cross guard and pommel that could be used as a skull crusher. The lower knife has a somewhat smaller blade. This knife has a thick aluminum cross guard and pommel. Collectors value (top) $275.00 (Wright Collection) (lower) $350.00 (Ballard Collection)

Two WWII horse head Bowie Knives are pictured above. The larger knife to the left has a 10" blade that is 1 7/8" wide and 3/16" thick. This knife comes with a hand crafted fringed leather sheath. The horse head pommels of both knives were hand crafted and cast out of aluminum. The Bowie to the right was made using a standard issue U.S. Navy MK2 blade. The original fiberglass MK2 sheath is inside the hand made leather sheath. Collectors value (left) $675.00 (right) $450.00. (Wright Collection)

This WWII Bowie Knife has a blade that is only 6 1/4" long, but it is 1 3/4" wide. The quality is outstanding in fit and finish. It has an aluminum cross guard and pommel. The handle has red and black Micarta spacers. The sheath has the name "SGT. E.G. STONE" stamped into the back. Collectors value $425.00. (Wright Collection)

The quality Bowie pictured above was made during WWII. The 7 7/8" blade has a high polish. This knife has a stainless steel cross guard and aluminum pommel. The handle was made using Bakelite, Micarta, and Plexiglass, with copper and aluminum as spacer materials. The quality of the sheath matches that of the knife. Collectors value $300.00. (Wright Collection

The blade of the left knife has a 1/2" thick forged bolster at the bottom of the blade. The 7 3/4" blade then quickly tapers to 1/16" thick the full length of the blade. The knife has a stainless steel cross guard and pommel. The center knife has a 7 1/4" blade that is silver soldered to a stainless steel cross guard. The knife and sheath to the right was purchased in Eugene, OR. I was told that "it was made locally during WWII." Collectors value (from left to right) $275.00, $225.00, $200.00. (Wright Collection)

This knife has a highly polished 7" clip point blade with a sharpened false edge. It has a steel cross guard and an aluminum pommel. Brown, red, and black Micarta, as well as aluminum were used to make the handle. Collectors value $300.00. (Wright Collection)

The top knife has a blade that is 6 3/4" long, 1 1/2" wide, and 5/32" thick. The lower knife has a 6" blade. The handle has patriotic red, white, and blue spacers. Collectors value (top) $150.00 (lower) $225.00. (Wright Collection)

The knife pictured above has a 6 7/16" blade. This high quality knife has a mirror finish blade. It has a nickel sliver hand guard and pommel. The use of nickel silver on a WWII knife is rare, because nickel was a regulated war commodity. The body of the handle was made using alternating red and black Micarta spacers. Collectors value $175.00. (Wright Collection)

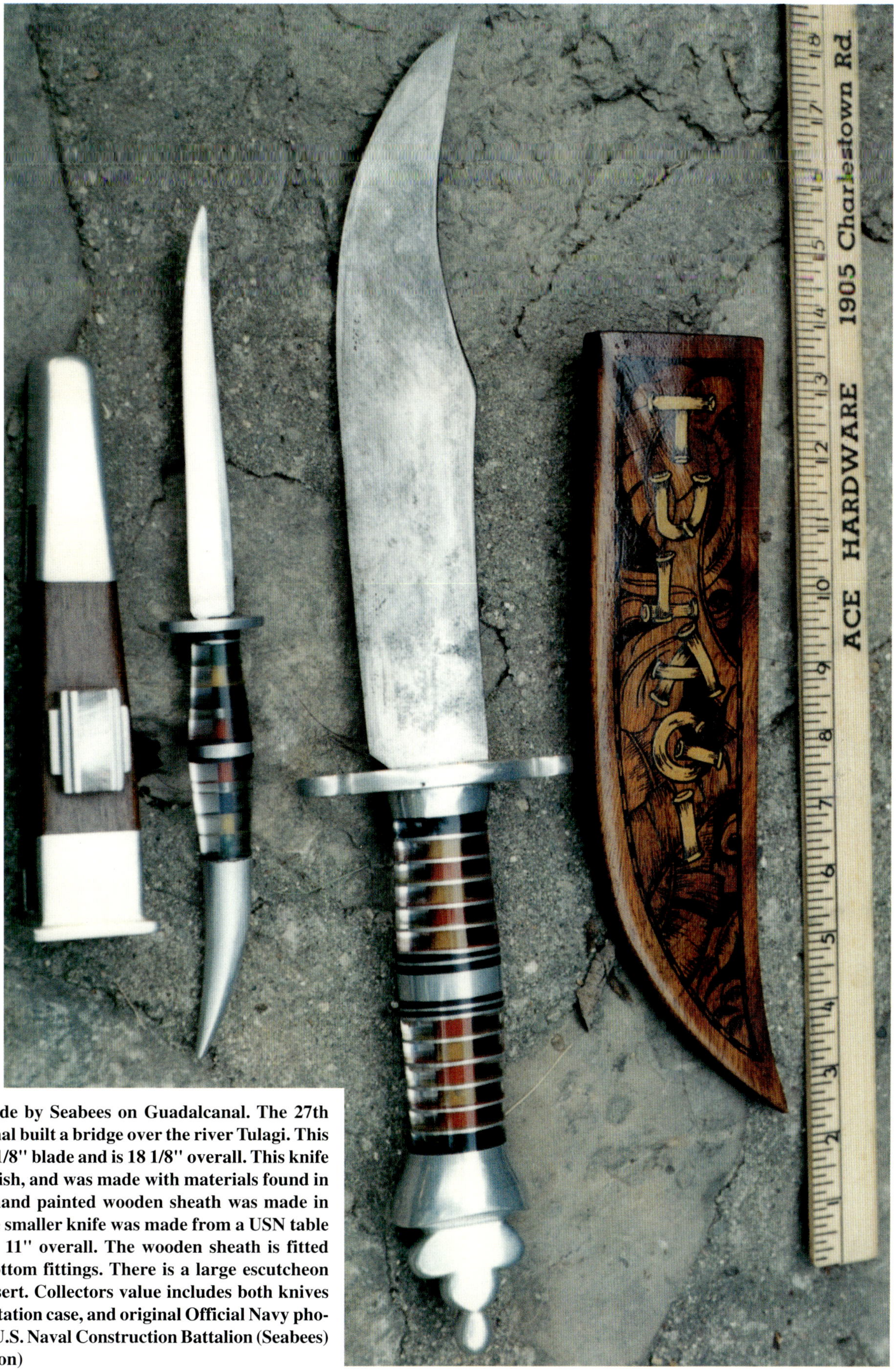

These two knives were made by Seabees on Guadalcanal. The 27th Seabees while at Guadalcanal built a bridge over the river Tulagi. This large Bowie Knife has a 10 1/8" blade and is 18 1/8" overall. This knife is high quality in fit and finish, and was made with materials found in this Theater of War. The hand painted wooden sheath was made in two pieces. The blade of the smaller knife was made from a USN table knife. This knife measures 11" overall. The wooden sheath is fitted with aluminum top and bottom fittings. There is a large escutcheon plate with a black pearl insert. Collectors value includes both knives with sheaths, an oak presentation case, and original Official Navy photographs taken by the 27th U.S. Naval Construction Battalion (Seabees) $1,500.00. (Wright Collection)

Pictured on this page are Theater Knives that vary in shape and design, however, I would consider most as being small Bowie Knives. Collectors value (top Left to right) $175.00, $150.00, $100.00, $100.00 (lower left to right) $125.00, $125.00, $100.00, $175.00. (Wright Collection)

This large Bowie type knife does not have a long blade. The blade measures 7" long, 1 3/4" wide, and 1/4" thick. The aluminum cross guard and pommel are curved to fit the hand. The handle is made using a variety of materials that include Micarta, brass, and aluminum. The front of this heavy-duty sheath is embossed with designs. Collectors value $400.00. (Wright Collection)

Three-quality WWII hand made Bowie type knives are pictured above. The blade lengths measure (from left to right) 7", 8 1/4", and 7 7/8". All three have thick, well made blades. Collectors value (left to right) $300.00, $250.00, $150.00. (Wright Collection)

4

Identified Knife Makers

The knives in this chapter will be identified as to their maker. In some cases individuals made their own personal fighting knife. In other cases they also made knives for other people. Some of the knives shown in this chapter were made and sold by custom knife makers of the day, who have since become famous. Other knives that are identified were made in factories and machine shops large and small. The owners and employees made a number of these knives on their own personal time. Many of these knives were donated to employees or their family members that were headed to war. Some were donated in small quantities directly to military posts and knife collection campaigns, such as "Save a Life with a Knife." Everyone donated whatever he or she could to the war effort.

John Carlson and Sons Inc., Springfield, MA, were manufactures of ice skates. The knife pictured above was made by them during WWII. The blade of this knife, which is 6 5/8" long, appears to have been made from the blade of an ice skate. This knife has a stacked leather washer handle. It has a steel cross guard and a flat piece of steel on the end that holds the handle together. This flat piece of steel is turned up on the bottom side, and is drilled to form a hole for a lanyard. In this case a lanyard is a cord or strip of leather that is attached to the knife. The owner's wrist goes through this so that the knife will not be dropped when being used. Collections value $350.00. (Wright Collection)

Right: The blades of these WWII Bowie Knives are marked "SMITHS." It is believed they were made in New Zealand. There are several different patterns of "SMITHS" Knives known, which include Bowies, daggers, and knuckle knives. The aluminum handle knife pictured above is cast in the form of a Tiki. In New Zealand the Tiki represents an ancestor. Both aluminum and brass Tiki handle knives are known. The blades of the knives pictured above measure 6 3/4" and 7". Collectors value (Tiki) $500.00 (stag Handle) $350.00. (Wright Collection)

Ernest Warther of Dover, OH, made this knife in 1943. He made a little more than 1,100 knives during WWII. His knives came with brass and aluminum cross guards and trim. He used woods like ebony and cocobolo, as well as genuine ivory for handle materials. His knives were unmarked; however, the sheaths, which were made out of copper on the front and stainless steel on the back, were marked "E. WARTHER, DOVER, O. U.S.A." The blade length on the above pictured knife is 6 3/4". The overall length is 11". Today these knives are rare and highly sought after by collectors. Collectors value $5,000.00 (Wright Collection)

The engraving on the 7 3/4" double edge blade of this WWII knife reads, "Made By John Barlock 438 E. Front St. Dover, Ohio." The back is engraved "P.F.C. Earl McDaniels A.S.N. 35381989 Co. D 32nd Bn 8th Regt." The total length of this knife is 13". It has a German silver cross guard and aluminum pommel that is secured with a 1/4" steel pin. The handle was made using copper, aluminum, and red and black Micarta spacers. The sheath has a copper front and a brass back with an aluminum belt holder. John Barlock made both knife and sheath, however, Ernest Warther from Dover, OH, must have influenced him. Collectors value $1,000.00 with sheath. (Wright Collection)

ROEBUCK WORKS KNIVES

The One Man Operation of Howard Cole

Written By Roger Ballard

Howard Cole, the noted author and collector, has been the recognized leader and authority of U.S. Military knives for the past 50 years. It was truly the end of an era when Howard's untimely death took him away from his many friends and fellow collectors. Howard is well known for the four outstanding books that he authored on U.S. Military Knives, and the knives that he made during and after WWII in his home workshop. He is known world-wide for his accomplishments. His last book was all about one of his first loves—the Skinning Knife.

Several years ago I asked Howard how he got started making fighting knives during WWII. He told me that one of his friends came to visit him in the early 1940s and wanted to show him a knife that he had made. It was a homemade knuckle knife that he had just constructed (see page 79 in Cole's book I). After his friend had gone, Howard told me that after thinking about it, he believed that he could make a knife a little better than the one he had just seen. The knife that had been brought by a friend had actually inspired Howard to create a fighting knife that is now established as a key component in any advanced U.S. Military Knife collection.

Roebuck Works was the name assigned to Howard Cole's home workshop where he constructed fine knives and home furniture during and after WWII. Roebuck is a section of the city in Birmingham, Alabama, near Howard's home residence. "Roebuck Works" was stamped on most of his post war knives, along with his initials, MHC and /or MH Cole.

During WWII he produced knives completely void of all markings. Howard made over 300 knives, and most of them were brass knuckle fighting knives. Approximately 50 of these knives have nine points, and the rest had eight points on the knuckle guard. None of the knives or sheaths were marked during the WWII time period. Only after WWII did his name, initials, and /or "Roebucks Works" appear on his products.

Collectors are still seeking Cole knives that were made during or after WWII. Most of the knife collectors that I know seem to think that to own a Cole knife is to own a piece of history.

One interesting event occurred when Howard and I traveled north a few years ago to attend the Allentown Gun Show in Pennsylvania. On a side trip, before the show, we paid a visit to the American Military Edged Weapons Museum in Intercourse, PA. Located in the rear of the building on one of the display walls was a section devoted to M.H. Cole and his WWII knives. When Howard saw this his surprised reaction was, "Well—I never thought that I would make it to a museum!"

Howard not only made it to a museum, but his impact on collectors of U.S. Military Knives has been indelible. He has made a lasting contribution to the collecting world with his five books and his willingness to share information with others, and with his passing it is, indeed, an end of an era.

See August 1992 issue of the Blade Magazine and February 2000 issue of Knife World for more information on Howard Cole and his Roebuck Works Knives.

Above, Right: Pictured is the scarce first model 9 point knuckle knife made by M.H. Cole during WWII. He reportedly made 50, but no more than 75 of these 9 point knives. Most of these knives were sold without sheaths, however, when a sheath was needed Cole ordered them from Blackhorse Leather Works in Birmingham, AL. Collectors value $5,000.00. (Wright Collection)

Below, Right: The two M.H. Cole knives pictured were made during WWII. The top knife is the second design, 8 point knuckle knife with a Blackhorse sheath. The bottom knife is very unusual and rare. It, too, has a Blackhorse sheath. Collectors value (knuckle knife) $5,000.00 (double edge dagger) $3,500.00. (Ballard Collection)

E.W. Stone Sr. Knife

Written By: E.W. Stone, Jr.

The Stone knuckle knife started out as a crude set of brass knuckles acquired from an old sailor who had spent much time in China. In this original pattern, the skull was not very well done and detail on the cobra was lacking. The skull was revamped, and the cobra handle was given much more detail. The first castings were done in Darwin, Australia. A total of six knives were made there. Of the knives produced, all were of good quality in the castings. In those early attempts to get the method of casting to an artistic stage, low quality handles were melted off so none would leave the foundry.

The early pattern knives are characterized by a lighter, thinner cobra, which comprises the guard and knuckles. The integrity of the castings is not compromised since the detail and pattern improvements are present, but the strength of these components was thought to be too flimsy. This perceived weakness was corrected in the next stage of development.

Invasion knives were made in large numbers. Propellers from Mitsubishi seaplanes were recovered to supply the duraluminum to make the alloy used in the castings of the knife handles. At the same time, some chrome molybdenum steel struts were removed to provide the material for forging some high quality blades. These castings had heavier guard and knuckles, as well as increased detail in all areas of the casting, since techniques for getting a consistent product had been worked out. The easiest way to identify knives of this period is not the casting but the detailing, finishing, and polishing.

With the invasions of Saipan, Tinian, and Guam looming, there was no time for a great amount of finish work. Many Marines needed their knives done by the next day! Some Marines said not to even bother with anything but the basic casting work that would render the knife usable. They would do the rest themselves. At this point a new feature enters the picture. Marines, since the battle of Guadalcanal onward, were called "Mud Marines," or "grunts." Although these terms are related to pigs the Marines adopted them as a compliment to their toughness. Who else could live and fight in the mud so well?

As a tribute, a few knives were made with "pig noses" on the skull, instead of the standard form. The "pig nose" configuration is, as it sounds, a round, flattened structure. This change was an instant success, and the Marines wanted knives with this feature. The exact number of pieces made in this way is not known, but it is one of the less common variations seen. Unfortunately, the highest casualties occurred among this group of the assault troops.

Later war knives comprised the final evolution of the knife pattern. With more lead-time to prepare for upcoming campaigns, these knives appear to have even more detail.

The fact is that with more time for finishing and polishing the castings, detail was greatly enhanced. In the post- Saipan, Tinain, and Guam period another change took place. This time it was not the handle, but the blade used that differed. With D-Day over and the war in Europe winding down, new troops with new equipment were making their way to the Pacific. The first M3 Trench knives began to appear. Before only Ka-Bar and a few Pal blades had been used in the Stones knives. About ten knives were made using the M3 Trench knife blade.

Most knives were cast in the foundry aboard the sub tender USS Holland, where E.W. Stone was the chief molder. The reason for the development of the cast aluminum handle was the extreme conditions in the Pacific Theater. Marines wanted a grip that would not slip, twist, mildew, or rot. They were also interested in knuckles, and an efficient skull crusher. About a quarter of the knives had the knuckles removed for faster access. Most of the knives were cast on issue blades, as discussed earlier, and utilized the standard sheath. Total production of Stone knives of all varieties for the WWII was 250-300.

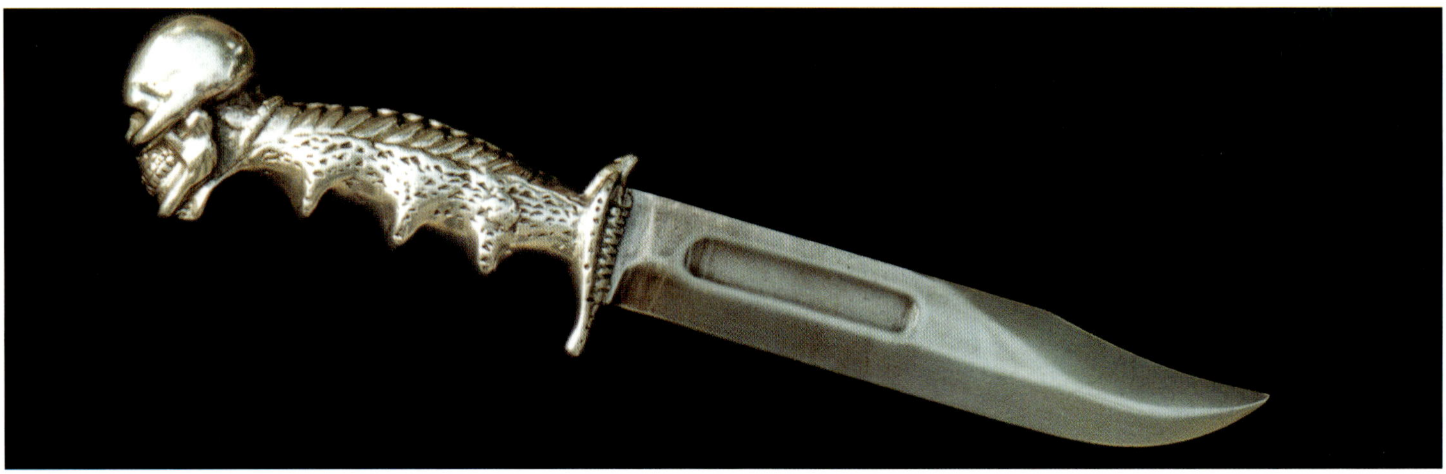

The knife pictured above was not only made by E.W. Stone, Sr., but was his own personal WWII fighting knife. This knife is still in the family today and not for sale.

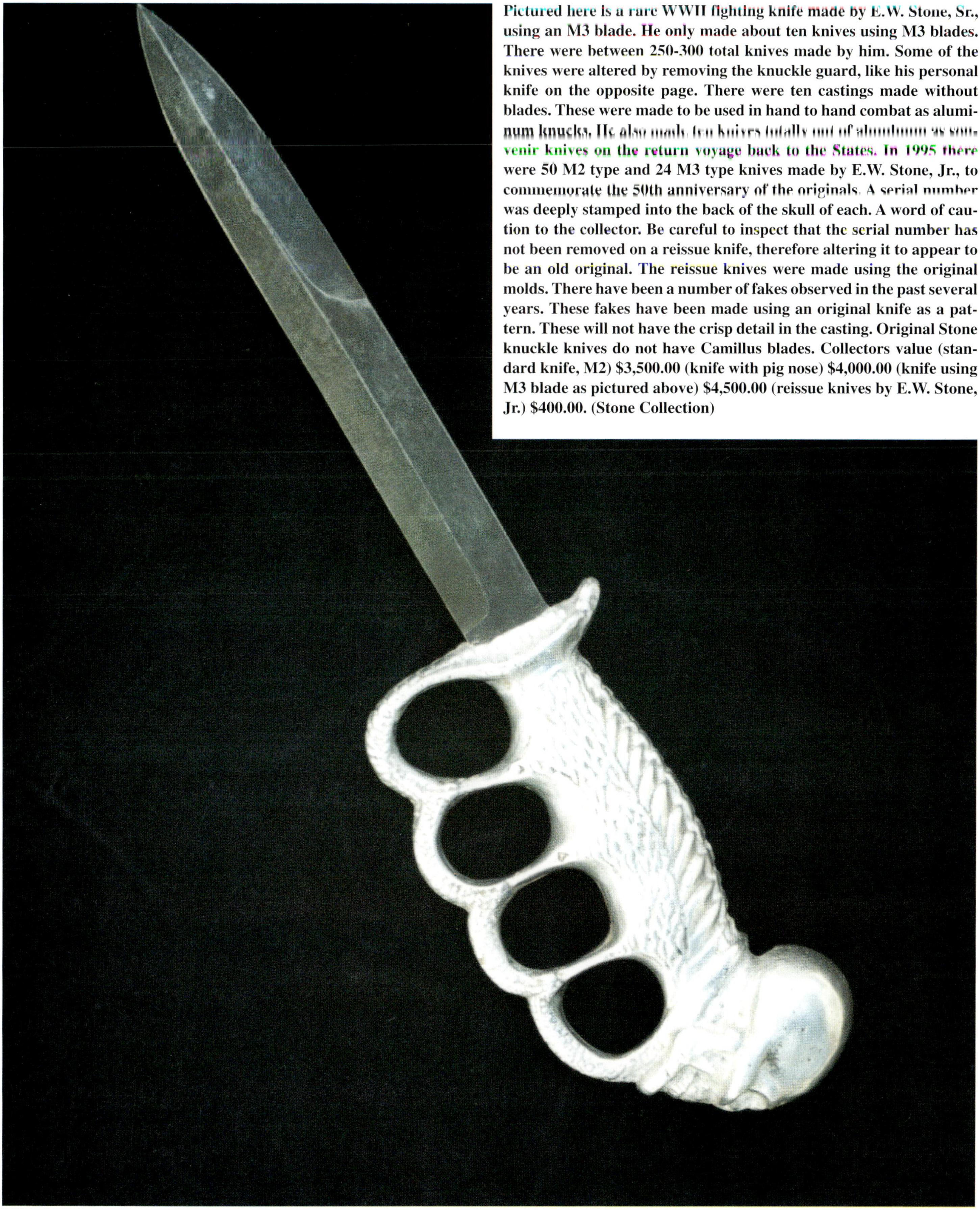

Pictured here is a rare WWII fighting knife made by E.W. Stone, Sr., using an M3 blade. He only made about ten knives using M3 blades. There were between 250-300 total knives made by him. Some of the knives were altered by removing the knuckle guard, like his personal knife on the opposite page. There were ten castings made without blades. These were made to be used in hand to hand combat as aluminum knucks. He also made ten knives totally out of aluminum as souvenir knives on the return voyage back to the States. In 1995 there were 50 M2 type and 24 M3 type knives made by E.W. Stone, Jr., to commemorate the 50th anniversary of the originals. A serial number was deeply stamped into the back of the skull of each. A word of caution to the collector. Be careful to inspect that the serial number has not been removed on a reissue knife, therefore altering it to appear to be an old original. The reissue knives were made using the original molds. There have been a number of fakes observed in the past several years. These fakes have been made using an original knife as a pattern. These will not have the crisp detail in the casting. Original Stone knuckle knives do not have Camillus blades. Collectors value (standard knife, M2) $3,500.00 (knife with pig nose) $4,000.00 (knife using M3 blade as pictured above) $4,500.00 (reissue knives by E.W. Stone, Jr.) $400.00. (Stone Collection)

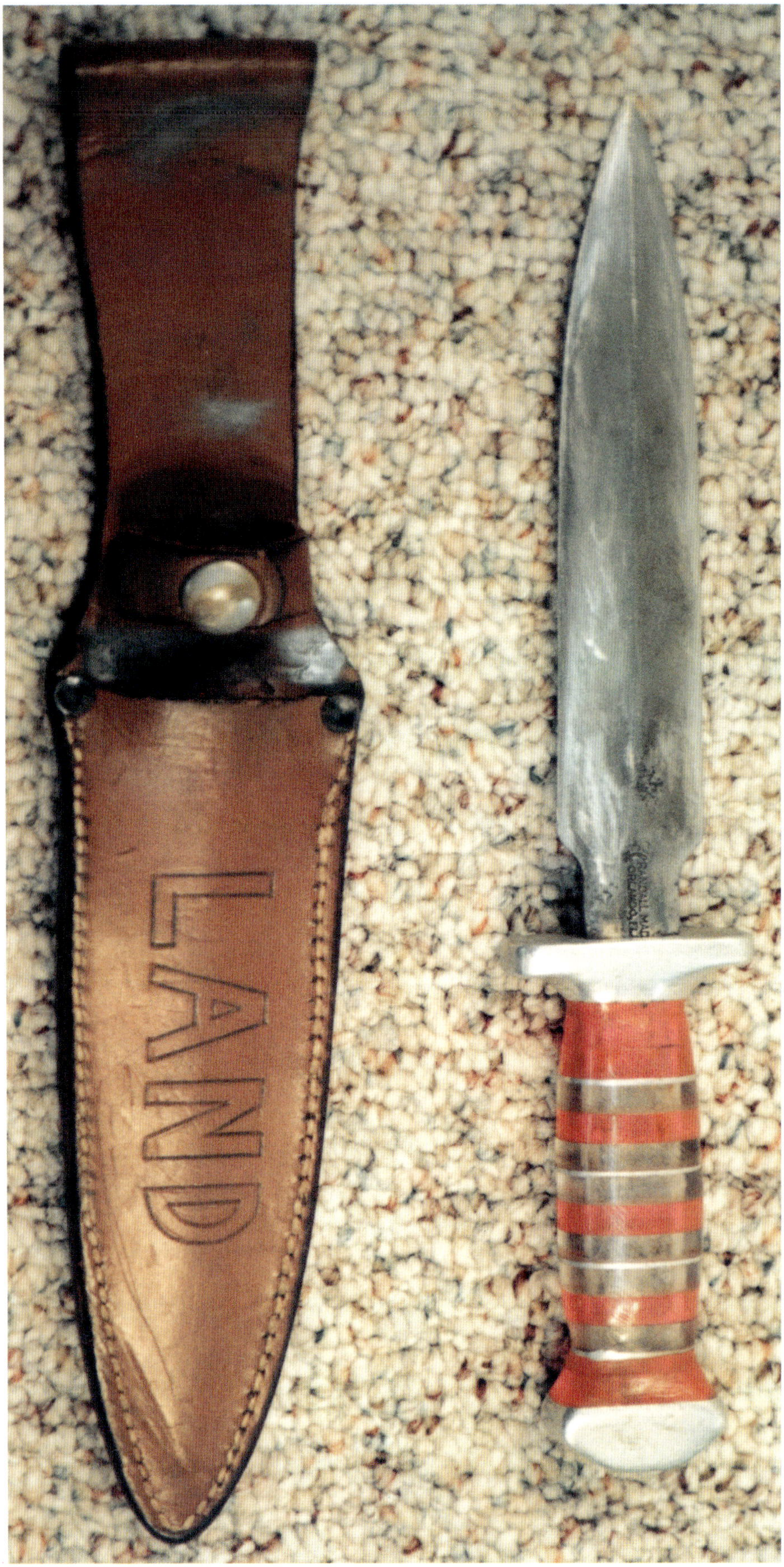

This WWII Randall Knife has been Theater Altered. A Plexiglass spacer handle and heavy-duty aluminum cross guard and pommel have been added to the original Randall 6 5/8" double edge blade. The hand made leather sheath has the word "LAND" cut into it. The back of the snap on the retaining strap is marked "UNITED CARR." This marking is on a lot of WWII sheath retaining strap snaps. Collectors value $1,000.00. (Wright Collection)

The above pictured WWII fighting knife is marked "RANDALL MADE, SPFLD. MASS." Bo Randall, of Orlando, FL, did not make these knives. Bo Randall and William F. Larsen, of Springfield, MA, entered into a partnership on May 20, 1943. Randall would provide the original design and some parts of his knives to be copied. Larsen would have the knives manufactured, sell them, and pay a royalty of $0.50 per knife to Randall. Because of wartime production problems the knives were slow to be made. According to records a total of 1,389 Springfield Randall knives were made mostly between mid-1943 and mid-1944. It is believed that Northampton Cutlery Co. finished and assembled the rough parts furnished by Larsen. It is not known where Larsen got the rough parts. The end of the war came in August 1945, and there was no longer any need for fighting knives. Larsen's last letter to Randall is dated 8-28-45. Stated in the letter he, William Larsen, would be ending the partnership. At that time he reported to Randall that he had forging dies, rough-forged blades, wrist throngs, and 200 knives left. Larsen offered to sell these items to Randall and he declined. It is not known what happened to these left over items. Pictured above is a Randall Springfield Knife. Pictured below is a knife that is believed to be an unmarked Randall Springfield Knife. Collectors value (top) $2,750.00 (below) $1,500.00. (Wright Collection)

The dagger on the top has an 8 1/2" blade and is 13 1/4" in overall length. This knife was used and carried by T/SGT Don Fanti. He was in the medical detachment of a signal warning battalion. He participated in the invasion of Africa, going in at Casablanca. He later served throughout Europe as a Master Sargent. The two clip point knives below were made from machete blades. Sterling Wortham of Birmingham, AL, made these two knives when he was assigned to the Mediterranean Allied Air Force in Bari, Italy, in 1944. The sheaths are marked "STERLING WORTHAM AIR CORPS." To see a picture of Sterling Wortham look in U.S. Military Knives Book IV by Howard Cole, P. 66. Collectors value (dagger) $375.00 (clip point knives) $150.00 each. (Ballard Collection)

The knives at left were made by Everitt. It is unknown who Everitt was or where he made the knives, however, the knives and sheaths were professionally made. The knife on the top is a standard production knife. Removing the knuckle part of the grip has modified the bottom knife. There are other known modified knives like this one. Collectors value (standard) $600.00 (modified) $350.00. (Wright Collection)

There have been several knives like this one showing up in recent years. I have another knife with the same handle that has a Vietnam era jet pilot's blade in it. That blade is marked "MILPAR." The man I got the knife from told me he that he "got the knife at the Milpar Factory." With this knowledge I think the above pictured knife was made by MILPAR during WWII. This knife has a 5 3/4" blade. Collectors value $175.00. (Wright Collection)

This is not a WWII Theater Knife. It was made a few years ago using an old PAL RH36 blade by Roland Delaune of Passadumkeag, ME. It is a custom knife made as an interpretation of the famous Stone Knuckle Knife that was made during WWII. The cost of the knife was $100.00 from the maker. (Wright Collection)

Merrill E. Brown made this knife in 1944 at the Brown Machine Works, located at 314 3rd Street New Albany, IN. Some of the blades were hand forged in a blacksmith shop across the alley behind the machine shop. Brown then finished the blades and took them to the New Albany Aluminum Works, located on rear Market Street, where the handles were cast onto the blades. After receiving the knives back from the foundry he ground, filed and polished the handles, also sharpened and put the final finish on the blade. Charley K. Brown, Merrill's son, helped make the sheaths. The knives were given to the military installation at Fort Knox, KY where they were distributed. There were several designs of the knives, all of which had a one piece cast aluminum handle with an eagle head pommel. Some had the words NAVY KNIFE or ARMY KNIFE in a shield on the front of the cross guard (for examples of these knives see P.84, Knives of the United States Military, World War II, by Mike Silvey). Others were marked U S in the shield. There are different blade designs that include several styles of clip, spear, butcher and double edge blades. Merrill Brown knives are RARE today, rough estimates of 300 were made. I only know of 9, which are held in private collections. The Brown Machine Works made 4 items for the government during WWII. They made: 1. Ring Bolt Hitch (trailer hitch) for Jeeps and trucks. 2. Fin Lock Ring for a 500lb. Bomb. 3.Bomb Base for a 4.2 mortar shell. 4. Valve Stem for plumbing on ships and submarines. A special thanks is given to Charley K. Brown for the above information. The Merrill Brown knife pictured here has a 9 7/8" clip point blade that is 1/16" thick, 1 1/8" wide and is not hand forged. The overall length of the knife is 15 5/8". The blade appears to be made from a piece of scrap steel that was too rough and pitted for standard military production use. The blade is hand ground to remove the pitting and to form the edge. This blade is very sharp and hard (if the blade is hit it rings like a bell). The cast aluminum handle has an eagle head pommel that is stamped 1944 on the top and has the rare U S in the shield on the cross guard (only 2 known). Collectors value $1500.00 (Wright Collection)

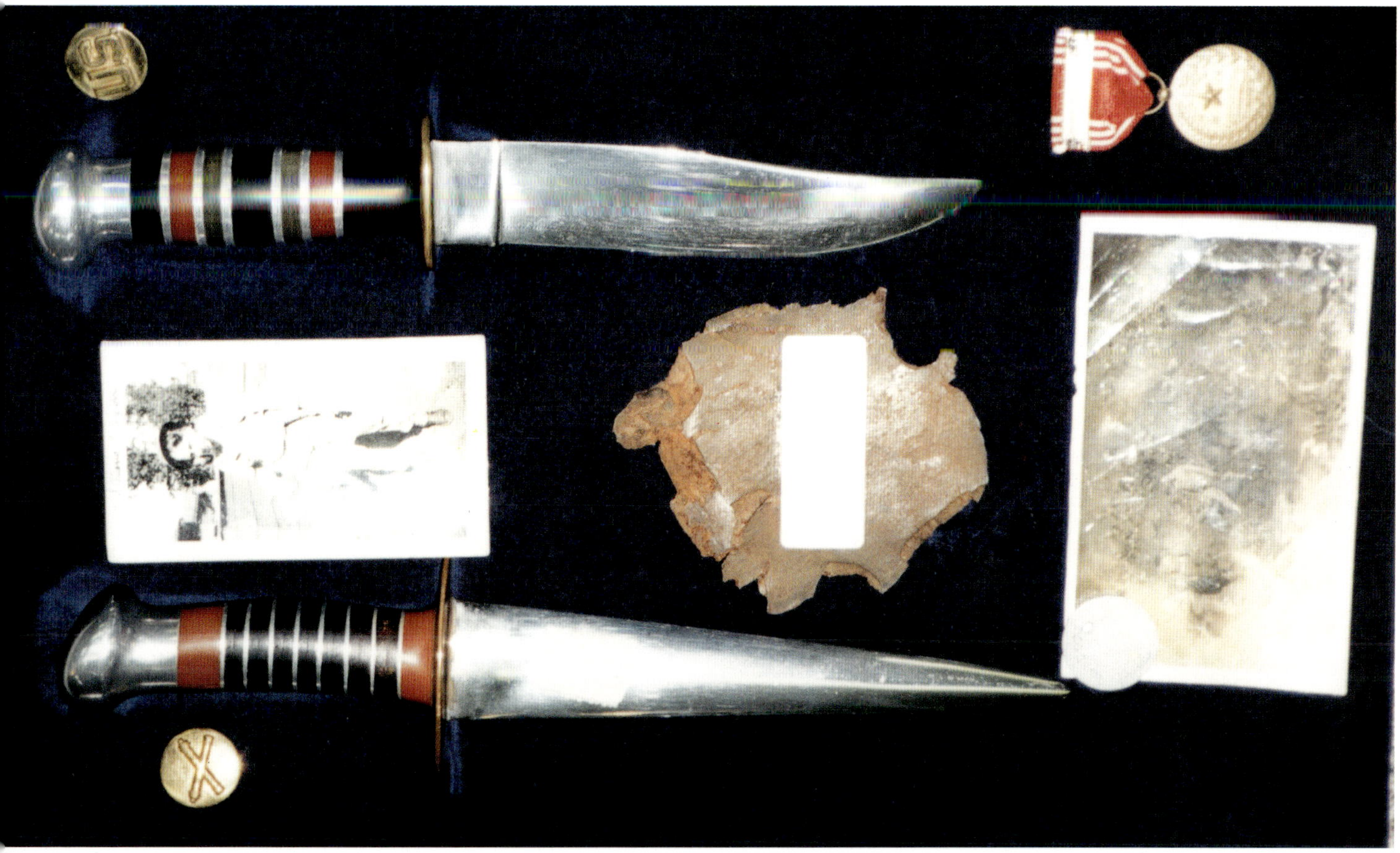

These three knives were made by Cecil H. Doty, who was stationed at Fort Stevens, OR, in 1942. Also pictured above is his photograph and a picture of a large crater. Fort Stevens was the only military base in the U.S. that was bombed by the Japanese during WWII. A fragment of the bomb, and some of his personal effects, such as uniform buttons, a dog tag, and a medal are also pictured. Daggers in the top and bottom pictures both have 7 3/16" blades and are 12 7/16" overall. Both daggers have the same type of copper oval cross guard and a similar handle design using the same type and color of materials. All three knives have colorful handles and exhibit superior quality and craftsmanship. Collectors value for set pictured above without sheaths $1,500.00. (Claussen Collection) Knife pictured at bottom with sheath $750.00. (Wright Collection)

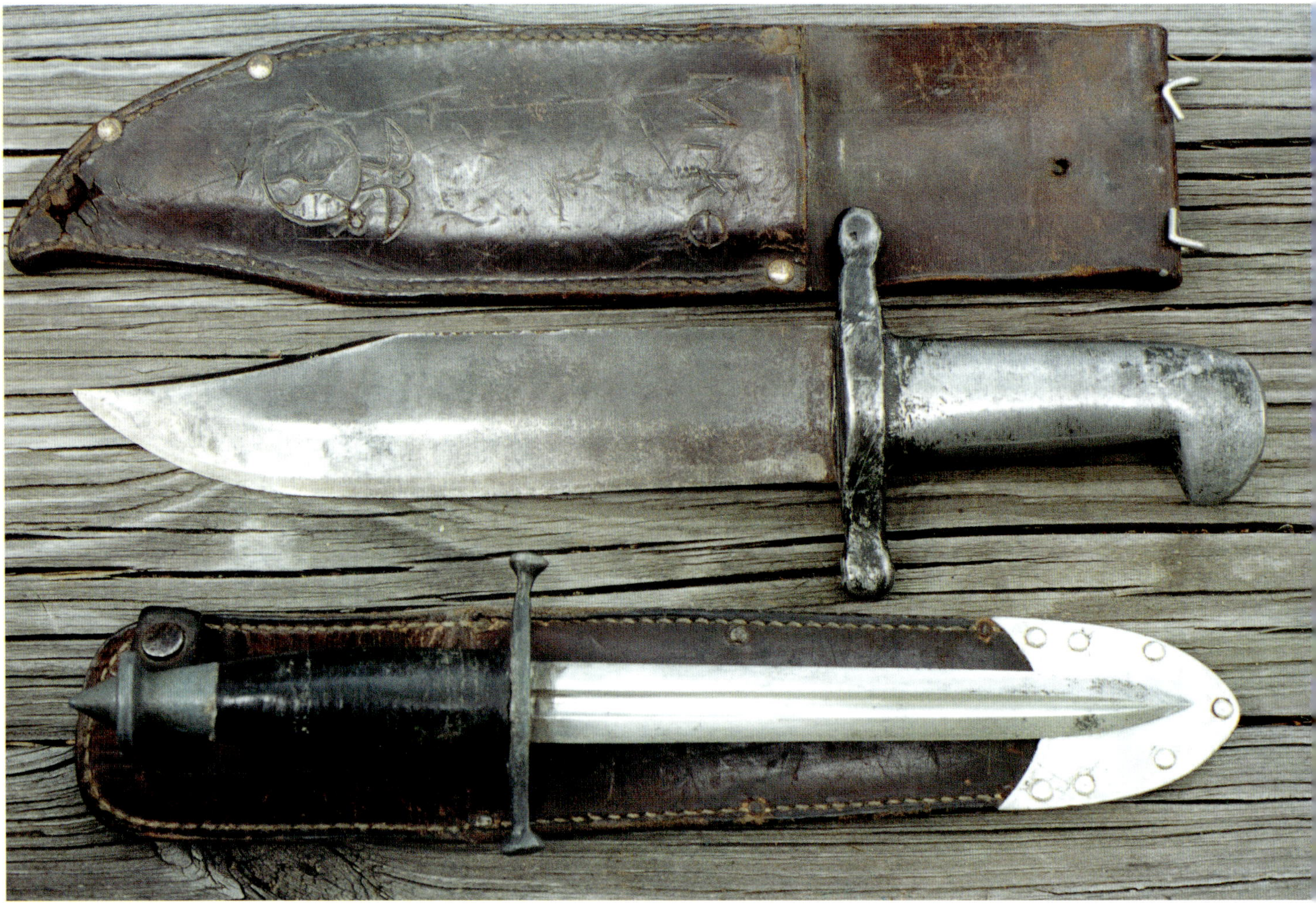

MOORE
MPLS.

Above, Left: Pictured is a clip point knife with a cast aluminum handle. There were 1,000 of these knives made in New Zealand for the 1st Battalion 21st Marines. The original sheath has the name MIKE and the Marine Insignia cut into it. The bottom knife could have been made out of a Patton sword. It was carried by a member of the 1st Special Service Force. Collectors value (top) $3,500.00 (bottom) $275.00. (Ballard Collection)

Below, Left: Donald W. Moore of Minneapolis, MN, made these two aluminum handled knives. He gave them to servicemen during WWII. Kennedy Arms Co. of Minneapolis sold knives made by Donald Moore. The top knife has a 6 5/8" blade and the bottom knife has a 5" blade. Collectors value (top) $300.00 (bottom) $250.00. (Ballard Collection)

Right: This knife was made by Ben Rocklin of Chicago, IL. His shop was located at 746 South Halsted Street. Before the war Rocklin made bread knives and hunting knives. He thought war was coming so he bought up all of the steel files he could. Rocklin then started to make double edge fighting knives like the one pictured to the right. By some accounts he made and sold 6,000 knives to servicemen. The knife pictured here has a 7 9/16" blade, hollow ground from a file. It has a steel cross guard and ferrule. The design of the wooden handle came from the bread knives he made before the war. The sheath is plain, but very sturdy, being both stitched and riveted. Collectors value $450.00. (Wright Collection)

This knife was made from an M1 bayonet by Bennie Hamilton, USN, in 1944. He was a machinist at the "U.S. Naval Repair Base at San Diego CA.," which is engraved on the front of the blade, along with a submarine. Included with this knife is "Bennie's" photograph and other personal papers pertaining to his service during WWII. Collectors value $375.00. (Wright Collection)

Carl Rinker made this knife in 1943 or 1944. It is not clear to me whether he owned or was employed at Alliance Machine Steel Casting Co. Linden Ave., Alliance, OH. This knife has a 5 1/4" hand forged blade. The top and bottom ends of the handle are heart shaped. Several other examples of this knife exist. Collectors value $200.00. (Wright Collection)

This is a very fine example of a Theater Knife, made in Dayton, OH, in the machine shop of the National Cash Register Co. This knife exhibits exceptional craftsmanship in design, fit, and finish. It has a 7" double edge blade and is 12 1/2" in total length. The blade is expertly ground and finished to a high polish, and has a thin fuller on each side of the blade. The guard and pommel are cast of aluminum and then finished and polished. The handle is made using 36 colorful spacers, individually cut and stacked. Knives were made at many businesses during WWII. They were usually made out of scraps and discarded materials. I own one more knife very similar to this one. Collectors value $500.00. (Wright Collection)

This large, well made double edge knife has a 10 7/8" blade, which is 1 3/16" wide and 1/4" thick. The blade appears to be made from a large file and chrome plated to help prevent it from rusting. The overall length of the knife is 16 7/16". The short steel cross guard has been welded to the blade and plated. The handle is made from 1/4" Plexiglass and has a large aluminum spacer next to the cross guard. The pommel appears to be an aluminum knob from another part of an aircraft. The well made sheath is sewn and has 25 rivets holding it together. Both knife and sheath are marked with the owner's name and "USS Nevada." This knife was made and used by Cpl. John H. Merriman, USMCR, while aboard the USS Nevada. Merriman served on the Nevada from March 1943 to April 1945. The USS Nevada was damaged at Pearl Harbor December 7, 1941, and was towed back to the Brooklyn Navy Yard to be repaired. This battleship was part of the bombardment fleet for the D-Day invasion. Collectors value $450.00. (Wright Collection)

This group of WWII fighting knives was made by Simon. The blades are engraved "MADE BY SIMON LIMA." I think these knives were made in Lima, OH, and I do not think the maker's last name is Lima. These knives are very well made and are above average in design, fit, and finish. The body of the handles is made from Birdseye Maple. The sheaths are all alike and are sewn and riveted with brake lining rivets marked "3-5." I have seen other knives like the top two knives, but only one fighter. Collectors value (top) $375.00 (center) $400.00 (bottom) $750.00. (Wright Collection)

There are a good number of knives like the one pictured above. A thin 5 1/2" blade is cast directly into an aluminum handle that has finger grooves. These knives have been linked to knife maker Frank Richtig. I have not found credible evidence that Richtig was the maker of these knives. This type of sheath is most often found with this knife. Collectors value $175.00. (Wright Collection)

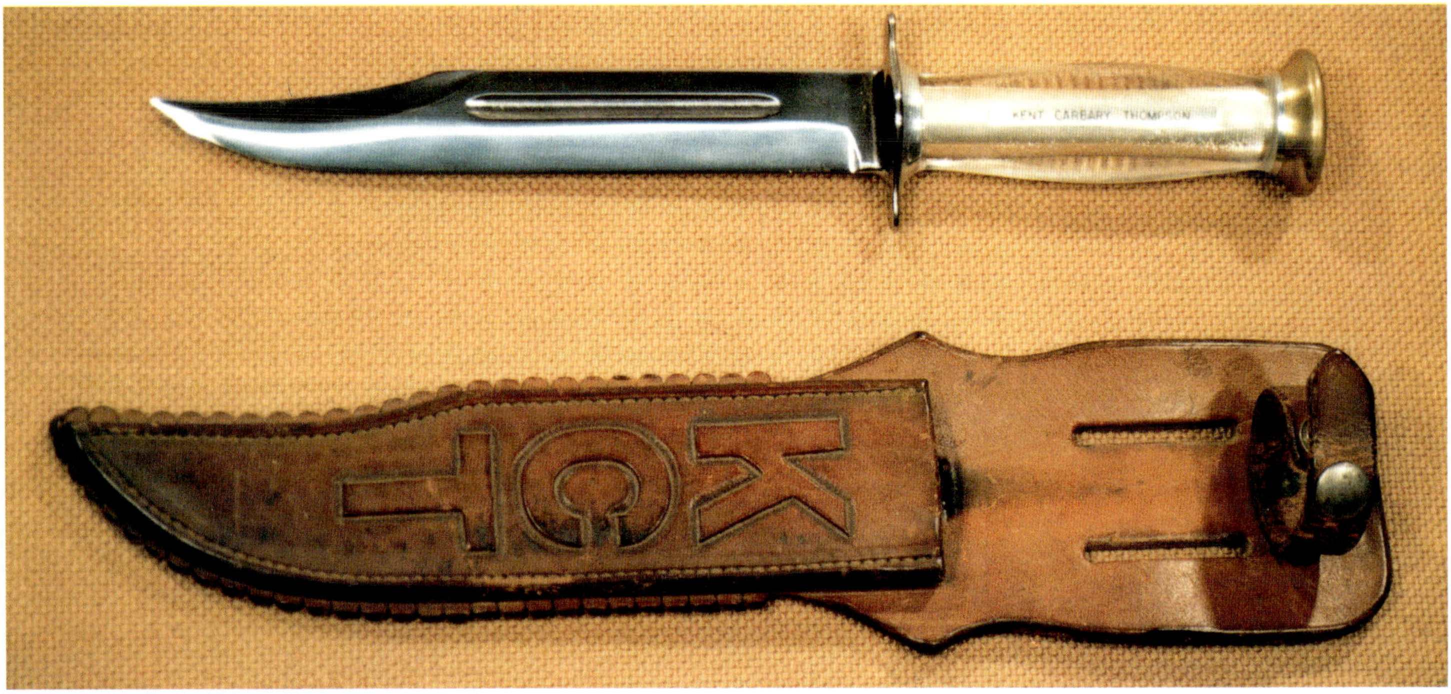

Kent Carbary Thompson made and used this very high quality WWII knife in FT. Myers, FL. His name and "1911162, USNR –A, T-12-42" is imprinted on the tang of the knife under the one piece Lucite handle. The 7 3/4" clip point blade has a sharpened false edge. The blade has a blood groove machined into each side. This high quality sheath, although unmarked, was made by Alfred Cornish of Omaha, NE, and has the letters "KTC" embossed into it. Collectors value $1,000.00. (Wright Collection)

These two knives were made in Kansas City, MO. The knuckle knife has a triangular blade. The knuckle bow is marked "DECKER MFG. CO. K.C. MO.," and the blade is marked "JOHNSON" with an arm holding a hammer. The Bowie Knife in this picture has an 11 3/8" blade that is 3/16" thick and 1 3/8" wide. The blade has a sharpened false edge. This knife has an aluminum cross guard and a rounded steel pommel. The handle is made from leather spacers. The blade is deeply stamped "SOLAS MACH. CO K.C. MO." Collectors value $300.00 each. (Wright Collection)

The two knives pictured here were made by Rudy Ruana of Bonner, MT. The double edge fighter is unmarked, and was likely made between 1938 and 1943, because Ruana did not mark his knives during that time period. In 1943 Ruana started marking his knives on the aluminum handle frame. The marking was "R.H. Ruana, Bonner, MT." This double edge fighter has a 6 3/4" blade and is 11" overall. The sheath has the early style belt buckle keeper strap. Both knives have square handle inserts that are made of deer horn. Square handle inserts were used between 1938 and 1944. The knife on the left is called a Deluxe Sticker™ pattern and was made in 1943 or 1944. It has a marked handle frame and square handle inserts. In an early advertisement Ruana called this pattern the "Serviceman's Favorite Emergency Weapon." The original sheath carries a sharpening stone. Collectors value (right) $1,200.00 (left) $1,000.00. (Wright Collection)

Floyd Nichols of David City, NE, made the knife on the right in this picture. This knife has a 7 5/8" blade and is 13 1/4" overall. The handle is made of brass brazing rod and finished with a pommel that sometimes was inset with an Indian Head Nickel or Indian Head Penny and the name "NICHOLS" stamped above the coin. Nichols decided not to put a coin in the pommel of this knife, but decided to stamp it "NICHOLS DAVID CITY.. NEBR.". These letters were hand stamped one at a time. Alfred Cornish of Omaha, NE, made the sheath. It is common to find the name and serial number of the owner to be stamped into a Nichols knife, as well as the sheath. The knife on the left was made by Robert Riggs of Fife, WA. Collectors value (Nichols Knife) $3,000.00, (Wright Collection) (Riggs Knife) $1,200.00 without sheath. (Ballard Collection)

Pictured here is a knife made by "Uncle Bob Riggs" of Fife, WA, which is close to Tacoma. He called his knives "Jap Stabbers." Bob Riggs was born in 1861 in Indiana and died on February 7, 1946, while chopping wood at his home in Fife. Riggs was a machinist and tinsmith by trade and retired in 1937. At that time he made knives for sportsmen as a hobby in his small machine shop at his home. By March 1943 Riggs was 81 years old when he started to make knives for servicemen. Working 8 hours a day he could make a knife every two days. It has been estimated that he made between 150 and 300 knives. One report states that he charged $4.00 for his knives. His knives differed a little in style and length. The knife pictured here is typical of "Uncle Bob's" work. It has an 8 1/8" clip point blade that is saber ground and has a blood groove on each side. This knife is stamped with a large "V" for "VICTORY" on the front side of the blade. There is a heavy brass cross guard and six large copper pins that hold the elk horn handles in place. Some of the Riggs knives I have seen have sheaths that are tin or copper lined. It is not known if "Uncle Bob's" knives all came with sheaths. Collectors value $1.500.00. (Wright Collection)

The blade of this knife is engraved "Virginia Grant June 1944, Compliments of the Keen Cuter Dept., Cone Auto matic, June 1944." The Cone Automatic machine shop was a large business in Windsor, VT. They started business in the early 1900s and held several patents, including the patent for the automatic screw machine. They were in business until recently when they filed for bankruptcy. During the war they had over 1,000 employees that worked three shifts. A long time employee told me that workers made these knives on their own time, at lunch, or before or after work. They made these knives out of scraps and gave them to servicemen headed for war. Collectors value $275.00. (Wright Collection)

This knife was made at the "Vocational School, Fond du Lac, WI," and is so marked in script on the blade. Marked on the backside is "Donald Lauzon" (student and knife maker). The leather sheath is tin lined and marked Beaker (?) Built. The blade is 8 3/8" long, and the total length is 13 3/8". The wooden handle slabs are held on with three large brass rivets. The S shaped steel cross guard is 1/8" thick. There are several of these knives and sheaths known. Collectors value $650.00. (Wright Collection)

Both knives pictured above are made by "L.NEVILL." This maker could have been located somewhere in Oklahoma or Texas. It was reported to me that a serviceman from Oregon carried the knife on the right in WWII. This knife has a 6 3/4" blade and is 12 1/4" overall. The pommel and the unusual light colored handle spacers are made of elk horn. The sheath was originally a pancake style, but has been trimmed. The quality and the style of designs cut into the leather suggest that Heiser of Denver, CO, made the sheaths, however, the sheaths are marked "NEVILL." There are several other known knives similar to the knife on the right. The knife on the left appears to be modeled after Russell Bowie Hunters of the 1890s. The blade length is 7" and is marked "NEVILL." The overall length is 11 1/2". The sheath for this knife has a floral design on the back, which is similar to the front of the other sheath. To date there are only two knives known of this type (knife on left), however, other styles and patterns may exist. Collectors value $850.00 each. (Wright Collection)

This rare prototype Taylor Huff Knuckle Knife has a knuckle bow with two rows of six teeth. This knife has a 9 3/8" blade and is 14 3/8" overall. The wooden handles, which are likely pine, have a long steel plate on each side that is riveted together. The length of the knuckle guard extension on the back is longer than the Patented Taylor Huff Knife. It is known that Taylor Huff made several designs before he decided on his final design and patented it. These knives were made at Fort Knox, KY, and he sold them to servicemen for $0.01. This appears to be the original sheath, but differs from the patented model. Collectors value $3,000.00. (Wright Collection)

The Taylor Huff Knuckle Knife pictured above is what I would call the 2nd design. The teeth on the knuckle guard are reduced in number from six to five in each row. This model still has wooden handle slabs with steel support plates on each side. The front plate on this knife is marked "MADE AT FORT KNOX KY." The knuckle guard extension has been reduced in length from 1 7/8" to 1 1/4". It is not known if this is the original sheath, as other known 2nd models have a variety of sheaths. Collectors value $3,000.00. (Wright Collection)

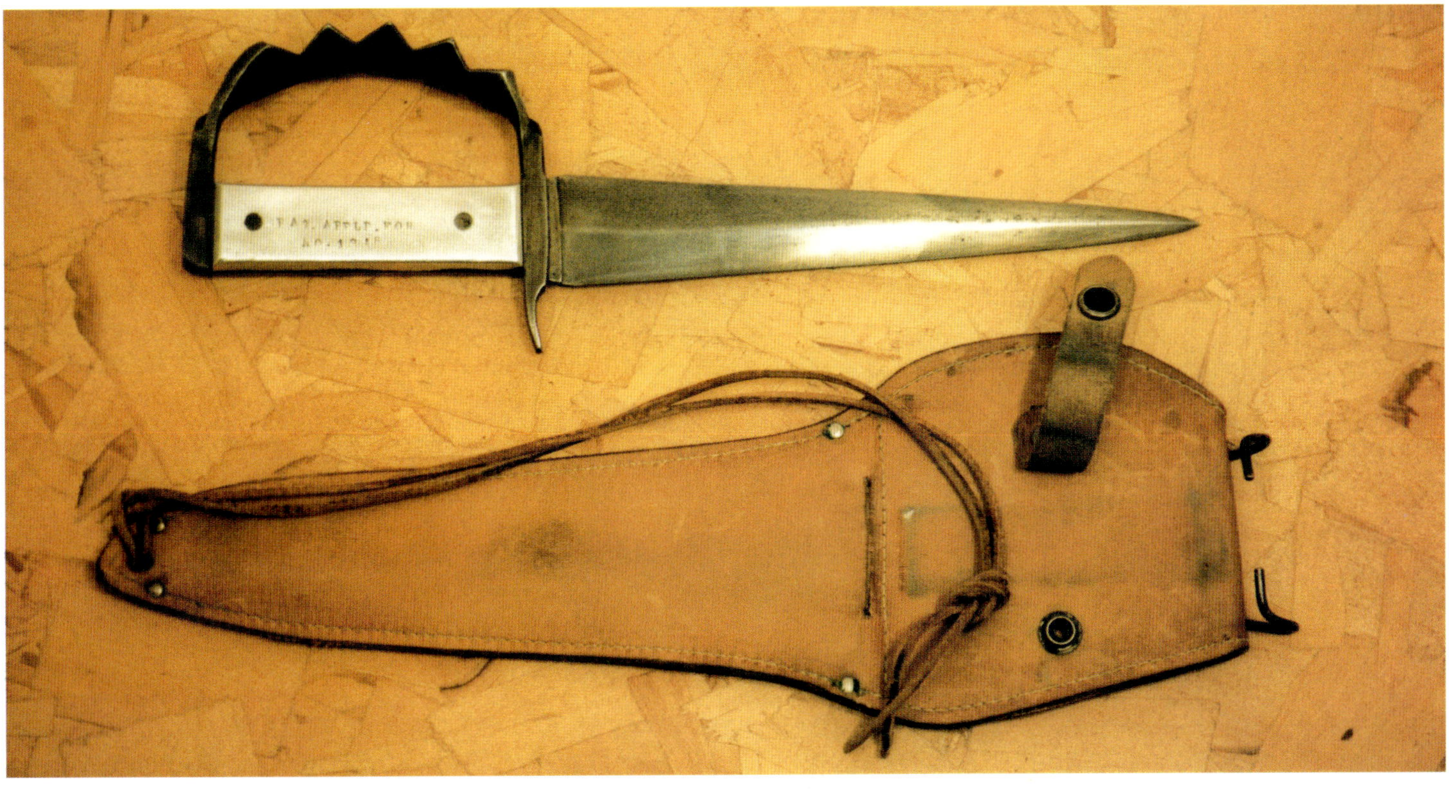

This is the 3rd model, and it is the one that was patented. The difference between the 2nd and the 3rd models is the 3rd model has aluminum handle slabs, which are marked on the front side "PAT. APPLD. FOR" and the serial number of each knife. The markings on all Taylor Huff knives are stamped with individual letter and number stamps. Collectors value $3,000.00. (Wright Collection)

Three high quality Theater Knives are pictured above. The top knife has an 8 9/16" blade that is 1/4" thick. The blade on the center knife measures 8 3/8" and is 1 5/8" wide. This knife was made at Armco Steel, located in Middletown, OH. The lower knife has a 6 7/8" blade. This knife was made and carried by Thomas Albert Hurlbert. He was with the 22nd Marines in the Battle of the Marshall Islands and was decorated for gallantry. He was wounded in the Battle of Guam with shrapnel in his left shoulder. He was at the Battle of Iwo Jima and Okinawa with the 6th Marines and returned home in December 1945. Collectors value (top to bottom) $500.00, $500.00, $675.00. (Wright Collection)

The knives on this page were made on the Island of New Caledonia during WWII. Markings are usually on top of the cross guard and are in script. However, I have seen one marked on the bottom of the guard and several marked in block letters. The markings are New Caledonia and Noumea. I have seen knives that are unmarked, however, some will have either or both markings. Noumea is the capital city of New Caledonia and was a staging area for U.S. Marines during WWII. At this time it is not known if one person made all of the knives, or if they were made in a cottage industry on the island. The knife pictured below has an 8 1/2" blade. It is marked under the cross guard and is the only known knife of its kind. The knives pictured above have blade lengths from 7 1/2" to 8 3/4". They are typical New Caledonia knives. All known knives made there have deer horn handles. The antlers came from deer that were native to the island. Collectors value as pictured (top, left to right) $550.00 (without sheath), $800.00, $750.00, $800.00, (below) $850.00. (Wright Collection)

The top knife in this picture has a very unusual blade. All of the grinding was done on the front side; the backside is absolutely flat. The blade is 7 3/8" long and the total length is 12 3/4". Similar knives are known and can be traced to Florida. The lower knife was made by Christian Smelling, who worked for General Electric in Syracuse, NY, during WWII. Several other Smelling knives are known. Collectors value $350.00 each. (Wright Collection)

Sidney Baxter & Co. of Boston, MA, made this knife. It has a 6 1/16" blade that is installed into a brass handle frame. There are other known knives similar to it. To see other knives marked "VICTORY or COMMANDO" see Cole's book "IV," p. 169, and Silvey's book "Knives of the United States Military WWII" pp. 82-83. Collectors value $450.00. (Wright Collection)

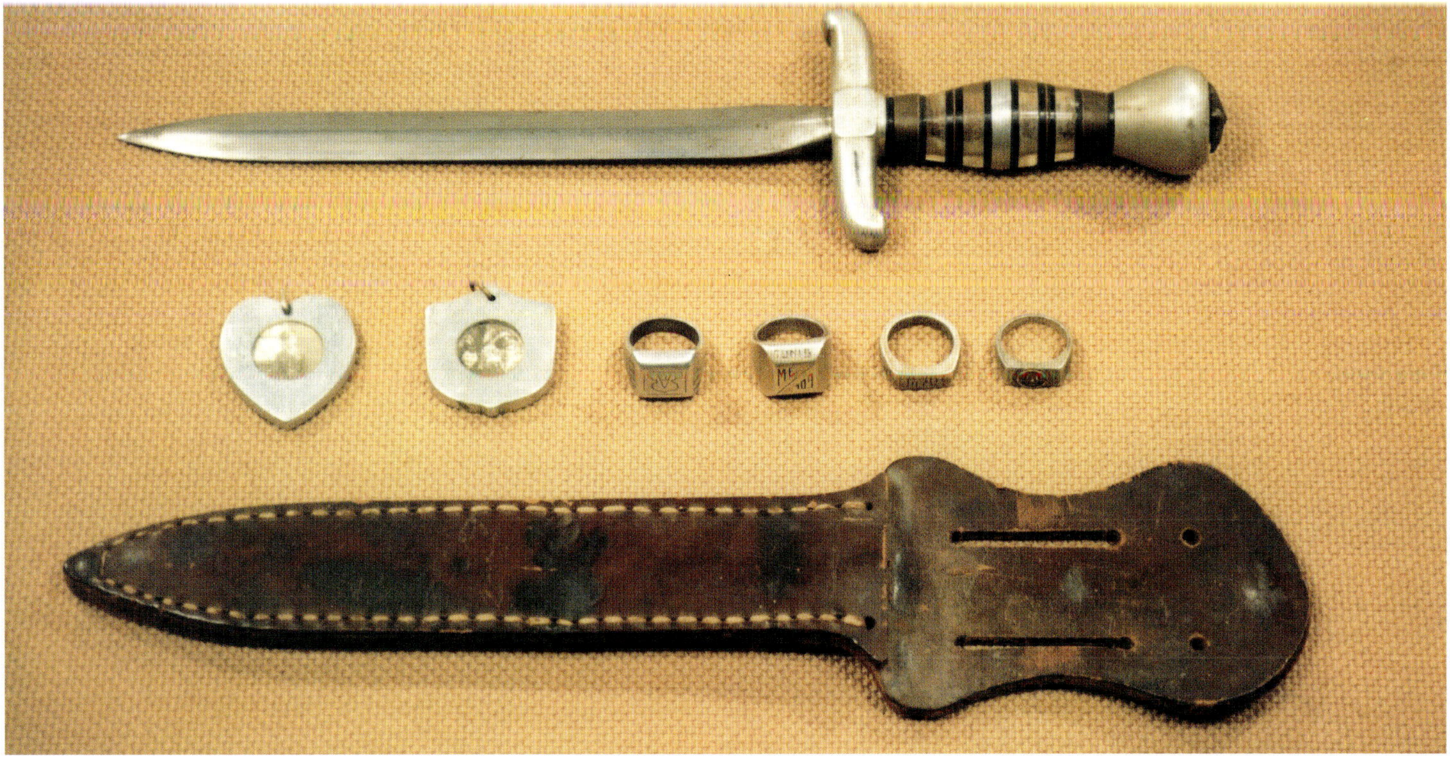

Loren T. Kruger of North Webster, IN, made the knives, rings, and lockets pictured here. He served in the 5th Army in Italy, France, and North Africa as an anti-aircraft gunner. He made most of these items with parts from the planes he shot down. The knife pictured above was made from a wing strut of a German Me 109. The 7 5/8" double edge blade is hand forged. The handle materials, including Plexiglass, came from the windshield of the same plane. The sheath for this knife was made from the gunnery belt. There is a star on the pommel that came from the pilot's lapel. The aluminum lockets have pictures of Kruger and his wife. He wore the one with his wife's picture, and his wife wore the one with his picture. Engravings on the rings show dates, places, and the type of aircraft they were made from. Pictured below are three other knives made by Kruger. The top and bottom knives were made out of German bayonets. The center knife was made out of a wing strut. Loren Kruger made, sold, and traded his custom knives, as well as other items that were made by him. He was depicted in the Stars and Stripes magazine as a cartoon character shooting down aircraft. Then, with a hacksaw in hand and wrench in his belt, headed for the aircraft to rob parts to make his knives. Collectors value with history and all items pictured $1,500.00. (Wright Collection)

Frank J. Richtig from Clarkson, NE, is one of the most famous knife makers in American history. His secret tempering process gave his knives the ability to hold an edge, which is unsurpassed today. His first knives were made in 1925 with cast aluminum handles. He primarily made kitchen and hunting knives, and traveled to county and state fairs demonstrating his knives. Richtig demonstrated the quality of his kitchen knives by hammering a knife through a buggy axle. The knife would remain sharp without nicking the edge. A demonstration of this kind earned Richtig a place in Ripley's "Believe It or Not" in 1936. Today, Richtig's knives are some of the most prized items in the field of knife collecting. His leather handle custom fighters and hunters are the ones most sought after. He usually sold these without sheaths, but for an additional charge offered a custom made sheath by Alfred Cornish from Omaha, NE. It is difficult to identify the knives he made during WWII because some are unmarked. Some of these knives might be unmarked because he did not have the proper permission from the War Production Board. The War Production Board controlled all raw materials, new and scrap, as well as the price that could be charged for the finished product. Another reason that his knives were unmarked might be that he did not want to sell them at the War Production Board's allowed price. Pictured on this page are WWII Richtig fighting knives. The upper knife has an 8 1/4" blade with brass cross guard and pommel and an unmarked Cornish sheath. Below is a knife with a 7 1/2" blade, brass cross guard, and thick aluminum spacer and pommel, as well as a sheath by an unknown maker. Collectors value (above) $6,000.00 (below) $4,500.00. (Wright Collection)

The same family ordered these two WWII Bowie Knives directly from Frank Richtig. No other history is known, nor is the reason why they are still near mint condition. The top knife has a 7 1/8" blade and is 12 1/4" in overall length. The brass cross guard is 4" long. The lower knife has a 6 15/16" blade and is 11 13/16" total length. This knife has a 3 1/16" brass cross guard. The sheaths are original to the knives. As previously discussed, most Richtig Knives were sold without sheaths, and it was up to the new owner to provide one. Collectors value (top) $6,000.00 (lower) $5,500.00. (Wright Collection)

Frank Richtig made these three small WWII fighters. The blade measurements are (left to right) 5", 5 1/16", and 4 13/16". Collectors value (left to right) $3,500.00, $3,000.00, $3,000.00. (Wright Collection)

This knife is marked "WICHITA MACHINE TOOL CO WICHITA KANSAS." Marked on the backside of the handle is "WICHITA MODEL SP 3." This knife has a 10" blade and cast aluminum handle. Collectors value $300.00. (Wright Collection)

This knife was made by "Red Hooper," custom knife maker from Burbank, IL. It was made during WWII and was one of his first. The 7 3/8" blade is 3/16" thick and has been bright blued. The Bakelite and Plexiglass handle has finger grooves to give a better grip. The quality sheath is hand embossed with a floral design. Collectors value $300.00. (Wright Collection)

Robert A. Van Adrstin made this WWII fighting knife in the Township of Little Wolf, WI. The knives are stamped A.J. Van Adrstin, which was Robert's grandfather. A.J. Vanadestin was a blacksmith passing his trade down from generation to generation. The stamping die that was used on this knife was made during the Civil War. Robert made knives before, during, and after WWII. He made hunting knives and kitchen knives, however, he only made fighters during WWII. It is believed he made 1,000 knives during his lifetime with wartime production numbers unknown. The blades of his first knives were made using grist mill stone picks. Later on he used worn out files from the brake division of the nearby 4–wheel drive plant. Some of his knives were sold at VL&A in Chicago, IL. There may be some evidence that Robert Van Adrstin knew William Scagel, and one may have influenced the other's designs for WWII fighting knives. The knife pictured to the right belonged to Gerald W. Sloan of Ft. Smith, AR. Sloan is a Pearl Harbor survivor. This knife has a 7 3/4" blade and has an overall length of 12 3/4". The aluminum cross guard and pommel were cast directly onto the blade. The wooden handle slabs are held on with two large copper pins. Collectors value $1,500.00. (Wright Collection)

The two knives pictured above were made at the Anaconda Copper Smelters of Great Falls, MT. It was reported to me that these knives were made and only given to employees that went to war. They were not given to family members of employees or anyone else. The top knife has a 7 5/8" blade, and the lower knife has a 7 7/8" blade. The topside of the blade is sharpened about 2". Collectors value (bottom) $400.00 (top with sheath) $500.00. (Wright Collection)

The top knife in the picture to the left is marked "MURPHY COMBAT" on the cast aluminum handle. It was made by David Z. Murphy of Portland, OR. Frank Barteaux, who was a friend and neighbor of Dave Murphy, made the bottom two knives. They are similar, but not the same as the top knife. It is my understanding that they sometimes worked together, and Barteaux used some of Murphy's scraps and reject blades to make his knives. Collectors value (top, Murphy) $750.00 (lower Barteaux) $400.00 each. (Wright Collection)

Fighting knives like the three pictured (to the right) were offered in the 1944 firearms catalog of Thomas Woroniecki. His business was located at 47 West 44th Street, New York, New York. These knives were advertised as "Commando Knives for servicemen only." The ad continued "Parents or friends, place the order with us, and we will ship directly to serviceman's camp." These knives originally sold for $12.50 to $15.00. The blades of the top and bottom knives were made from 1848 English Brunswick Bayonets. The top knife has a 7 1/2" blade cast aluminum knuckle guard, one-piece wood handle, and a steel skull crusher pommel. The center knife has an 8" double edge blade, aluminum cross guard, leather spacer handle, and a cast aluminum skull crusher pommel. The lower knife has a 9 1/16" blade and a heavy brass cross guard and pommel. The handle is made with aluminum spacers and Micarta. Collectors value (top) $800.00 (center) $375.00 (lower) $600.00. (Wright Collection)

The same talented knife maker made all three of these WWII knives. The only clue to the maker's identity is the smaller knife to the right is engraved on both sides "Hand Made 12-1-42 By O'le Mac-1," and "Howard B. Jacques 646 92 82" (the owner of the knife, and his serial number). These knives are made similar to the knives made in early San Francisco. Another known knife by O'le Mac can be traced back to San Francisco in 1945. All three sheaths are made from very hard heavy leather held together using small brass rivets. All of these sheaths have the same style of stainless steel belt holder, which is attached with brass rivets. Underneath the stainless is a piece of leather to keep the belt from being cut. The blades are hand forged and finished to a high polish. Both small knives have a 6" double edge blade and are 10 3/16" overall. Both of the small knife blades are 3/16" thick, and the large knife is 1/4" thick. The larger knife has a 9 1/8" blade and is 13 3/4" overall. The knives have either thick brass or copper cross guards. Collectors value (small right) $750.00 (large) $675.00 (small left) $600.00. (Wright Collection)

It was reported to me that this high quality knife was made in the machine shop of the Weyerhaeuser Corporation in Longview, WA. This knife and others were made and given to employees and their family members that were going into military service during WWII. The unusual 6 1/2" blade is 1/4" thick and 1 5/16" wide. It has a heavy-duty aluminum S shaped cross guard with a wedge shaped brass spacer at the cross guard and aluminum pommel. The quality leather sheath is embossed with an eagle in a tree and a bear climbing rocks. The outside of the sheath is braided with thin leather lacing. Collectors value $500.00. (Wright Collection)

Pictured here are two knives marked "KEPHART." The marking is deeply stamped into the wood slab handle. Above is a double edge knuckle knife with a 7 1/2" blade. Below is a clip point Bowie Knife with an 8 1/2" blade that has a sharpened back edge. Another Kephart Bowie knife is known with a slab leather handle that is also marked. The "Kephart Knife Works" was in Des Moines, IA. I have a letter that is personally signed by A.R. Kephart. He gave the address of 511 School St. next to his name. The letterhead itself does not have a street address. It is not known if 511 School St. is Kephart's home or business. The letterhead states that they were "Manufactures of hand made cutlery and tools, hand forged from a special grade steel, tempered by the best process known to science. Each and every knife or tool is fully warranted, and anyone found imperfect will be replaced by a new one." Also stated is, "We manufacture butcher knives, razors, cold chisels, punches, and anything you want to order." The letterhead continues "We have a complete forging and grinding plant." This letter is dated September 14, 1920. The date A.R. Kephart started or closed the business is not known at this time. Collectors value (above) $875.00, (Ballard Collection), (below) $675.00. (Hunt Collection)

The four knives pictured here came from an antique shop in San Diego, California. It was reported to me that the lady who owned the knives said they had belonged to her husband. She said her husband got them just before he entered into the army, and they were so nice he did not want to use them and sent the knives home. When the lady was asked if she knew who made the knives, she said her husband told her they were made by the guy that makes knives for all of the servicemen. It is not known what date the knives were made, but her husband served in WWII. These knives have a handle design similar to the early knives made by Hoyt or Al Buck. Levine's Guide to Knives 4th Edition says Al Buck settled in San Diego in 1940 and Hoyt moved there in 1945. Levine's Guide also states that early Buck knives have Lucite handles and the blades are made from old files or power hacksaw blades. These knives have Lucite handles and blades the right size to have been an old file or power hacksaw blade. It has not been proven who made these knives, but whoever it was did a fine job. The knife to the right has a 9 1/8" blade that is 1 1/2" wide and 1/8" thick. The next knife has a 4 1/2" blade that is 11/16" wide and 1/16" thick. The other two smaller knives have 2 3/4" blades that are 1/2" wide and 1/32" thick. Collectors value not known at this time. (Wright Collection)

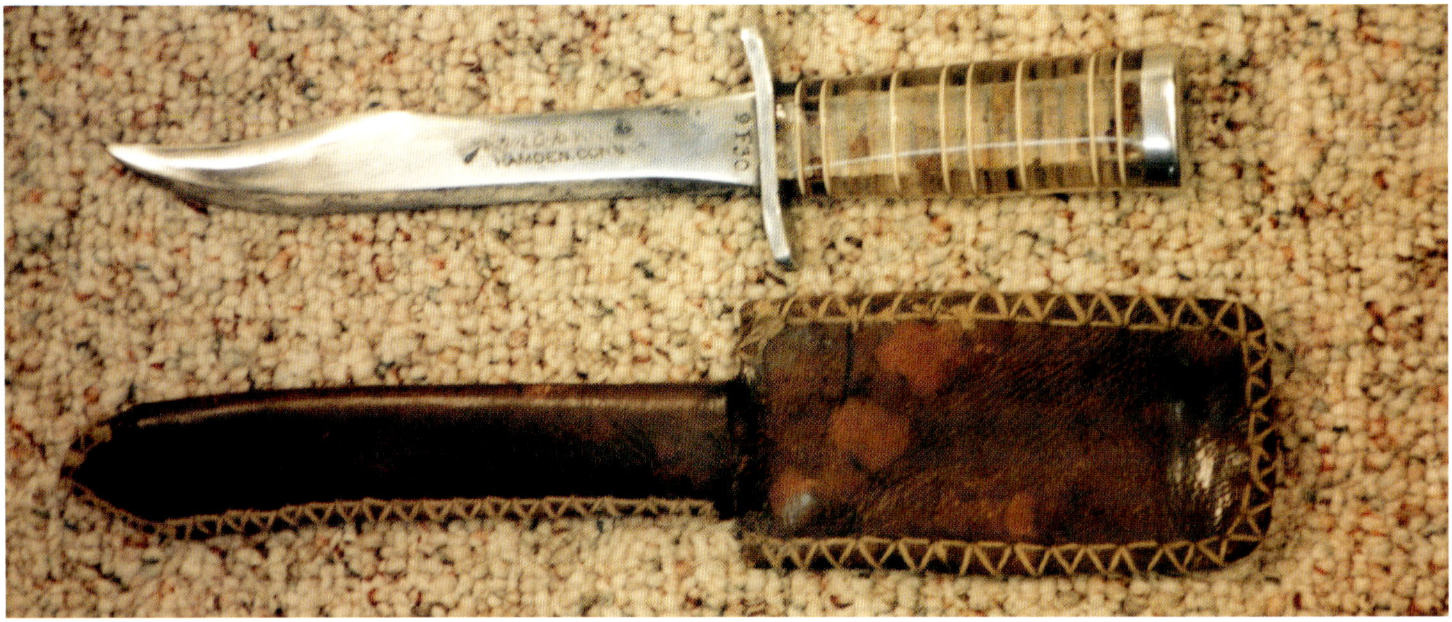

John Ek of Hamden, CT, made the knives on this page. Ek only sold knives to active duty military personnel. He kept a record of each serial numbered knife matched to the serviceman's name. The serial number is a code. The first number is the model of the knife. The second letter represents 1,000 made, and the last 3 being the number less than the next 1,000. The knife serial numbered 1c784 means it is model #1, knife #3784. It is reported that John Ek made 100,000 knives during WWII. The top knife has been Theater Altered. The wooden handle was replaced with a Plexiglass spacer handle, aluminum cross guard and pommel. Collectors value (top) $500.00 (bottom left to right) $650.00, $575.00, $750.00. (Wright Collection)

These two double edge fighting knives are of superior fit and finish and were made by the same maker. Both sheaths are marked "Made by Wm. E. McDonald, Butler, PA." It is not known whether McDonald was the sheath maker or the knife maker. Either way, he did a wonderful job. The knife to the left has an 8 1/4" blade and a cast aluminum handle. The sheath was marked with the owner's name, "WENDEL REARICK U.S. NAVY 251-21-87." The knife on the right has a 7" mirror polished blade. The handle is made from Lucite and Micarta. This is another knife that I really like. Collectors value (right) $500.00 (left) $375.00. (My Collection, Bill Wright)

S A
1913

Right: Knife Crafters of Philadelphia, PA, made this WWII knife. They converted Patton Sabers and Civil War swords into WWII fighting knives. There are several different styles of Knife Crafters knives known. This knife has a 7" blade measured from tip to guard and was made out of a section close to the end of a sword blade. The construction of this knife is typical of Knife Crafters' knives. A small section was cut from a sword blade, brazed into a steel bolster with a cross guard, then attached to a hollow steel tube. The handle was then covered with leather and sewn up one side. This quality sheath is typical for Knife Crafters' sheaths. The front of this sheath has been hand carved with the words "FRANCE, OMAHA," and the beginning of the letter "B" (BEACH?). This knife was likely at the D-Day invasion. See chapter 6 for other Knife Crafters knives. Collectors value $750.00. (Wright Collection)

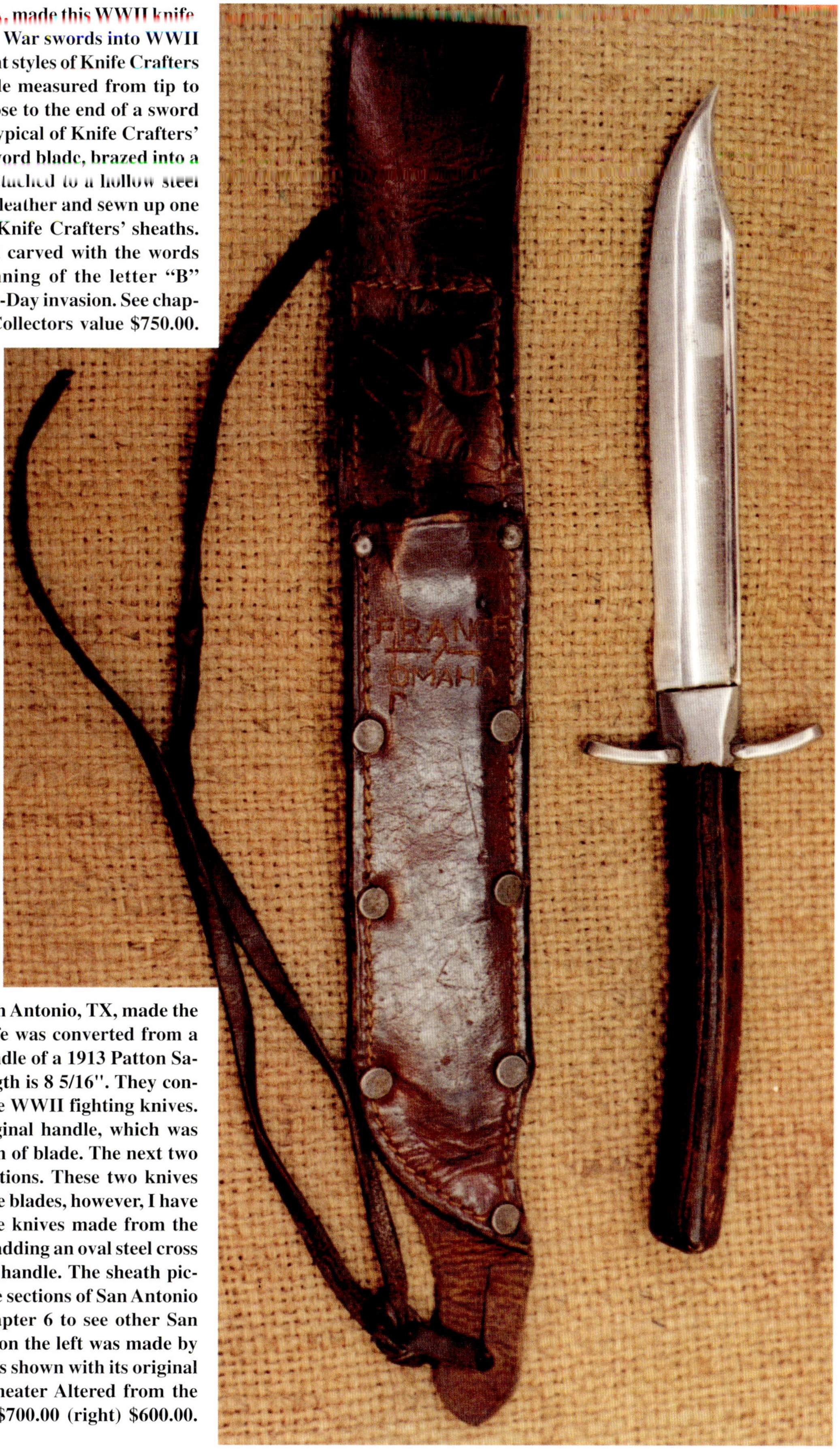

Left: The San Antonio Iron Works of San Antonio, TX, made the knife and sheath on the right. This knife was converted from a bottom section of blade and original handle of a 1913 Patton Saber serial numbered 625. The blade length is 8 5/16". They converted one WWI Patton Saber into three WWII fighting knives. The first knife was made from the original handle, which was slightly modified, and the bottom section of blade. The next two were made from the center and tip sections. These two knives usually will have double edge dagger style blades, however, I have seen several with a clip style blade. The knives made from the center and upper sections were made by adding an oval steel cross guard and a roughly fashioned wooden handle. The sheath pictured to the right is the type that all three sections of San Antonio Irons Works knives came with. See chapter 6 to see other San Antonio Irons Works knives. The knife on the left was made by Knife Crafters of Philadelphia, PA, and is shown with its original sheath. The handle and pommel are Theater Altered from the original design. Collectors value (left) $700.00 (right) $600.00. (Wright Collection)

5

Personally Identified & Presentation Knives

Some of the knives in this chapter will be identified by the name and or serial number found on them or their respective sheaths. Family history or other items that came with the knives will help make some identification possible.

This WWII fighting knife has an 8" blade with an overall length of 13 1/4". The walnut handle is inlaid with pewter. The knife and heavy-duty leather sheath are above average quality. Richard L. Croop, from Massillon, OH, carried this knife. Personal effects, such as dog tags, patches, and other personal items add from 20% to 200% to the value of any WWII knife and sheath. Value for grouping as shown above $250.00. (Wright Collection)

The top knife in this photo is a heavy well made fighting knife. The handle is marked "Stephen P. Novosel Jr. 552608-USMC," owner and possibly maker of this knife. The double edge blade is 8" long. It has an unusual S shaped cross guard and bottom knuckle guard. The bottom knife has a 7 3/16" double edge blade that is 1 1/2" wide. It has a very unusual leather D-guard or knuckle bow with 12 brass spikes attached. The knife belonged to "Marvin Wernick ASN1107404." Collectors value (top) $375.00 (bottom) $400.00. (Ballard Collection)

The top knife belonged to "Francis Lee Bradley." He was a Private in the USMC during WWII. The 9 3/8" blade has a sharpened false edge. The bottom knife is marked "T-5 Henry M. Goyette 31215264-HD Q BTRY 45th R.R.A. GROUP." This knife has a 7 1/8" blade and is 11 7/8" overall. Both knives are high quality. Collectors value (top) $350.00 (bottom) $275.00. (Ballard Collection)

A wonderful example of a hand forged file blade knife is pictured above. The blade is 7 3/8" long, 1 1/2" wide, and 3/16" thick. There is a brass cross guard and pommel with the tang sticking out the back to form a skull crusher. The handle is made of stacked leather washers, likely made out of the same leather as the sheath. The sheath is marked "C.E. BARR U.S. A.A F." (United States Army Air Force), and is hand laced with heavy leather, possibly a boot string. This sheath was made out of a leather belt used in machine shops to drive the machinery. The back of the sheath is marked "RUN IN THIS DIRECTION" with a large arrow (to show the direction the belt should run on a pulley) and "THIS SIDE TO PULLEY." Collectors value $250.00. (Wright Collection)

This heavy-duty double edge Theater Knife is made from 3/8" steel. The blade length is 7 3/8", and the overall length is 12". The knife has a brass cross guard and pommel. The handle is made of leather, wood, and red Micarta. The well made leather sheath has a belt buckle type keeper strap and is marked "DONALD F. TRYON, USN." Collectors value $500.00. (Wright Collection)

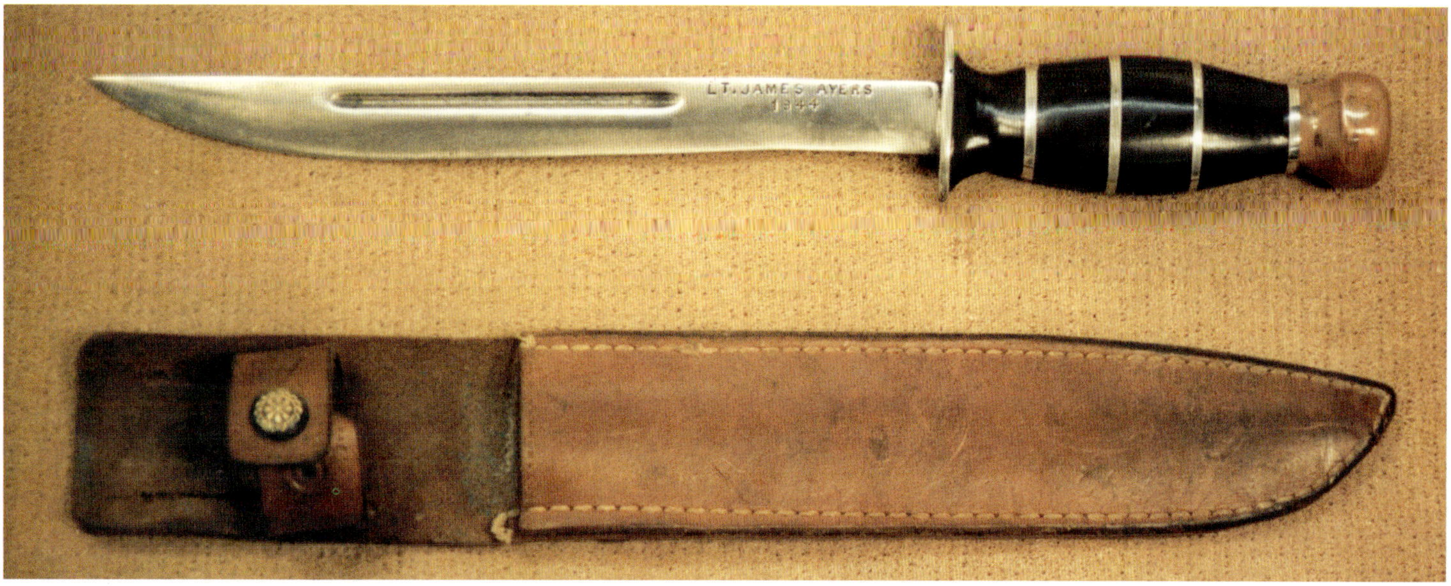

Pictured above is a knife with a blade marked "LT. JAMES AYERS 1944." The 8 11/16" blade was made from a file. The cross guard is made of stainless steel and the pommel is copper. The handle is made of thick black Micarta spacers divided by thin aluminum. The hand made leather sheath is sewn with heavy white string. Collectors value $325.00. (Wright Collection)

This knife belonged to Sargent George Jackson of New Albany, IN. It was expertly converted from an 1899 Craig bayonet into a WWII fighting knife. The 7 1/8" blade is razor sharp, top and bottom. The heavy-duty sheath is of the best quality. Knife and sheath are in near mint condition. Collectors value $200.00. (Wright Collection)

The same unknown maker made the above two daggers. I have seen several more knives like these, which are similar to the famous British Fairbairn-Sykes commando knives. The top knife has a 5" blade and is 9 1/2" overall. It has a stainless steel cross guard and hexagon nut pommel with the handle being wrapped with green cord. The bottom knife is made the same as above, except it has a 7" blade, is 11 15/16" overall, and the handle is wrapped with a black cord. The bottom knife is marked "RAYMOND S. GREEN, ASN 336839." Collectors value $125.00 (top) $200.00 (bottom). (Wright Collection)

This pair of Theater Knives were made and used by "R.P. Moore, Belgium, 1944." The top knife has a 5 5/8" blade, possibly made from a bayonet, and is 9 5/8" overall. It has a brass cross guard and pommel, and a stacked leather spacer handle with thick Plexiglass spacers in the center. His name is visible through the Plexiglass on one side and red, white, and blue stripes are visible through the other. The second knife has a blade length of 6 5/16" and an overall length of 11". It has a brass cross guard and pommel, stacked leather handle with two aluminum spacers and a Plexiglass in the center. Collectors value $250.00 for the pair. (Wright Collection)

Ernest Warther of Dover, OH, made this knife for "G.W. JENSEN 1943." This is a typical 7" double edge knife and sheath made by Warther during WWII. For additional information see chapter 4 Identified Makers. Collectors value $5,000.00. (Wright Collection)

The 7 1/16" blade of this knife is marked "Leo F. Lauber 1943." It is not known if he was the owner, maker, or both. This knife has a heavy-duty aluminum cross guard and pommel. The handle is made from red and black Micarta, along with aluminum spacers. This quality knife and sheath is one of my first, and one of my favorite Theater Knives. Collectors value $275.00. (My Collection, Bill Wright)

The blade of this classic WWII Bowie Knife is marked "JOHN WILLIAM CONLEY," his serial number, and "UNITED STATES ARMY." The back of the blade is marked "FROM DAD TO JOHN, REMEMBER PEARL HARBOR." The blade is 7 1/8" long and 1 7/8" wide. The knife has an aluminum pommel and brass cross guard. The handle is made from red Micarta, as well as several nickel and leather spacers. The sheath is held together with what is likely a long bootlace. Collectors value $300.00. (Wright Collection)

This well made knife has a 7" blade that is ground from the center to bottom and from center to top, forming a central median ridge that makes the blade sturdy and lightweight. The heavy aluminum hand guard and pommel were cast in a mold, then hand finished before being installed on the blade. The handle is made up of thin and thick Plexiglass, with two wood and five aluminum spacers. The two dog tags that came with the knife indicate the knife belonged to "LELAND G. BACKES DENVER COLO." Collectors value $200.00 (knife and dog tags). (Wright Collection)

The 8" blade of this WWII double edge fighter is marked "TO ROY FROM MARTY 4-6-45." The quality hand made pancake style sheath is marked "FROM SWANEE." It is not known who these people were, but all had something to do with this knife. The unusually long handle measures 5 13/16" and has finger grooves. Collectors value $300.00. (Wright Collection)

This knife was made using an E.G. Waterman blade. The blade length is 7 5/16". The knife has a stainless steel cross guard and a cast aluminum handle. The hand embossed sheath has a medical insignia on the front. The back of the sheath is marked "N.F. Polen 7/27," along with his serial number. Collectors value $250.00. (Wright Collection)

The sheath of this knife is marked "Lt. Leo F. Olson." The blade is 5 7/8" long and 3/16" thick. The sculpted leather spacer handle fits well and makes the hand grip tightly against the brass cross guard. Collectors value $175.00. (Wright Collection)

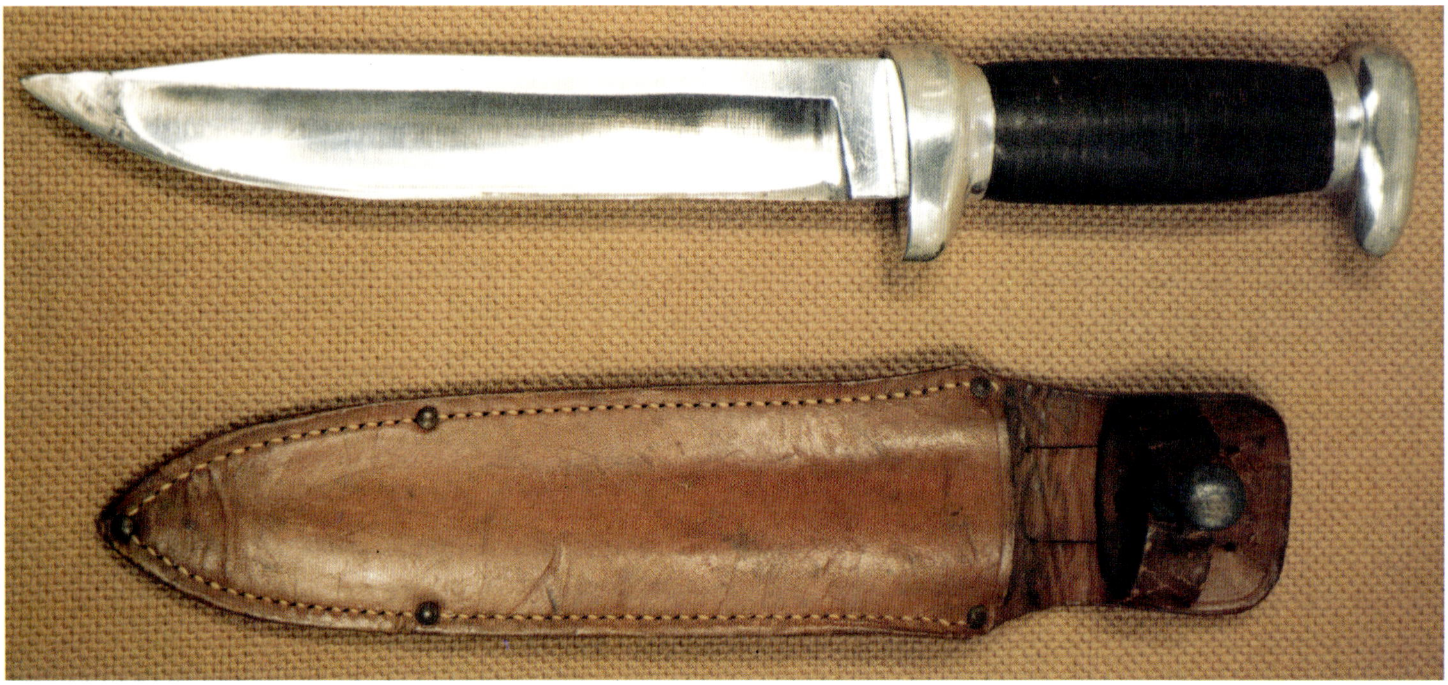

The blade of this knife is engraved "USN, 1943, DES" (the owner's initials). The 7 5/8" blade is hollow ground, 3/16" thick, and razor sharp. The pommel and hand guard are made out of heavy aluminum. The handle is made from leather spacers. The generic sheath is numbered "227S." Having a generic sheath might indicate the knife was brought from home or donated to the war effort without a sheath. Collectors value $250.00. (Wright Collection)

The 8 1/4" blade of this "Classic Bowie Knife" is floral engraved and has the name "Dr. J.H. Rose" on it. The heavy brass cross guard and pommel, as well as the brass handle spacers have been gold plated. The sheath is made of very heavy leather and is sewn and riveted. This knife is well above average quality. Collectors value $300.00. (Wright Collection)

This quality WWII dagger has the name "BOB LEONARD" scroll engraved around the pommel, and on the top "A.S. No. 15078701." A.S. is the abbreviation for army serial number. The aluminum guard is engraved with dots and scrollwork. The handle is made up of leather and aluminum disks. This is a large knife, with the blade being 9 1/16". The sheath is made of heavy leather held together by lacing tied into knots. This is a very good example of an identified WWII Theater Knife. Collectors value $325.00. (Wright Collection)

The back of this sheath is marked "MADE IN PEARL HARBOR 1941 I.D.O.Y.C." The sheath is sewn with black electric wire and bound with leather lacing. There is a German hunting badge on the front. The MK2 knife was modified by having its original handle and cross guard replaced with aluminum and Plexiglass. Collectors value $250.00. (Wright Collection)

This knife was likely Theater Altered from a standard issue MK2. The blade markings were removed, and a heavy aluminum hand guard and pommel replaced the originals. The 1/4" Plexiglass spacer handle has three aluminum spacers. The tang of the blade has been painted red for added color. The original MK2 sheath is marked "HILO 1944" on the front and "F.W. LODGE, C.B.M.U. 562" on the back. Small brass bolts help hold the sheath together. Collectors value $275.00. (Wright Collection)

The back of the sheath for this fine WWII fighting knife is marked "PVT. NORBURT H. BROWN, U.S.M.C.R., #543871, FROM FATHER, SEP 23 1944." The double edge blade measures 7 5/16", and the knife is 11 3/4" in overall length. The unusual S shaped brass cross guard is 4 1/4" long. The handle is made of different colors of Micarta. Collectors value $500.00. (Wright Collection)

This quality WWII double edge fighter is made from one piece of 1/2" steel. The blade is 6 7/8" long. The Micarta handle slabs are held on with large copper rivets. The cross guard is engraved "FRANK Q. WOLF." The two-piece leather sheath is held together with small nails bent over on the back. Collectors value $375.00. (Wright Collection)

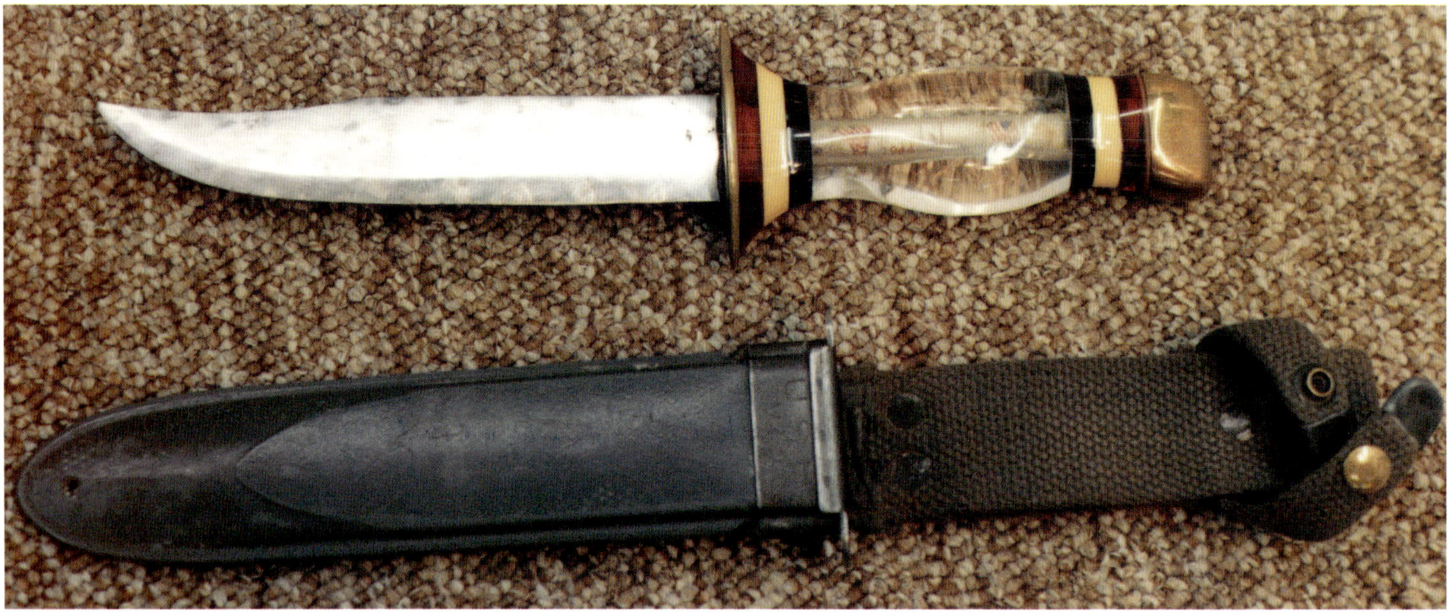

The handle of this knife was made using red, yellow, and black Bakelite. The name "JOHN GEARHART JR. 1944, VISALIA, CALIFORNIA" and two American Flags are visible inside the clear Lucite handle. The 6 1/4" blade has been polished by a method known as "engine turned." This knife has a USN MK2 sheath. Collectors value $275.00. (Wright Collection)

The unusual blade of this knife was hand forged from a file. The name "J.R. FISHER 850-89-46" is engraved on the back of the blade. The knife has a brass hand guard and pommel, with the handle made from leather spacers. The hand made leather sheath is marked "JRF" and has a web pistol belt hanger. Collectors value $250.00. (Wright Collection)

The two knives pictured above were likely Theater Altered from standard issue MK2 USMC and USN knives. The sheath for the knife on the right is marked "CHARLES MORTON, USS TEXAS, E-DIV." It is unusual to find two Theater Altered knives alike. This may mean an unknown maker could have made a small quantity of these knives aboard the USS Texas. Collectors value (left) $350.00 (right) $400.00. (Wright Collection)

The hand made 8 1/4" blade is made similar to the blade of a standard issue MK3 fighting knife, but is longer. It was reported to me that this knife has a Canadian history. No other details were given. There are several interesting markings on the handle. One is "COMPLIMENTS OF 718 R.O.B." I was told this stands for Royal Ordnance Battalion. The other marking is "COL. A.E. STODDARD 1st M.R.S." I do not know what M.R.S. stands for, but it has been suggested that it might be Marine Raider School. If anyone has information about this I would appreciate knowing of it. Collectors value not known at this time. (Wright Collection)

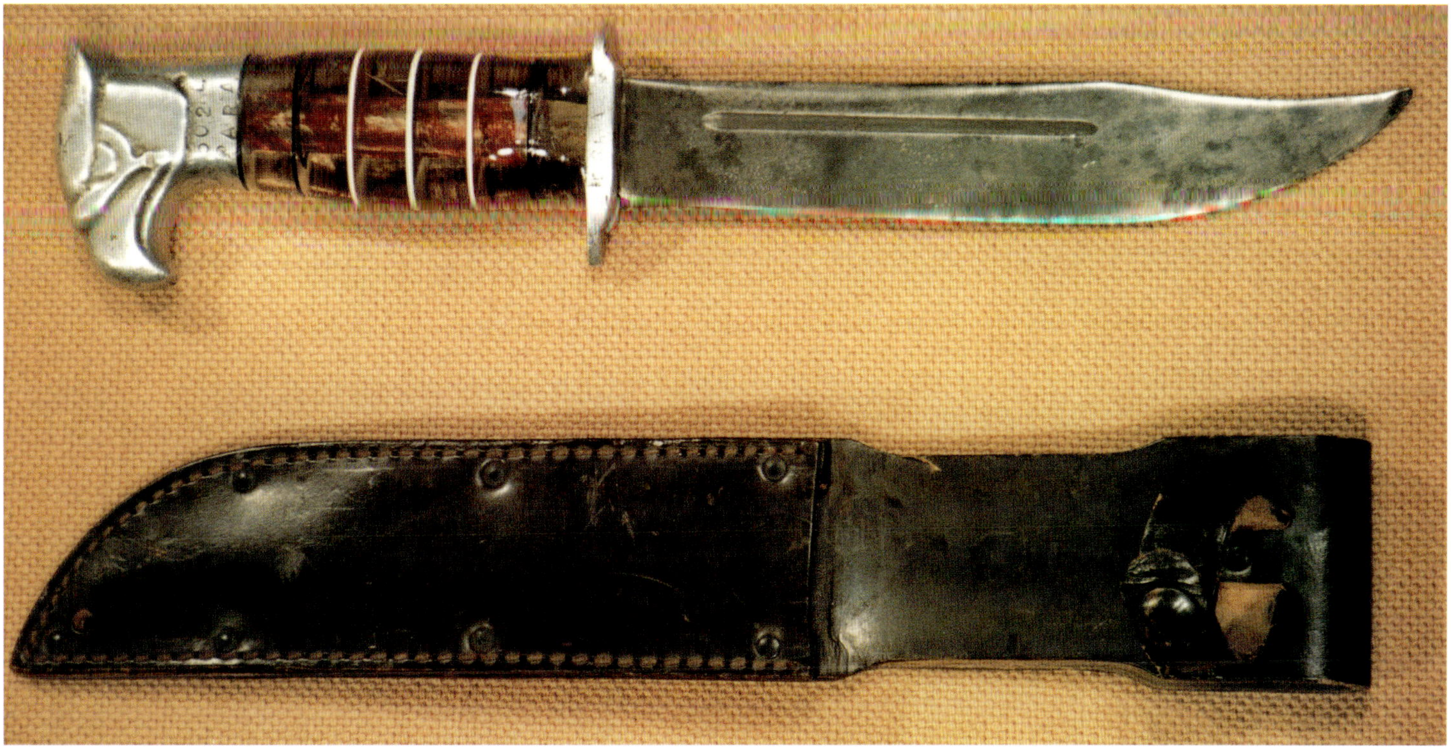

This great WWII fighting knife has a large cast aluminum eagle head pommel. Markings on the eagle are "502nd PARA BATT." Marked on the cross guard is "LT. CHA." This knife has a 7 1/2" blade and is 13" overall length. The handle was made using 1/2" Plexiglass and white and black spacers. Collectors value $500.00. (Wright Collection)

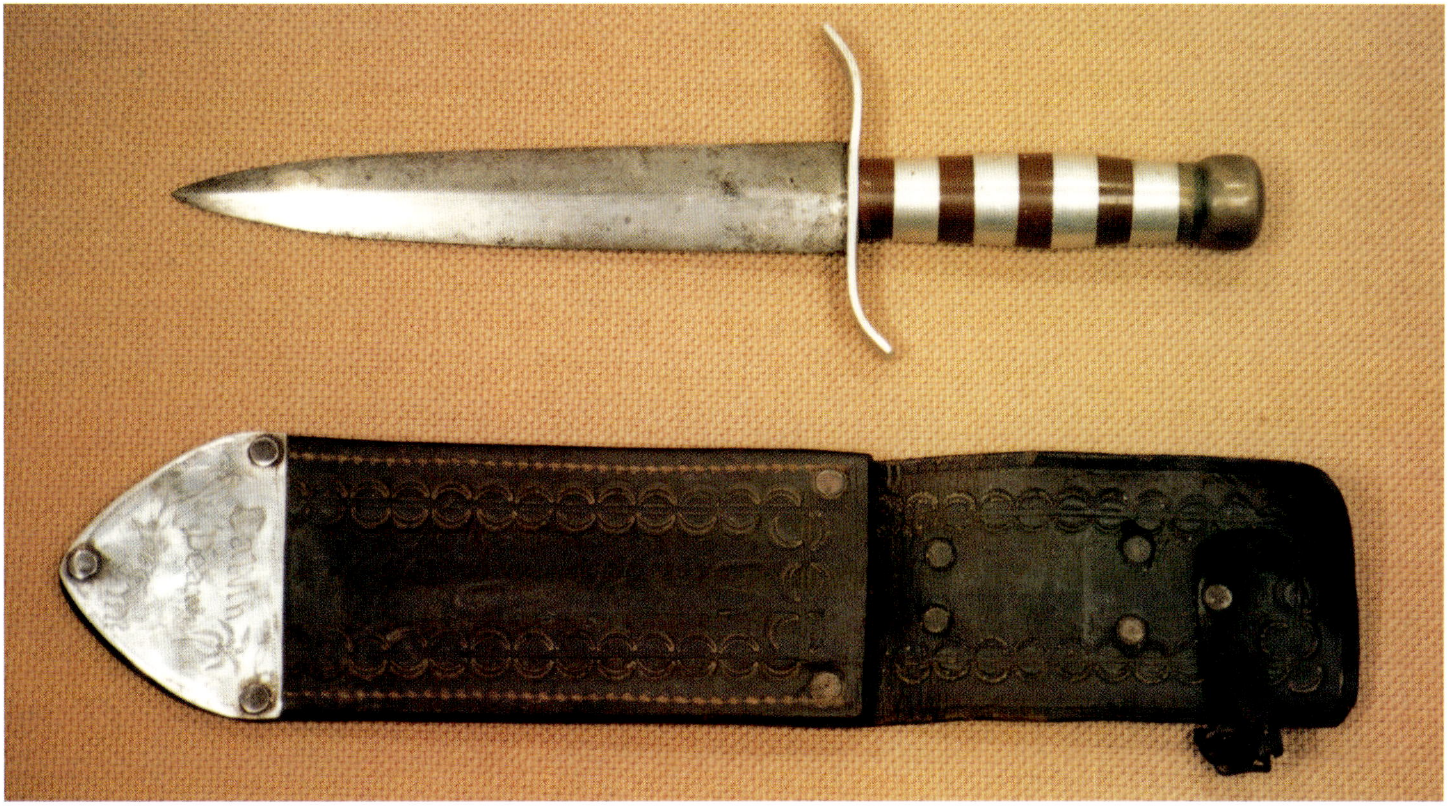

The 7 3/8" double edge blade of this quality knife is 1/4" thick. This knife has a long S shaped aluminum cross guard and brass pommel. The handle is made from red Micarta and aluminum. The quality hand embossed and engraved sheath is marked "CALVIN DEAN, SOUTH PACIFIC, 1943-1944, GUADALCANAL." Collectors value $500.00. (Wright Collection)

This unusual knife was made and carried by "CORPORAL WILBURN NEVINS." It was reported to me that he made this 9 1/4" blade from a Nazi half-track leaf spring. The brass cross guard is securely brazed to the blade. The handle was made using leather and aluminum spacers. The heavy-duty sheath is engraved with his serial number, the initials "WEN, 136 ord- A," and a horse. Collectors value $500.00. (Wright Collection)

This large double edge fighter was carried by "A.L. FAUVER, U.S. ARMY," and is so marked on the pommel. This knife has an 8 1/4" blade that is 1 3/4" wide. It has a brass cross guard and pommel. Brown and red Micarta, along with aluminum and brass spacers were used to make the handle. The sheath has a skull and crossbones painted on it. Collectors value $775.00. (Wright Collection)

Because fighting knives were in short supply, many types of knives were modified and used. Pictured here are butcher knives modified into fighting knives. The same unknown person or company likely modified both knives, because they each have the same type of cross guard. The top knife has a 9 3/8" blade with sharpened back edge, and an aluminum cross guard that has been screwed into the top of the wooden handles, as well as having finger grooves cut into it. The sheath is marked "RICHARD CLEMENTS 552422 USMC." The lower knife has a 6 7/8" blade with the back edge sharpened all the way back. Generic sheaths were used for both knives. Collectors value (top) $250.00 (lower) $150.00. (Wright Collection)

This knife is one of my favorites. The 5 3/4" blade is very well made and has a high polish. Aluminum was used for the pommel and cross guard. The handle was made using Micarta, leather, and aluminum spacers. The blade is marked "E.M. WENTZEL 33230495." His dog tags accompany the knife, which indicate he was in the Air Force. The sheath is marked on the back "WO495." This is a laundry number that was commonly marked on most personal items of WWII servicemen. This number is the first letter of the serviceman's last name and the last four numbers of his serial number. It is not known if Wentzel is the maker, owner, or both. Collectors value $500.00. (My Collection, Bill Wright)

This knife has a blade design that was popular in the 1840s, but it was clearly made during WWII. The 6 5/16" single edge clip point blade is very well made. The blade is marked "GEO. H. SCHAEFFER." Collectors value $350.00. (Wright Collection)

The 9 13/16" blade of this knife is marked "HAROLD J. LAHM, NO. 35592187." The blade is 1 5/8" wide and hand decorated on top. The leather spacer handle is accented with aluminum and brass spacers. The aluminum bird head shaped pommel is pinned to the tang of the blade. The hand made leather sheath is well made. Collectors value $250.00. (Wright Collection)

The sheath of this knife is marked with two names, "W.R. BIBBY" and "A.D. WHITE." We can only guess who these WWII servicemen were. The knife pictured here has an 8 13/16" clip point blade. Painted under the 1/4" Plexiglass spacer handle are the patriotic colors red, white, and blue. The aluminum cross guard is cast directly onto the blade. Collectors value $300.00. (Wright Collection)

Right: Both knives on this page belonged to "WARREN J. CLEAR, COLONEL U.S. ARMY." He was in WWI and retired from the army in 1935. When WWII came along he enlisted for active duty 4-26-1941. He then was in military service until 6-30-1946. Colonel Clear was awarded the Distinguished Service Medal, Legion of Merit, and the Purple Heart. The top knife has an 8" blade that is 1 3/8" wide and 1/4" thick. This knife has full tang construction, with the top visible between the one piece walnut handle. Other similar knives are known made by the same unknown maker, and are marked with the owner's name and or serial number on top of the tang between the wood handles. The lower knife has a 7 15/16" double edge blade. The aluminum cross guard and pommel were cast on to the blade. The wooden handle slabs are held on with brass pins. The blade is marked "A.J. VANADESTIN," a knife maker from Wisconsin (see chapter 4 for more details on this maker). The Collectors value for these knives is higher because the owner is identified and some of his military history is known. Collectors value (top) $1,200.00 (lower) $2,000.00. (Wright Collection)

Above: The same unknown WWII maker—who may have made the knives aboard ship—made these two knives. The top knife has a 7 3/8" blade that is 1 3/8" wide. The back of the sheath is marked "JOHN E. HALMO U.S.N.A.F." The aluminum cross guard is cast directly onto the blade. The dimensions and construction of both knives and sheaths are very similar. The collectors value is always more for a personally identified knife. Collectors value (top) $275.00 (lower) $200.00. (Wright Collection)

Left: The top knife is marked "WMJ to MG." I do not know who WMJ was, but MG is William M. Gemen of Wisconsin. This professionally made knife has a 6 5/8" blade that is 3/16" thick. The lower knife has an unusually shaped blade that is 8 1/8" long and 1/4" thick. It has a nickel cross guard and pommel nut. Collectors value $275.00 each. (Wright Collection)

COL. WARREN J. CLEAR

COL. WARREN J. CLEAR

This long blade Theater Knife was made from a large file that is 1/4" thick. The blade length is 11", and the overall length is 15 1/2". The knife has an S shaped brass cross guard and a sculpted aluminum pommel. The handle is made from black Micarta and aluminum spacers. The owner's name, "A.F. HOOD," is on the handle. The blade is marked "MADE AT U.S.N.A.S. ALOMEDA, CALIF." The sheath is made of heavy fiberboard and is screwed together. Collectors value $350.00. (Wright Collection)

These two high quality Bowie knives were made by the same unknown maker. It was reported to me that he was thought to be located in southern Illinois. I know of another, and all three are hand engraved with the owner's name. The top knife has an 8 5/8" long, 1 5/8" wide, and 1/4" thick blade with an overall length of 13 7/8". Both knives have similar brass teardrop shaped cross guards and round aluminum pommels. The handles of both knives are made of leather, Plexiglass, and brown Micarta spacers. The blade (top knife) is dated "5/3/44" and is engraved with the owner's name, "DONALD H. NEWZUEST U.S.N." The bottom knife has an 8 5/16" blade that is 1 1/2" wide and 3/16" thick, and has an overall length of 13". The cross guard and pommel are brass that has been nickel plated. The name "DWIGHT E. DRAGOO" is engraved on the blade. The high quality sheaths are similar and made by the same maker. The back of the sheath is made from two thin layers of leather, and the front is made from one layer. There is an unusual design impressed in the top of the sheath where the keeper strap is attached. Collectors value (top knife, unused condition) $500.00 (bottom knife) $400.00. (Wright Collection)

This unusual WWII knife has a 10 1/2" double edge blade. What is unusual? The blade is made out of aluminum. I own three Theater Knives with aluminum blades. The aluminum for these blades must be special high grade aircraft aluminum. I would not think aluminum would make a good blade, however, this knife has a good sharp edge on both sides. I decided to do a little test. I hit the cutting edge of this knife with another steel blade knife. Both blades had similar nicks. I think this might be a good fighting knife. The knife is marked "JERRY FENDER 39141748." It is not known if Jerry Fender was the owner, maker, or both. Whoever made it did a very professional job. Collectors value $750.00. (Wright Collection)

This grouping of WWII memorabilia belonged to "HAROLD G. NAGEL," who was a sailor aboard the "USS SOUTH DAKOTA." His Theater Knife was altered from a WWI Ross Bayonet. The hand made sheath is laced with wire and has his name cut into the front. Shown with the knife are the medals and ribbons awarded to him for his service during WWII. His dog tags are next to an old photograph of the ship USS South Dakota, and its official number "BB57." Another very interesting piece of memorabilia is a card presented to him that states: "USS SOUTH DAKOTA (BB57), Tokyo Bay, 2 Sept. 1945. This is to certify that Harold G. Nagel, was present in Tokyo Bay on board the USS SOUTH DAKOTA, Flagship of Fleet Admiral Nimitz, U.S.N., during the formal surrender of the Japanese Forces to the Allied Powers. Signed by W.F. Halsey, Admiral, U.S. Navy, Commander, Third Fleet." Also signed by "E.P. Forrestel, Captain U.S. NAVY, Commanding Officer." Collectors value includes all memorabilia pictured above and others not shown. Collectors value $1,000.00. (Wright Collection)

This unusual knife has a 5 3/4" double edge blade. The aluminum cross guard was cast on to the blade. The front of the handle is marked "CYRIL YOUNG," and "APPLETON, WIS" is on the backside. The bottom of the wood handle is marked "V" for victory. The leather sheath is held together with brake shoe rivets and has a belt buckle type keeper strap. Collectors value $300.00. (Wright Collection)

Several collectors have called this the "BEEHIVE KNIFE," because the pommel resembles a beehive. This high quality knife has a 6 1/4" blade that is 1 1/2" wide and was originally bright blue. Collectors value $1,000.00. (Wright Collection)

Pictured above is a knife that is very likely Theater Made. The 7" blade was made out of a bayonet, possibly Japanese. The knife has an aluminum hand guard and pommel. The handle has 1/4" thick Plexiglass spacers, which is the right thickness for some WWII aircraft windshields and canopies. The center of the handle is made of wood and has a woman's picture incased in aluminum and Plexiglass. Likely this is the picture of the owner's wife or sweetheart. The wonderful hand made sheath is sewn and held together with brake shoe rivets marked "5-5." The outstanding part of the sheath is the decoration. The front of the sheath is hand carved with "USN," the likeness of a sailor, the initials "JEA," and a palm tree. The back of the sheath is imprinted "JACK ARMIT 607-21-89." It is not known if Armit was the maker, owner, or both. Because of everything stated here, this knife and sheath make a very historic and desirable WWII collectible. Collectors value $650.00. (Wright Collection)

6

Sword Knives

The WWII fighting knives shown in this chapter were made out of a variety of old swords and sabers. Many of these were still held at U. S. Arsenals and storage facilities at the beginning of WWII. Most were of Civil war vintage, but some were from earlier times. Fighting knives were scarce and in great demand at the beginning of the war. The U.S. Government sold swords, sabers, and bayonets to companies and individuals to be made into the fighting knives our troops badly needed. A knife maker could make three knives out of one sword. The bottom section of blade usually incorporated the original handle, modified to the maker's own design. The center and top sections required new handles and cross guards to be made. There are several distinct varieties made by known and unknown makers. Several different kinds of sword, saber, and bayonet knives have been found in the same identical kind of sheath. This leads me to believe some unknown person or company was in the business of modifying them into fighting knives during WWII.

The top knife was made out of a 1913 Patton Cavalry Saber and has a wonderful tooled leather sheath. This sword knife was modified at the San Antonio Iron Works of San Antonio, TX. It has a blade length of 8 3/8" and is 14 1/2" overall. Both knives were made from bottom sections of blades using the original handles modified to the maker's design. The bottom knife was made out of a Civil War Cavalry Saber and has an 8" finely etched blade. The sheath pictured with this knife is of the kind previously discussed above. Collectors value (top) $600.00, (bottom) $350.00. (Wright Collection)

This knife was made out of an 1850 period French sword. The blade was cut down to a 6 1/2" Bowie clip point with a sharpened false edge (top of clip point sharpened). An oval cross guard has been brazed to the blade. The original sword handle, including its fancy brass ferrule and pommel, was left intact. The hand made sheath is stitched with white string. Collectors value $275.00. (Wright Collection)

This sword knife was made from the tip of a Patton saber at the San Antonio Iron Works and has a typical sheath made by them. The knife they originally produced had a two piece wooden handle. This knife was likely Theater Altered, possibly in the South Pacific Theater by a serviceman who changed the handle using Plexiglass and aluminum from a downed aircraft. Collectors value $300.00. (Wright Collection)

This group of WWII fighting knives was made out of Civil War swords by the same unknown maker previously discussed in the introduction of this chapter. The blade lengths are approximately 8". The bottom knife was originally a W. Clauberg saber made in Solingen, Germany, in the 1860s. It still has the original blade etching. The center knife was made out of a center section of blade, while the other two were made out of the bottom sections. This is the kind of sheath found with a variety of sword, saber, and bayonet knives. Collectors value (right to left) $375.00, $250.00, $450.00. (Wright Collection)

These two WWII fighting knives were made using the bottom blade section of the sword and their original handles. The top knife pictured above has a 10" blade with a sharpened top edge and is made from a French sword. The sheath was made from a belt sewn with a bootlace. The bottom knife has a 10" blade. Collectors value (top) $300.00 (bottom) $225.00. (Wright Collection)

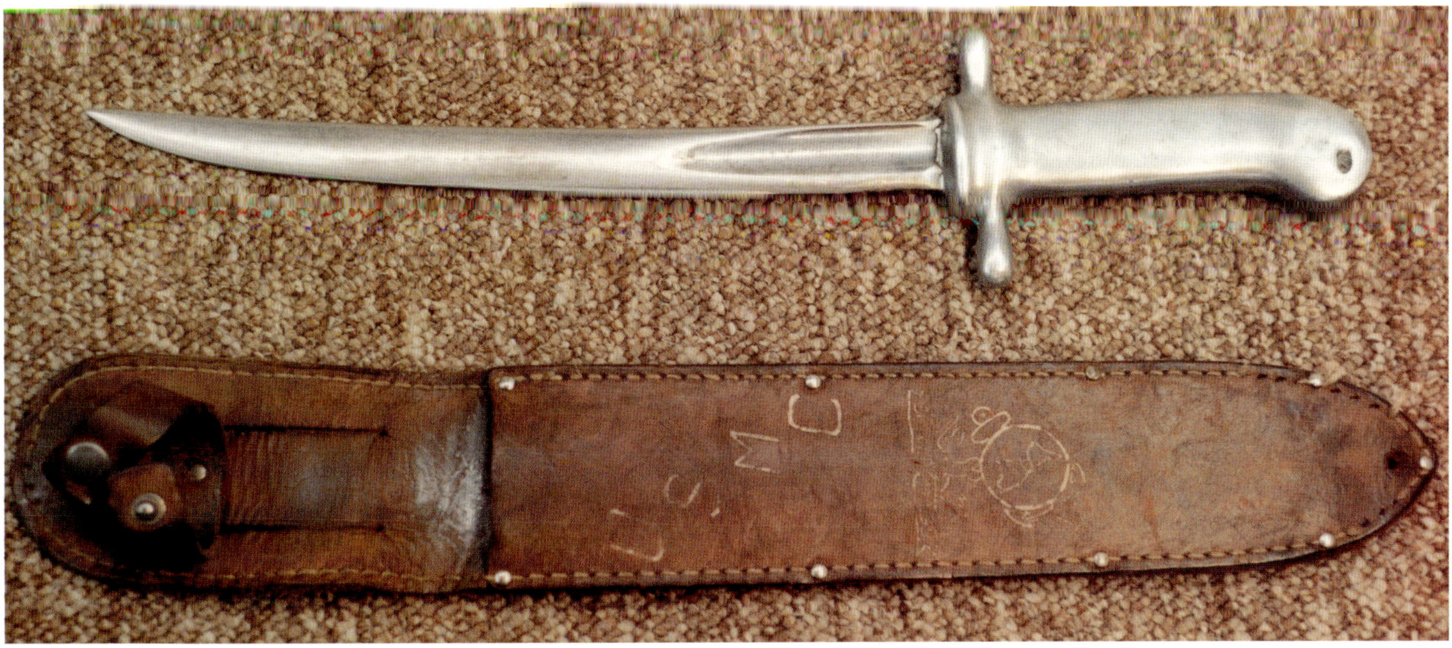

The tip section of an unidentified sword was used to make this WWII fighting knife. Because of the sheath that accompanies this knife I believe this is another style of sword knife made by the previously discussed unknown maker. The blade length is 10 1/2". The handle is made of aluminum and is cast onto the blade. There are other known knives of this type. Other knives exist with this style of handle, but have different blade designs. The sheath has been hand decorated with "USMC" and the "MARINE CORPS INSIGINA" Collectors value $350.00. (Wright Collection)

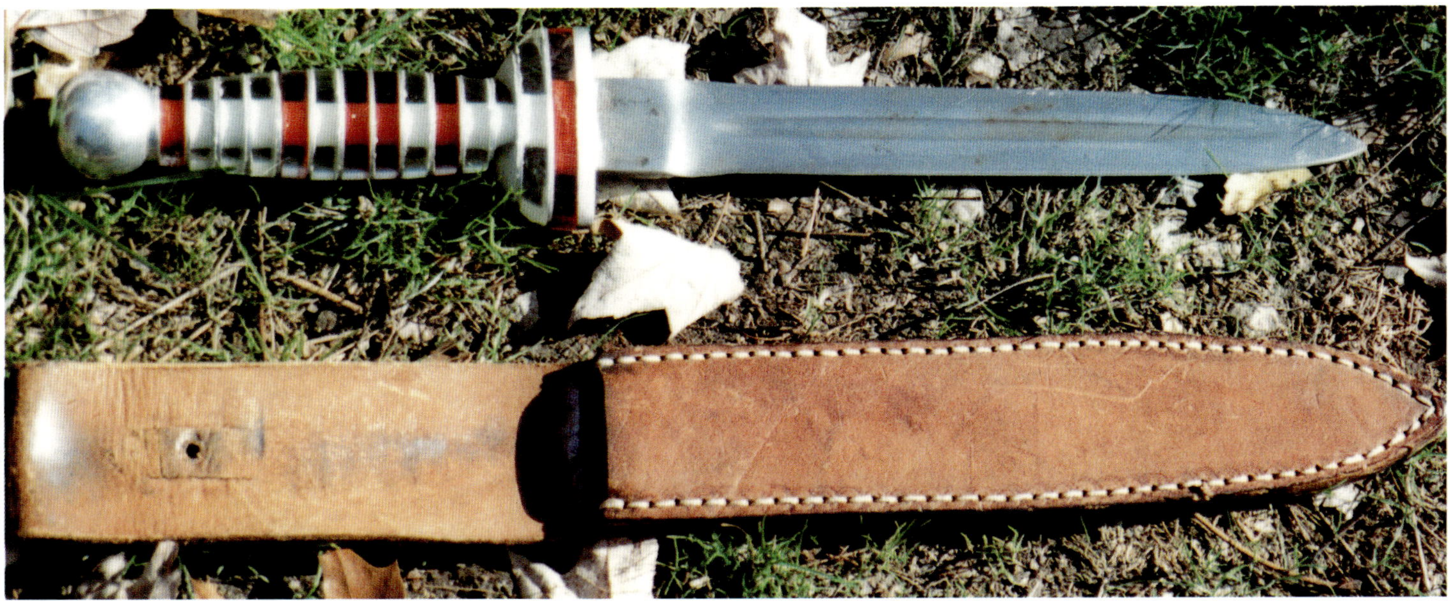

This Theater Knife was made from the bottom section of a Patton Saber with a blade length of 9" and has an overall length of 15". The double edge blade has been reduced in thickness to make the knife lighter in weight and easier to carry. The handle is made of 1/4" Plexiglass and thin aluminum spacers. The Plexiglass could be from an airplane window canopy. The thin aluminum is about the right thickness to be part of the outer skin of an airplane. A naval veteran told me that he made knives similar to this one aboard ship during WWII. He explained that they painted colors inside the Plexiglass handle to make the knives more colorful. Collectors value $300.00. (Wright Collection)

Knife Crafters of Chestnut Hill, Philadelphia, PA, made this impressive group of sword knives. The sheaths pictured here are typical of Knife Crafters' leatherwork and are original to their respective knives. The blade lengths range from 7" to 7 1/4". The top knife and sheath are marked with the Knife Crafters logo. The second and fourth knives were made from Civil War swords. The third knife has a double edge blade made from the center section of a Patton Saber. Notice the difference in the cross guards, particularly the bottom knife. Collectors value $750.00 each. (Wright Collection)

This WWII fighting knife was made out of a Civil War Saber imported from Germany by Horstman and Son from Philadelphia, PA. In the past collectors believed that these cut down sabers were altered during the Civil War. We now know that most conversions of swords to knives were done during WWII. The blade has been shortened to 8". I have seen other WWII altered swords, sabers, and bayonets with identical sheaths, which leads me to believe the same unknown knife maker altered all knives found in this type of sheath. Collectors value $300.00. (Wright Collection)

These two WWII fighting knives were made out of the tip section (bottom knife) and center section (top knife) of a WWI Patton Saber. These examples are another style of WWII Patton Saber knives made by another unknown maker, which are different from other knives previously discussed. The blade lengths are 7 1/2". The sheaths are typical for this type of knife. Collectors value $300.00 each. (Wright Collection)

Knives on this page were made from WWI Patton Sabers at the San Antonio Iron Works of San Antonio, TX. Three fighting knives could be made from one sword. Pictured above is a knife made by using the original hilt and bottom section of the sword blade. The lower picture shows knives made from tip sections (left and right) and center section (center knife). Knives made from tip and center blade sections typically have crude, rough wood handles. The sheaths for these knives are very nice, have embossed designs on the front, and are typical for San Antonio Irons Works knives. Collectors value (top) $600.00 (lower, right to left) $350.00, $350.00, $175.00 (without sheath). (Wright Collection)

Anderson of Glendale, CA, made the two center knives in the above picture. He used surplus Patton Sabers and could make three knives out of each sword. The knife on the left has a Theater Altered handle and was made at the San Antonio Iron Works. The knife on the right was also made from a Patton Saber. Collectors value (left to right) $300.00, $750.00, $600.00, $275.00. (Wright Collection)

Separate unknown makers made the two center knives from sword blades. The third knife from the left was made using a Patton Saber handle. The knife on the right is high quality. The 6 7/8" double edge blade is 3/16" thick. The left knife was made in France in 1944. Collectors value (left to right) $150.00, $200.00, $225.00, $250.00. (Wright Collection)

7

Bayonet Knives

Knives shown in this section were made out of bayonets, most of which were likely Theater Altered.

It was reported to me that a Canadian soldier took this Luftwaffe belt, buckle, and bayonet from a German prisoner in WWII. He modified the handle and wore the rig for the remainder of the war. Collectors value complete as shown $325.00. (Wright Collection)

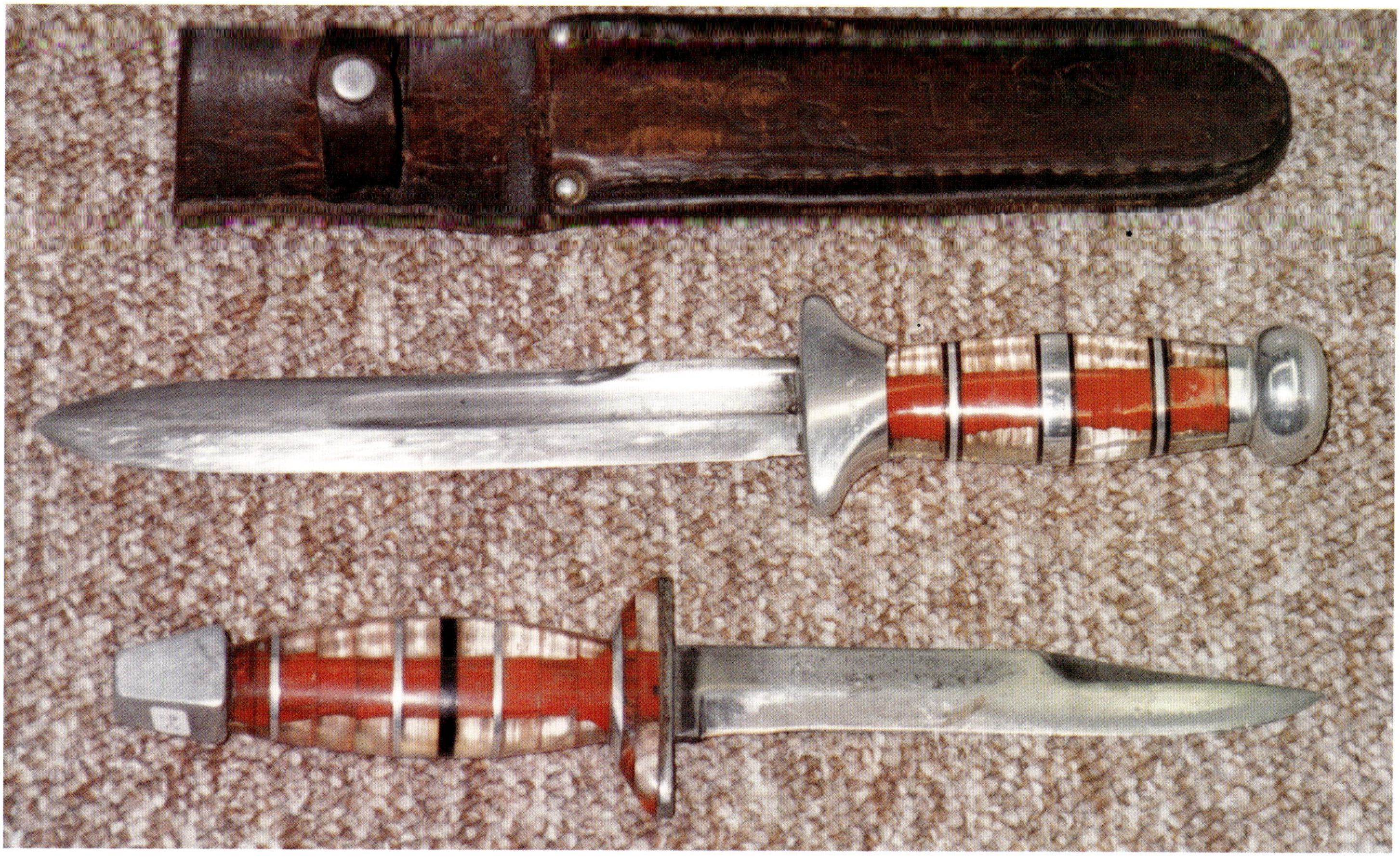

The two Theater Knives pictured above were made using standard issue blades and are of very good quality. An M1 bayonet was used for the top knife, while the bottom knife has an M3 blade possibly made by Aerial. The sheath for the top knife is marked "CARLSON." Collectors value (top) $275.00 (bottom) $150.00. (Wright Collection)

This WWII Theater Knife was made out of a German bayonet blade. The cross guard is S shaped and engraved top and bottom. The walnut handle has relief carving of a branch, leaves, and flowers. Collectors value $275.00. (Wright Collection)

The lower knife pictured above was made from an M1 Garand Bayonet and still has the original scabbard. Aluminum was used for making the cross guard and pommel, as well as spacers for the handle. The top knife was made out of an unidentified bayonet using materials the maker had at hand. Collectors value (top) $100.00 (lower) $175.00. (Wright Collection)

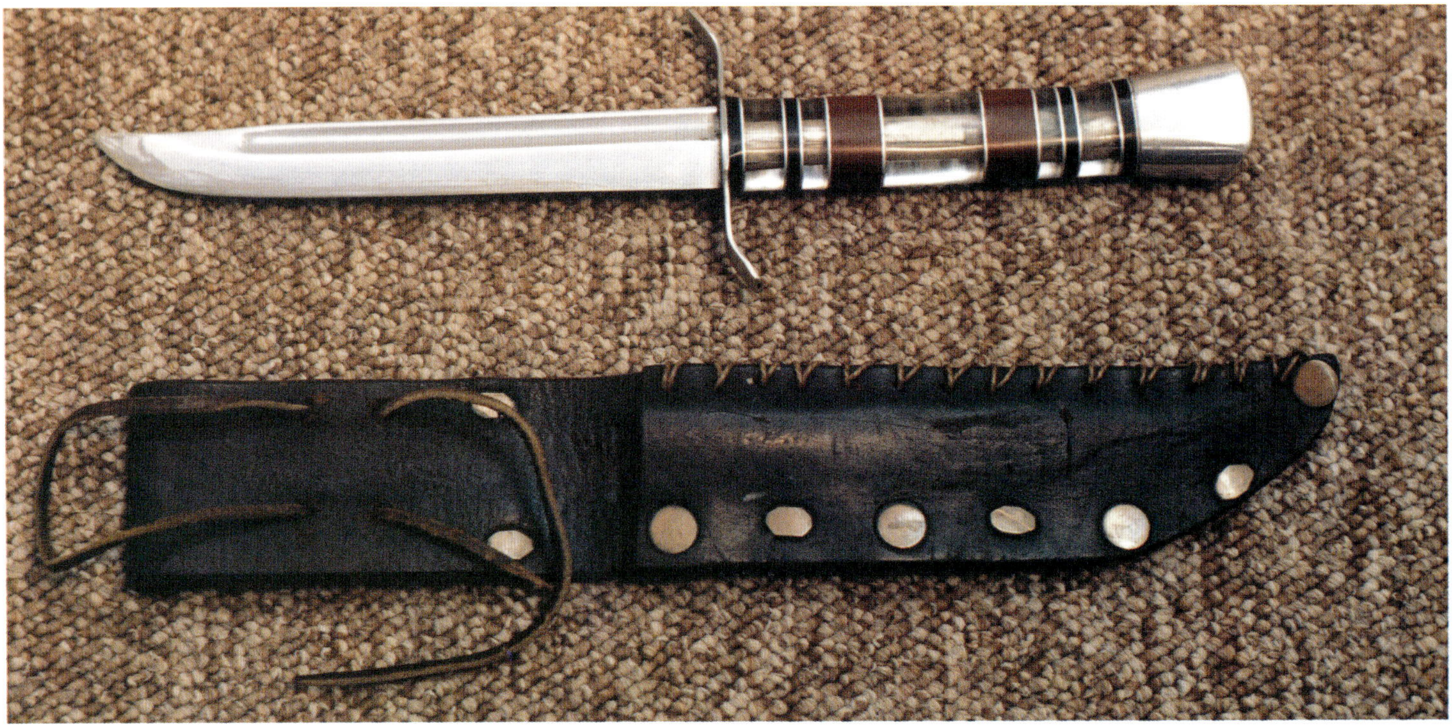

A Japanese bayonet blade was used to make the above Theater Knife. The blade is 6 1/2" long. The handle is unusually long at 5 3/8" and has a stainless steel cross guard and an aluminum pommel. The handle is constructed from Micarta, Plexiglass, and aluminum. The well made sheath is riveted and sewn with a coated heavy string. Collectors value $200.00. (Wright Collection)

This knife appears to be made out of a Model 1866 French bayonet. The 8 5/8" blade is inserted into a one piece brass handle frame. Thick slabs of red Micarta are attached with two brass pins. There are several other known knives similar to this one. I have several different sword, saber, and bayonet knives with identical sheaths. These are the same sheaths used with knives made by the unknown knife maker previously discussed in chapter 6. I know that some of these knives were issued to servicemen, however, it is not known if all were an issue item. Collectors value $250.00. (Wright Collection)

This Theater Knife was made from an M1 Garand bayonet made by Pal Cutlery Co. in Plattsburg, NY. The 6 5/8" upswept blade is finely crafted. The heavy steel cross guard was modified from the original. The handle was made using alternating black Bakelite and aluminum spacers. The knife and basket weave sheath are above average quality. Collectors value with sheath $225.00. (Wright Collection)

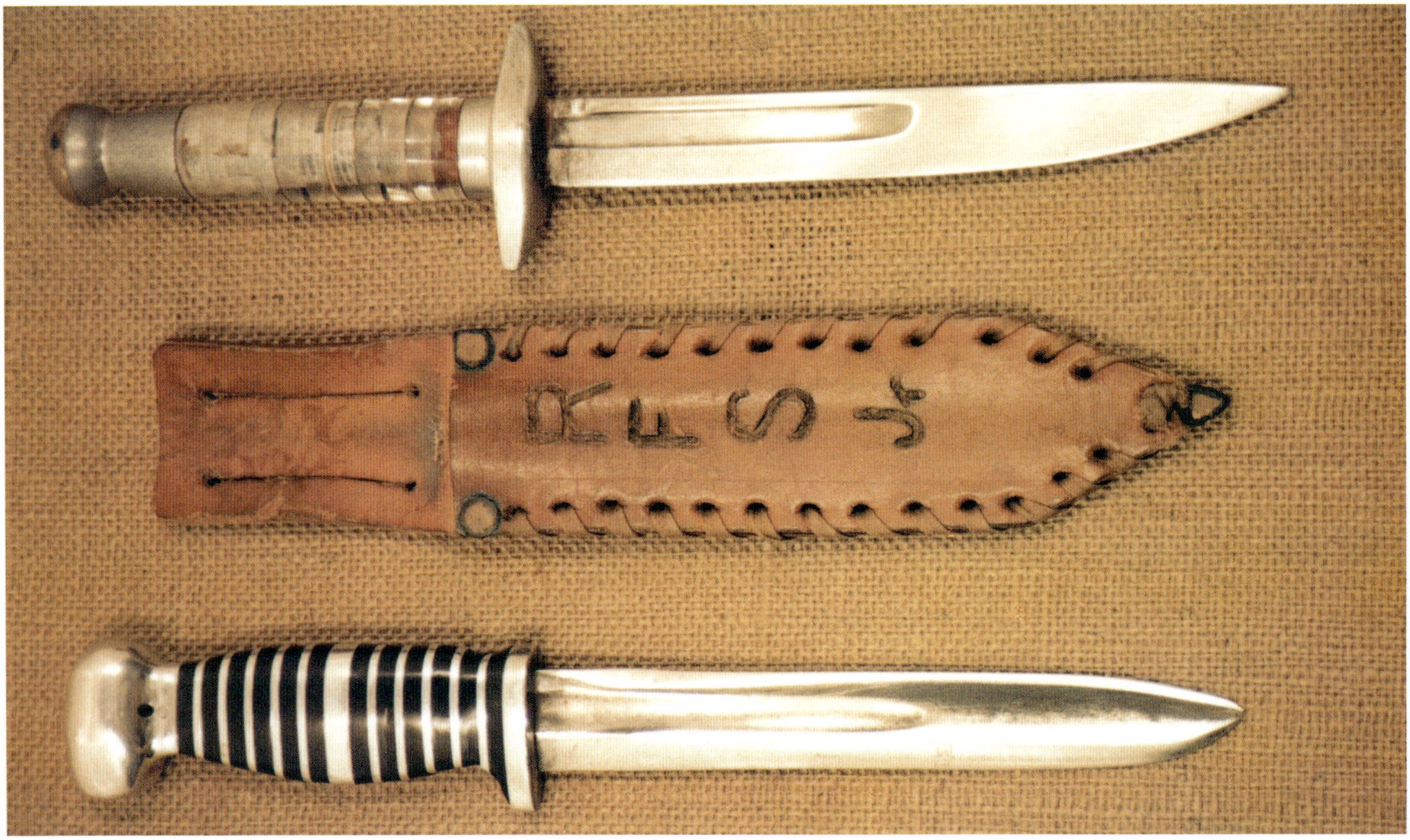

The top knife is made out of a Japanese bayonet blade that has been shortened to 7 1/8". The lower knife is made out of an M1 Garand bayonet blade and has been altered into a double edge fighter. The length of this blade is 6 3/4". Collectors value (top) $125.00 (lower) $150.00. (Wright Collection)

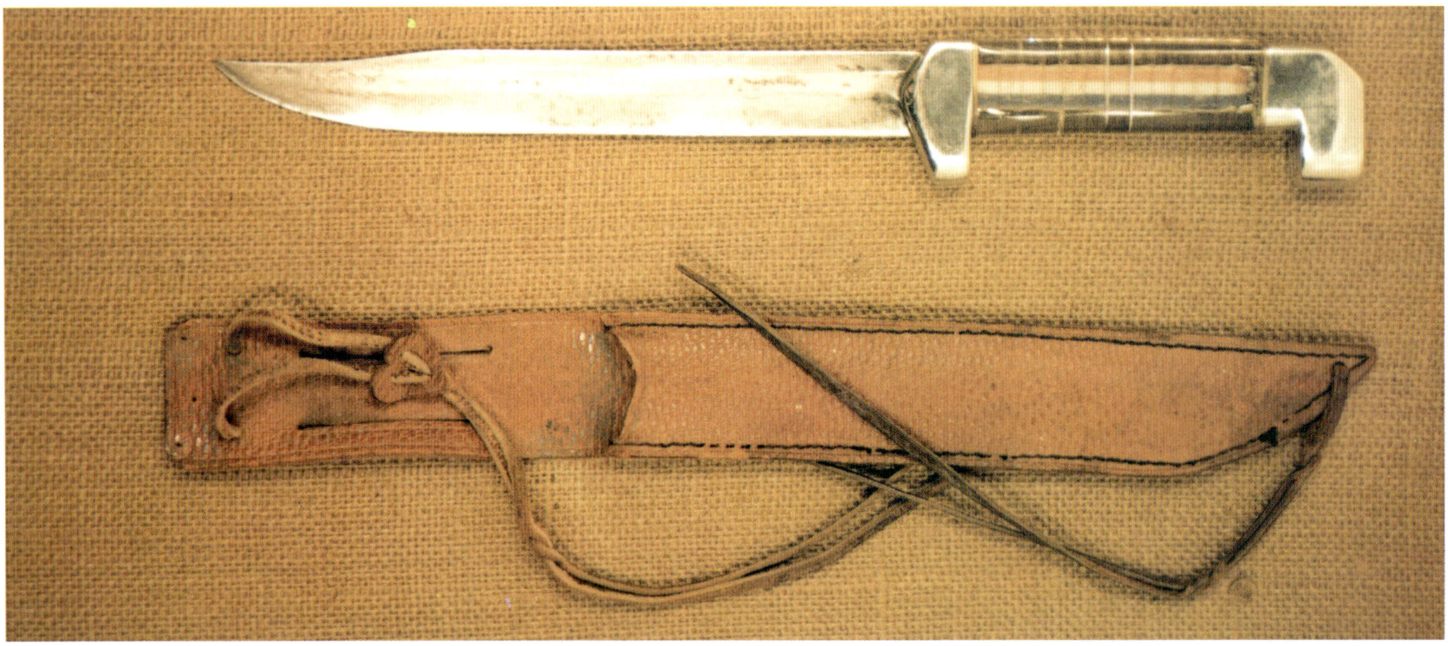

This WWII knife is likely Theater Made using a bayonet blade. The thickness of this 7 3/4" blade has been reduced to make the knife lighter in weight. The handle was made from 1/4" Plexiglass and has a cast aluminum pommel and hand guard. There is a patriotic red, white, and blue ribbon on the tang of the blade inside the Plexiglass handle. The back of the sheath is made out of two pieces of leather because one large piece was unavailable. Collectors value $275.00. (Wright Collection)

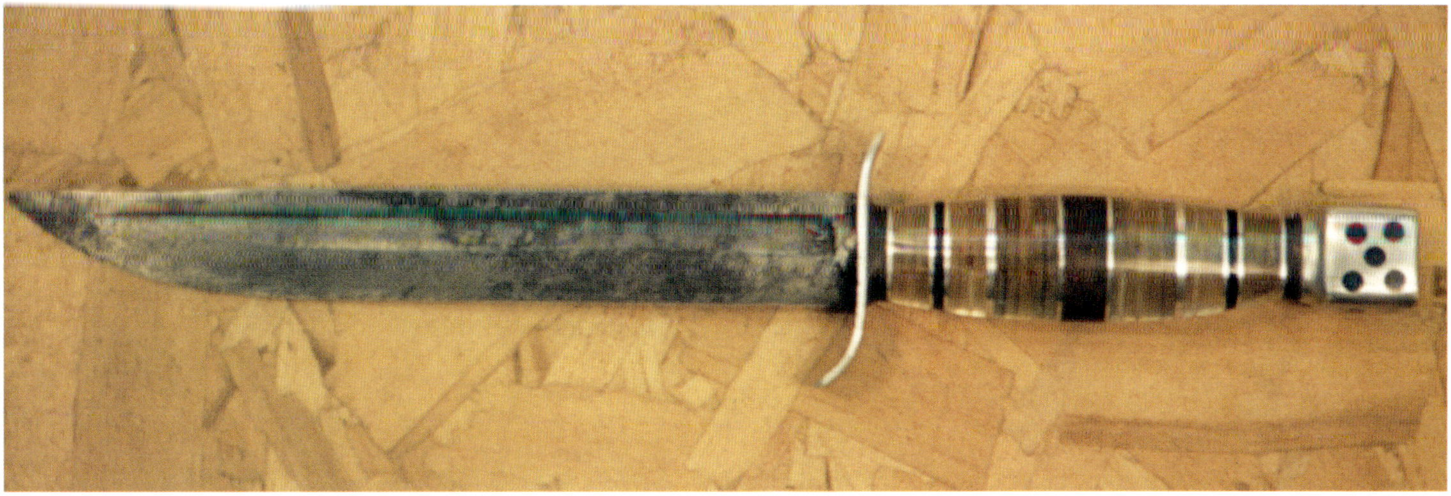

The knife above was made out of an unidentified bayonet or sword blade. The blade is welded to a round steel shaft to form the tang that holds the handle. The blade measures 7 1/2" and the total length is 12 1/2". The guard, as well as the unusual dice shaped pommel, is made out of aluminum. The handle was made of Plexiglass, aluminum, and black and brown Micarta. Collectors value $175.00. (Wright Collection)

This knife was made out of a WWII Japanese bayonet. The unusual brass cross guard is cast on to the blade. The handle is made of one piece of clear Lucite that is more than 3/4" thick. The sheath is made of leather covered wood with brass top and bottom mounts. Collectors value $275.00. (Wright Collection)

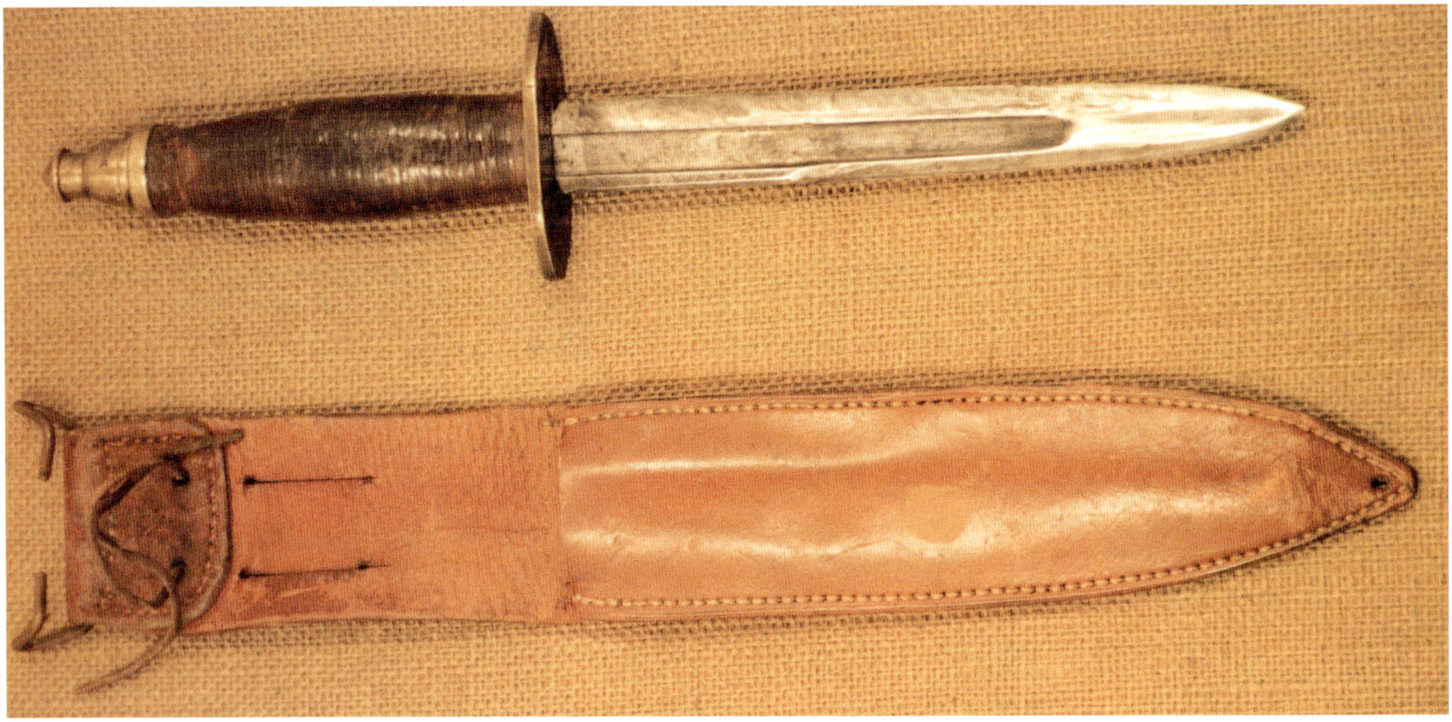

The 7 7/8" blade of this knife is made out of an M1 Garand bayonet and has a sharpened back edge. The knife has a thick oval brass cross guard and large skull crusher pommel. The handle is made of many thin leather spacers. Marked on the back of the sheath is "A-5113." Collectors value $175.00. (Wright Collection)

The top knife and sheath were made out of a Japanese bayonet and original scabbard. The two lower fighting knives were made out of English bayonets. Collectors value (top to bottom) $75.00, $100.00, $50.00. (Wright Collection)

The 7 9/16" blade of this knife was made from an M1 Garand bayonet. The name "LANDER" is engraved into the blood groove. It is not known if Lander was the maker, owner, or both. The sheath is marked "THIS SIDE TO PULLEY." Years ago machine shops were run by a series of overhead pulleys and leather belts. The belts were marked which side should run next to the pulley. Collectors value $225.00. (Wright Collection)

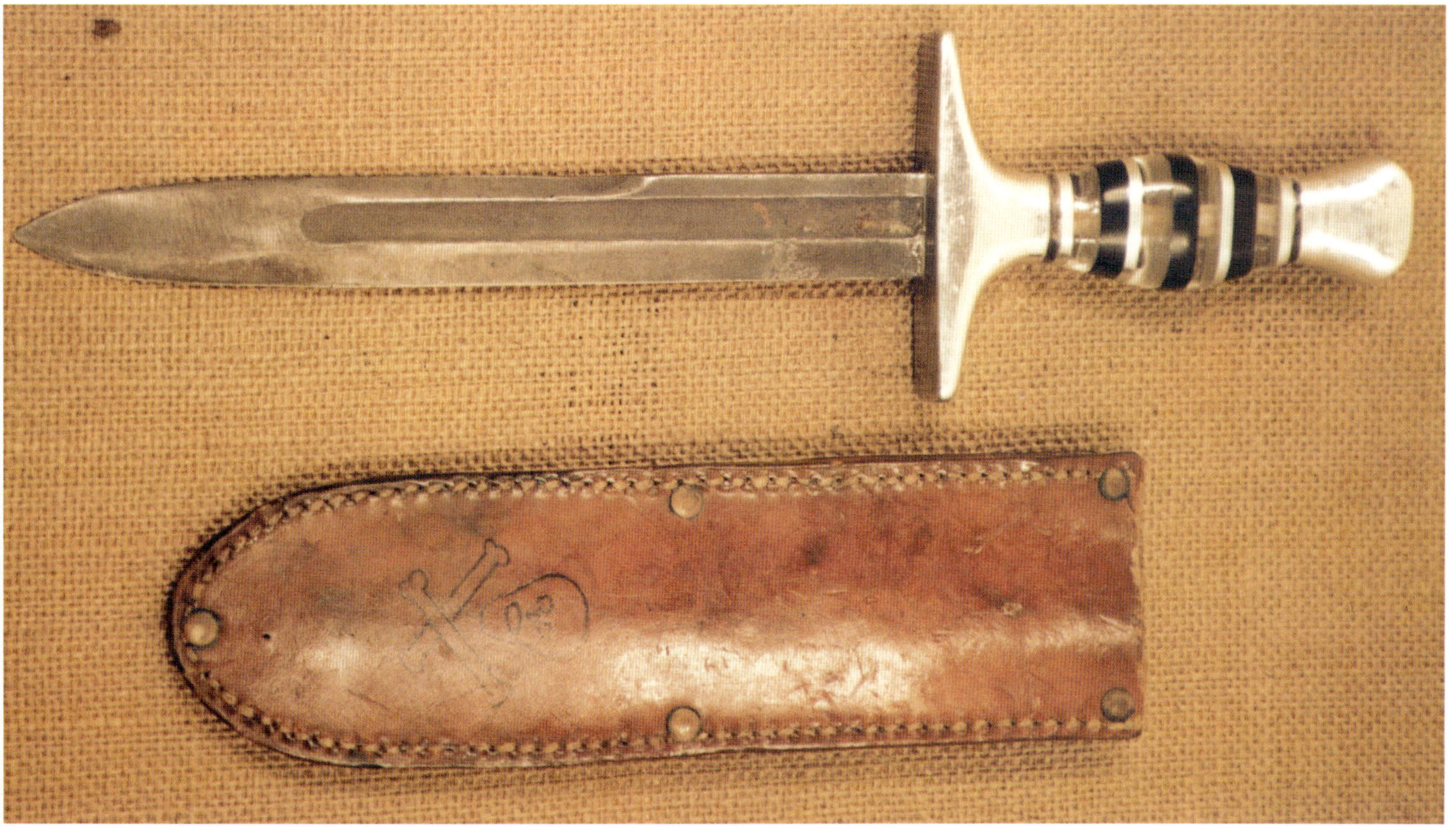

An M1 Garand bayonet was used to make this fighting knife. The 3 1/4" aluminum cross guard was cast directly onto the blade. On the front of the sheath is a "Skull and Crossbones," and on the back is the number "G-3899." Collectors value $175.00. (Wright Collection)

This WWII fighting knife was made out of a Model 1866 French bayonet. The back edge of the blade has been sharpened. The unusual hand forged cross guard has a large point made into the back. The handle is made of two thick slabs of Micarta held together with large brass harness rivets. The heavy-duty hand made sheath is stamped on the back side in an oval "G.W. McKIBBIN, SAN DIEGO- MAKER." Collectors value $375.00. (Wright Collection)

This fighting knife was made out of an M1 Garand bayonet. The back of the sheath is engraved "VOUZIER FRANCE MARCH 1945." "FRANCE 45" is carved into the front of the sheath. The bottom of the original bayonet scabbard is inside the leather sheath. The unusual handle, pommel, and cross guard were made from aluminum. Collectors value $500.00. (Wright Collection)

Ken Daurghty of Ottawa, IL, made this knife out of a bayonet blade while stationed in the Philippines during WWII. The handle was made using brown Micarta, wood, and water buffalo horn assembled and turned in a lathe to form the pattern. The cross guard and one handle spacer are made of aluminum. Collectors value $125.00. (Wright Collection)

This knife was made using an M3 or M4 blade. It has a brass cross guard and an aluminum pommel. The handle has red and green Bakelite, brass, aluminum, and leather spacers. The sheath is made out of stainless steel, with a Micarta liner and a spring to hold the knife in. Ernest Warther and Earl McDainels of Dover, OH, made similar style sheaths. Collectors value $400.00. (Wright Collection)

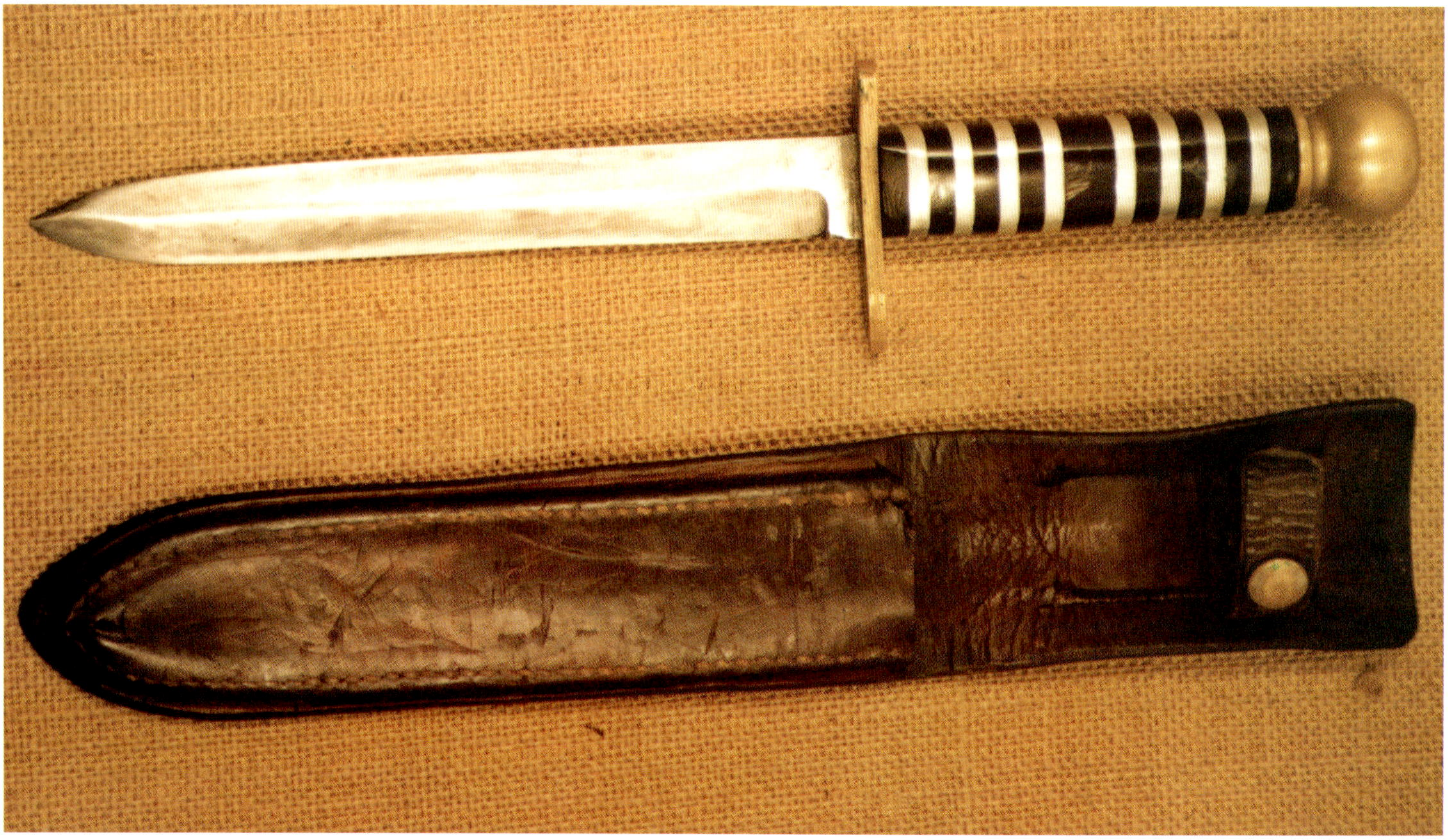

The WWII fighting knife above is made out of an English bayonet. It has a brass cross guard and large skull crusher pommel. Black Bakelite and aluminum were used to make the handle. Both knife and sheath are well made. Collectors value $275.00. (Wright Collection)

The top knife was made out of a Model 1866 French bayonet. The blade was shortened to 8 1/2". The tip section was likely made into another fighting knife. The lower knife was made out of a German sword. The blade is 8 1/4" long and has a sharpened false edge. This knife has a sheath of the same kind as previously discussed in chapter 6. Collectors value (top) $175.00 (lower) $200.00. (Wright Collection)

The lower knife was made out of a 1917 bayonet. It would be difficult to tell if this knife was altered during WWI or WWII, except for the fact that the handle is a 20 mm shell casting dated 1942. The top knife has an 8 1/2" double edge blade. The handle is made from Bakelite and Plexiglass. Collectors value (top) $200.00 (lower) $125.00. (Wright Collection)

8

Modified Factory & Issue Knives

The knives in this chapter were likely modified during WWII. It was reported to me by a number of veterans that in almost every case when you see a standard issue blade with aluminum and Plexiglass parts added, the knife was made aboard ship or in one of the various theaters of action. I refer to these knives as being Theater Altered. One of the reasons the handles were replaced was because the original leather handles would quickly rot off in the jungles of the South Pacific Theater. Another reason is the servicemen had spare time and did not want a standard issue knife.

The above two knives were altered from Cattaraugus 225Q knives. There are other known WWII Theater Knives with the same distinct pommel and hand guard as the top knife. There were some knives made in Torrance, CA, in the mid-1970s by Many Silva and Jim West. These were called Beaver Knives. They have a very similar pommel and hand guard as the top knife pictured here. Is this coincidence, or did one of these guys make Theater Knives during WWII? We will never know, because I have been told that both Silva and West are no longer with us. Collectors value (top) $225.00 (lower) $150.00. (Wright Collection)

The Cattaraugus Cutlery Co. of Little Valley, NY, originally made the above knives. The number designated for them was 225Q. This heavy-duty knife originally had stacked leather washer handles and a heavy steel pommel. They were one of the most commonly used knives of WWII. All of the above are Cattaraugus 225Q knives that were likely Theater Altered. They have very colorful handles and are well done. Collectors value $75.00-$125.00 with sheath. (Ballard Collection)

The group of Theater Altered knives pictured above was made using MK2 blades of various manufacturers. The knives pictured here are very good quality alterations likely done by soldiers in the field. Collectors value from $100.00 to $200.00 with sheath, depending on condition and quality of alteration. (Ballard Collection)

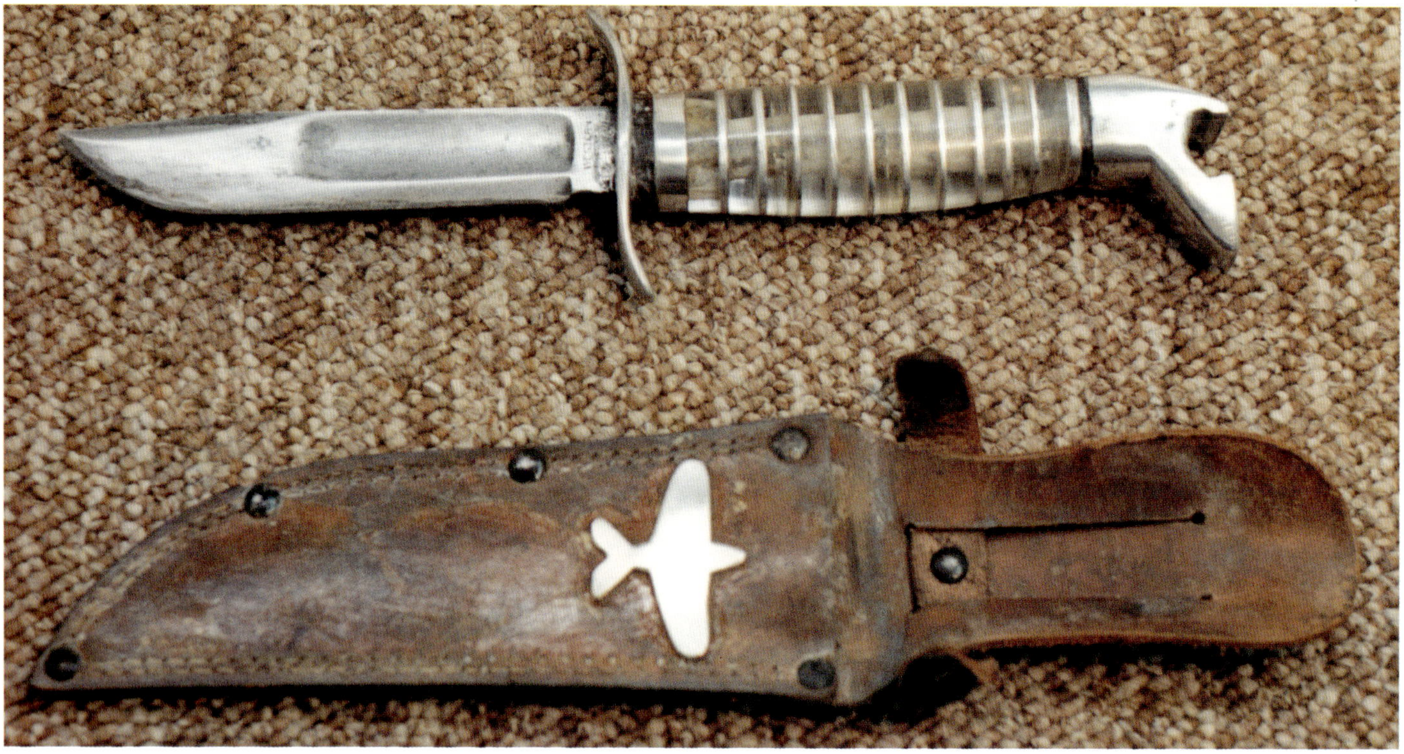

The above Theater Knife was made using a Marbles Ideal™ 5" blade. The cross guard and the boot shaped pommel have been made from aluminum. The handle was made using 1/4" Plexiglass and aluminum spacers. The sheath has a stainless steel airplane attached to the front. This unusual knife was likely altered using downed airplane parts. Collectors value $150.00. (Wright Collectors)

These two knives were likely Theater Altered using standard issue M2 knives and sheaths. The handles were altered using the materials the servicemen had at hand, which included aluminum, Plexiglass, and Micarta. This alteration was done with a lot of thought, artistic design, and skill. Collectors value (top) $200.00 (bottom) $150.00. (Wright Collection)

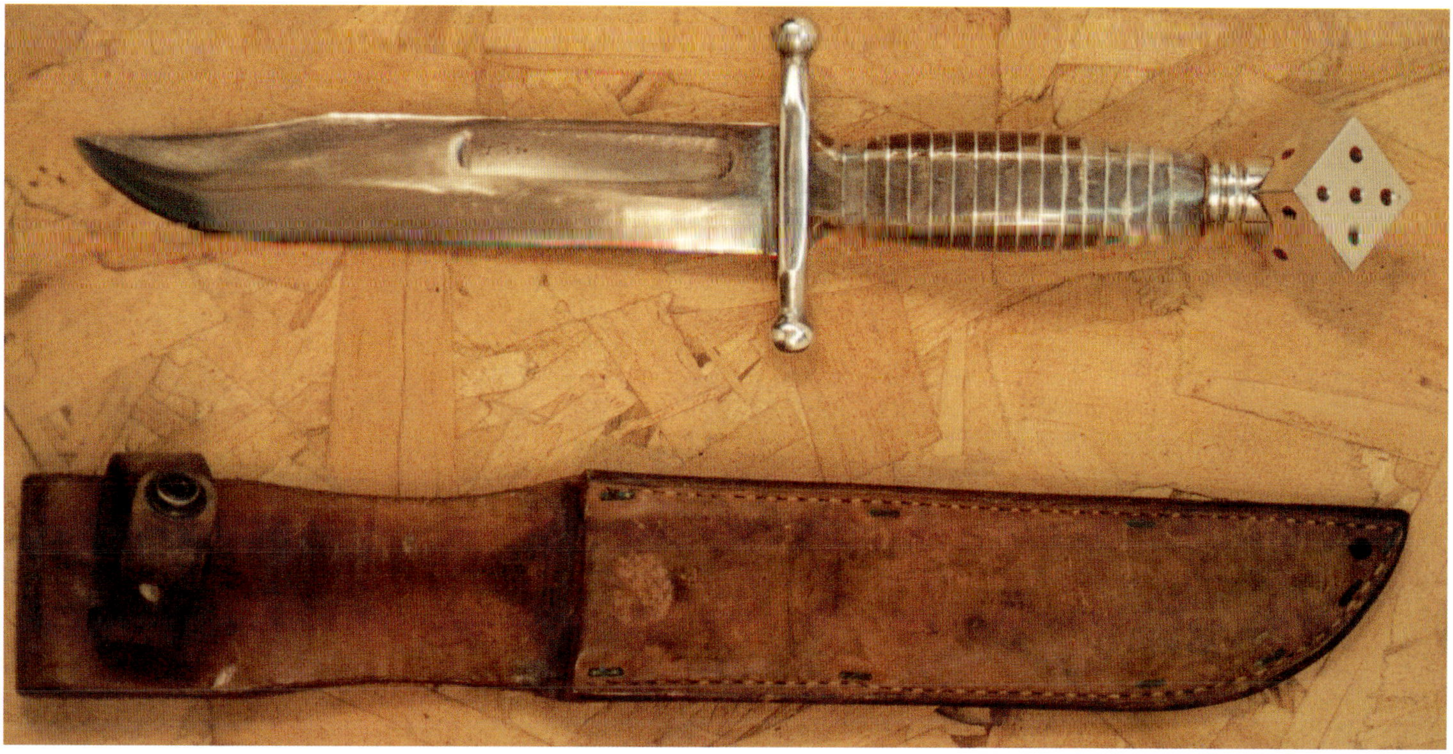

This is likely a Theater Altered knife using an unmarked MK2 blade. It has a cast aluminum hand guard and large dice pommel, which is not only decorative, but serves as a skull crusher. The handle is made of 1/4" Plexiglass spacers, which is the right size to be from an airplane windshield or canopy. Between each Plexiglass spacer is a thin aluminum spacer that is the right size to be from the skin of an aircraft. I have found from talking to servicemen who made and carried Theater Knives that most of the time when a knife has an issue blade and Plexiglass and aluminum handle it is almost positively Theater Altered (made or altered in one of the theaters of action). The sheath is an issue MK2 sheath that has the name "E.D. RICH" on the back. Collectors value $300.00. (Wright Collection)

The WWII serviceman that made this knife was very talented. He started out with an M3 or M4 blade. The M3 blade is from a standard issue fighting knife, and the M4 came from a bayonet that fit the M1 carbine. They are the same style blades and, as far as I can tell, there is no difference. The guard and pommel were cast from brass. The 1/4" Plexiglass handle spacers likely came from the canopy of a shot down aircraft. The sheath is cast from brass and then hand hammered. Collectors value $475.00. (Wright Collection)

This Theater Knife was created using a WWI LF&C trench knife blade. The attached tag has important information about the maker and owner. Unfortunately, part of the tag is missing. The handle conversion is of high quality and shows artistic ability. The sheath has a belt notch on the back, but could be hidden in a boot. Collectors value $275.00. (Wright Collection)

The top knife is made from a Cattaraugus 225Q blade. The handle is made of 1/4" Plexiglass slabs and has the American Flag proudly displayed on both sides of the handle. The sheath is hand carved and has the name "Ed." The bottom knife has a 6" blade. Painting the tang of the knife under the Plexiglass made the handle colorful. I know of another similar knife and sheath by the same unknown maker. Collectors value $250.00 each. (Wright Collection)

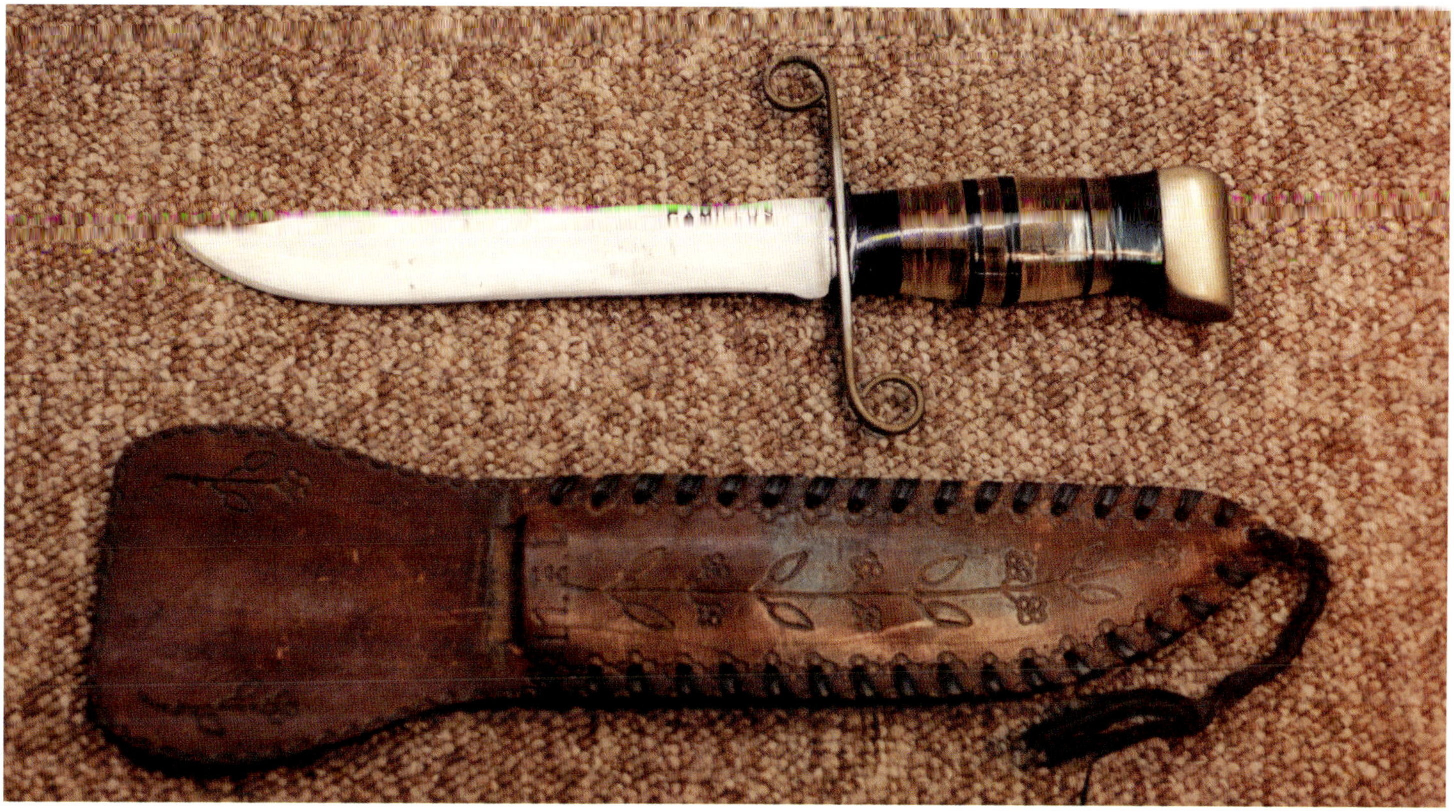

The 8" blade of this unusual Theater Knife was made from a Camillus butcher knife. The cross guard is 5" long. The quality sheath, which has the initials "M.E.L.," is hand decorated with a vine, leaves, and flowers. Collectors value $275.00. (Wright Collection)

The Ka-Bar Cutlery Co. of Olean, NY, made many different styles of knives during WWII, the most famous of which is the USMC MK2. The top knife was expertly Theater Altered using a Ka-Bar USMC MK2 blade and sheath. It has an aluminum eagle head pommel and heavy cross guard. The handle is made from Plexiglass and aluminum. The bottom knife has a 5 3/4" blade. It is not known if "G.W. WARD" is the maker or owner, but his name and "U.S.A. 1944" are nicely engraved on the handle. Collectors value (top) $400.00 (lower) $325.00. (Wright Collection)

The 8 3/4" blade of this Theater Knife was made from a Case XX™ machete and has a sharpened false edge. The handle is made of 5/8" thick Plexiglass and has finger grooves to give a better grip. The sheath is made of leather, with the front overlaid with a piece of thin aluminum. The sheath is stamped "LOAD ADJUSTER U.S. ARMY AIR FORCES" and has an extra wide keeper strap with two snaps. The snaps are marked on the back, "RAU FASTN. CO. PROV. (RAU FASTENER COMPANY PROVIDENCE, RI.). I have observed many WWII Theater Knife sheaths with this brand of snap. Collectors value $250.00. (Wright Collection)

The two knives pictured here are likely Theater Altered. The top knife has a CASE XX™ V-44 blade. It has a 1/4" thick cross guard and a heavy bird head shaped pommel. The sheath is a replacement. Below is a knife expertly altered from a CAMILLUS folding machete. The blade is 7 1/ 8", and the total length is 12". It has an aluminum cross guard and pommel. The handle has Plexiglass, aluminum, and brown Micarta spacers. The original sheath has the initials "REC Jr." stamped into the back. Collectors value (top) $250.00 (below) $225.00. (Wright Collection)

Some collectors might think that the above two valuable WWII items have been destroyed. I think this knife and sheath, that have been Theater Altered, are more personal to the owner than standard issue items. Therefore, this Fairbairn-Sykes knife and M6 sheath are valuable and desirable items today, especially to Theater Knife collectors. Collectors value $400.00 as pictured. (Wright Collection)

This WWII fighting knife was made from a U.S. Army 1940 Landers, Frary & Clark butcher knife. The maker has added a pair of wooden handles and a brass cross guard and pommel. The end of the blade tang has been altered to include a lanyard ring. The sheath is held together with brake shoe rivets. Collectors value $125.00. (Wright Collection)

This is a very rare knife. In 1941 the Wear-Ever pots and pans company approached the W.R. Case Cutlery Company to make a nine piece cutlery set. The order was made for 40,000 sets. Production had just begun when the attack on Pear Harbor happened. Within weeks W.R. Case had to cancel the contract and concentrate their efforts toward war production. These sets were only made for a very short time, and the number of knives made is unknown. The blade of the above pictured knife started out in one of those sets. This knife has an 8 5/16" blade that is marked "WEAR-EVER No. 55 PROCESS PAT No. 2147079." It has a double edge blade, with the top edge meant for chopping small bones when preparing food. It originally had a slab wood handle, but during the war this handle, pommel, and cross guard were added. The heavy leather sheath has been skillfully carved with crossed anchors, and the letters "USCG" (United States Coast Guard). Collectors value $500.00. (Wright Collection)

The 2 Theater Knives at left have colorful handles and are of high quality. Both were made from Cattaraugus 225Q knives. The knife to the left has a 3/8" thick aluminum cross guard and a handle made of 1/4" Plexiglass, aluminum, and wood spacers. The pommel was made from a Japanese mortar detonator that has the original tip, which can still be pushed up and down. The top of the sheath is covered with a thin aluminum sheet, likely from the skin of an airplane. The words "SOUTH PACIFIC" have been engraved into the aluminum. The knife on the right has a heavy cast aluminum S shaped cross guard and aluminum pommel. Collectors value (right) $200.00 (Ballard Collection) (left) $400.00. (Wright Collection)

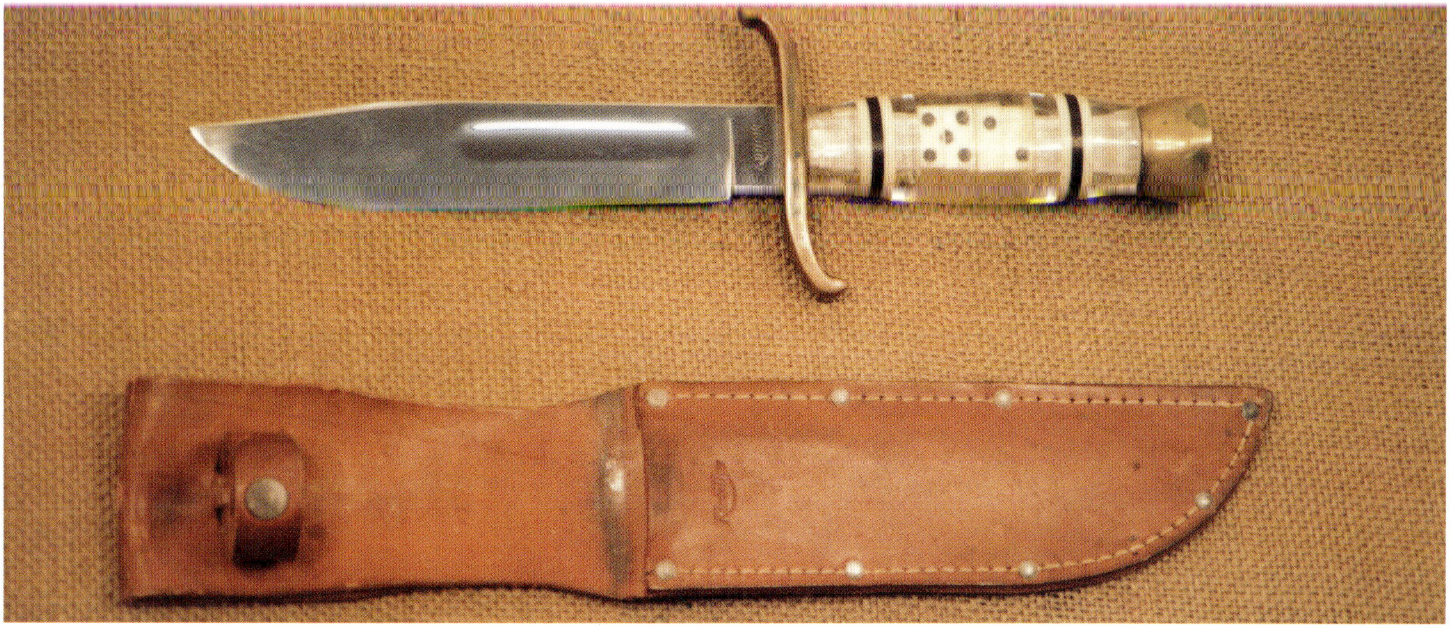

Pictured on this page are two WWII Kinfolks knives with original sheaths. Both knives were Theater Altered by the same unknown maker and came to me as a pair. The top knife has a brass cross guard and pommel. Encased inside the plexiglass spacer handle is a set of dice with 7s up for "good luck." The lower knife has an aluminum cross guard and pommel, and a Plexiglass handle with red, white, and blue spacers. Both knives and sheaths are in near mint condition. Collectors value (top) $225.00 (below) $175.00. (Wright Collection)

Left: These Theater Altered knives have original U.S. Government Issue blades and sheaths, and exhibit high quality craftsmanship in replacing their handles. Blade lengths are from 6" to 7". Collectors value, which includes sheath, (left to right) $150.00, $150.00, $275.00, $150.00. (Wright Collection)

The Pal Cutlery Co. of Plattsburg, NY, made the blade used in the knife pictured above. Pal designated the number RH36 to the original knife, which was one of the most commonly used knives of WWII. The original knife had a steel cross guard, stacked leather spacer handle, and an aluminum pommel. The replacement pommel is made from aluminum in the shape of a lion's head. This knife could have been made in the North African Campaign. Collectors value $200.00. (Wright Collection)

This M3 fighting knife is unmarked. An unknown craftsman did a fine job of rebuilding the handle, using different colors of Micarta and aluminum spacers and an aluminum pommel. Collectors value $175.00. (Wright Collection)

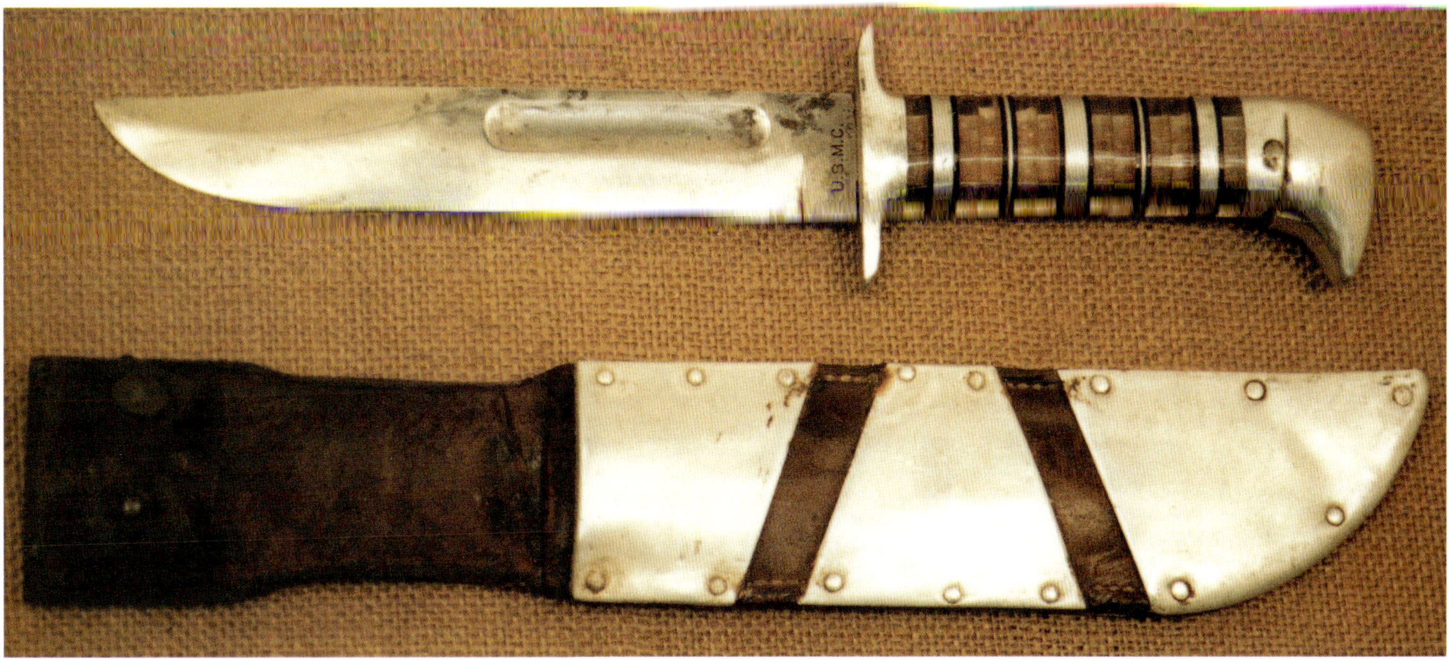

Pictured above is the rarest MK2 knife of WWII. It was made by the Robeson Cutlery Co. Rochester, NY, and marked USMC. Fortunately, or unfortunately, however the individual collector wants to look at it, this knife has been Theater Altered. The cross guard and pommel has been replaced with aluminum. The original leather handle has been replaced with Plexiglass and aluminum spacers. The sheath has been reinforced with thin aluminum that likely came from the skin of an aircraft. This is an excellent job of altering. Collectors value $500.00. (Wright Collection)

The above WWII knife is an MK2 made by the Camillus Cutlery Co. of Camillus, NY, and is marked USMC. Both knife and sheath have been Theater Altered. A brass S shaped cross guard has been added, as well as a brass skull crusher pommel. The handle is made from 1/4" Plexiglass and brass spacers. The back of the sheath has been opened up to make the knife hang lower on the leg for quicker accessibility. Collector value $275.00. (Wright Collection)

This KA-BAR Theater Knife started its life as a butcher knife. The 7" blade is 1 5/16" wide. Aluminum was used for the hand guard and eagle head skull crusher pommel. The tang has been painted yellow to give color to the clear Plexiglass handle. The back of the sheath is marked "BOB HILL TYPE –O V.M.R. 252." Collectors value $250.00. (Wright Collection)

The blade for the top knife came from a Cattaraugus machete. The 7 1/4" blade has been expertly reground with the intention of making the point strong. The aluminum hand guard was cast onto the blade. A piece of deer horn and aluminum for the pommel finished out the knife. The lower knife was altered from a Ross MK1 Bayonet by Pal Cutlery Co. Collectors value (top) $275.00 (lower) $200.00. (Wright Collection)

The two knives pictured on this page came from the same WWII veteran's estate. Both were Theater Altered using issue knife blades and other parts commonly found in the South Pacific Theater during WWII. The knife above was made using an MK2 blade. The cross guard was made using .45 auto. bullets, and a 30-06 round was used on the pommel. On one side of the pommel, which could have been a pressure gauge, is a picture of the soldier who owned the knives. On the other side is a picture of "IKE," Dwight D. Eisenhower. Also pictured in the Plexiglass handle is a woman, and on the other side an insignia depicting the "77th CONSTRUCTION BATTALION." The lower knife was made using a Cattaraugus 225Q blade and guard. The same woman's picture is in one side of the Plexiglass handle, and another woman's picture is on the other side. The pommel of this knife could have been made out of some kind of gauge and has the same insignia depicting the "77th CONSTRUCTION BATTALION." These knives are a pair and should not be separated. Collectors value $1,000.00 (both). (Wright Collection)

9

Sheaths

Quality sheaths, like the one pictured above, when combined with its proper Theater Knife, can increase the value of the combination 20% to 200%. Some sheaths are plain but very well made, while others have a tooled or embossed design, and still others can be highly hand carved. Some others may be carved more as folk art and are not so professionally made. Sheaths by themselves have a value, including the following: for plain well made sheaths $10.00 to $75.00; sheaths embossed or carved with designs $25.00 to $200.00+; and sheaths made by famous makers, such as Alfred Cornish and Heiser can be worth $200.00 to $500.00. Sheaths similar to the one pictured above are worth up to $200.00. (Wright Collection)

Bauch Leather Co., located in Wichita Falls, TX, made this very high quality sheath. They were in business from 1889 to 1950 and are listed as being saddle makers. The hand tooling on this sheath is of the highest quality, and is marked with the maker's mark and the owner's initials "W.B.C." Quality sheaths similar to this, which can be identified as to maker, are very desirable. Collectors value for sheath alone $250.00. (Wright Collection)

The collectors value given is for the sheaths without knives. Collectors value (from left to right) Large plain well made sheath $75.00, folk art carved sheath $100.00, sheath embossed with designs $75.00, sheath with large brass studs $75.00, sheath with embossed design made for San Antonio Iron Works Patton Saber Knife $100.00, sheath covered with woven colored bamboo $85.00, plain well made sheath with small design $50.00. (Wright Collection)

The sheath pictured above is very well made and embossed with floral design. Sheaths of this quality are rarely encountered. Pictured below are sheaths that are common to WWII Theater Knives. Collectors value (top) $150.00 (below, left to right) $40.00, $35.00, $25.00, $50.00, $25.00, $20.00. (Wright Collection)

The sheath above is made to hold a knife with a blade up to 8 3/4" in length. It has a nice tooled design and is bound on the outside with heavy leather lacing. Pictured below are common sheaths made for larger knives. They will accept blades from 7" to 12" depending on the sheath. Collectors value (top) $75.00 (below, left to right) $50.00, $50.00, $65.00, $20.00, $55.00, $50.00. (Wright Collection)

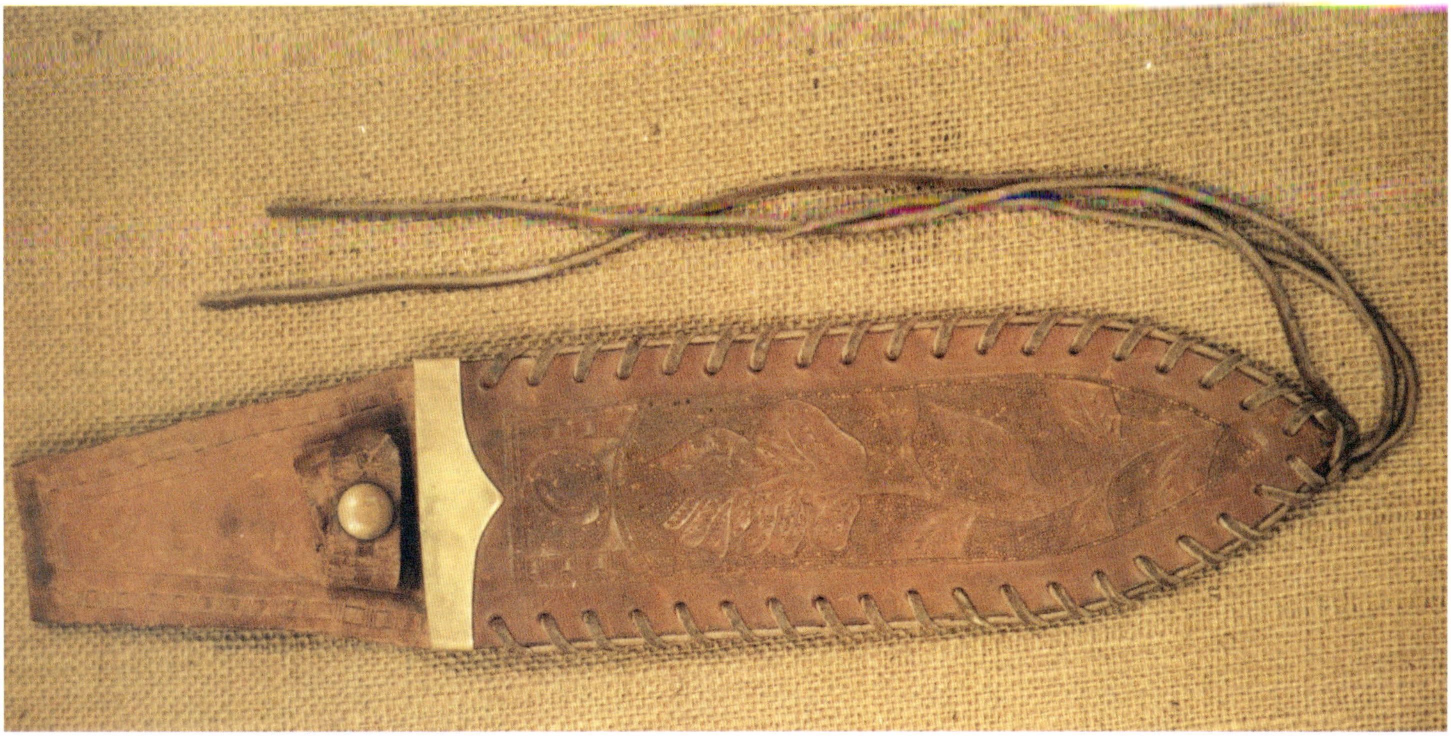

The quality sheath above was made for a very special knife with a 9" blade. Pictured below are two sheaths that have thin aluminum sheeting on them. This aluminum came from the skin, or outside covering, of an aircraft. Aluminum sheeting was used to strengthen, repair, or decorate sheaths during WWII. Collectors value (above) $125.00 (below, top) $125.00 (below, lower) $75.00. (Wright Collection)

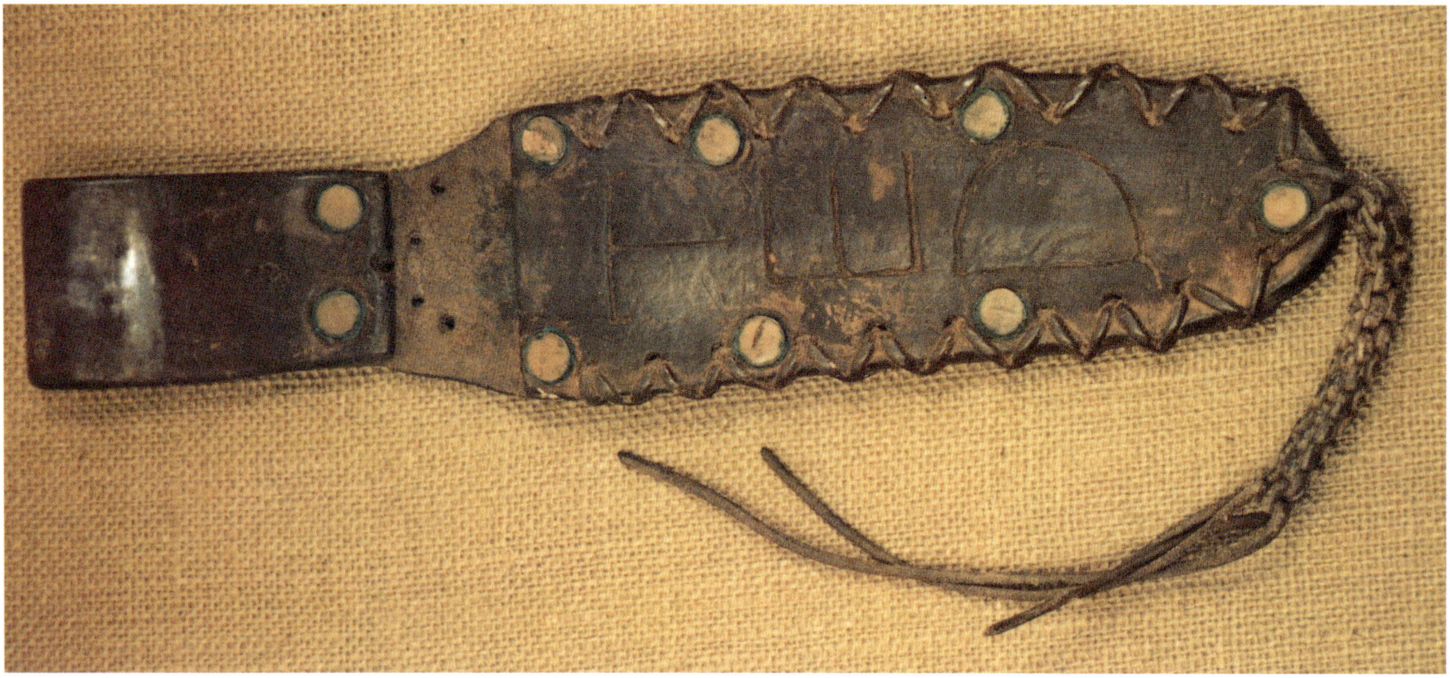

The sheath above is made to accept a knife blade up to 7 1/2". This sheath is heavy-duty, riveted with large copper harness rivets, and sewn with thick leather lacing. Pictured below are sheaths common to WWII Theater Knives. Collectors value (top) $75.00 (below, left to right) $45.00, $85.00, $35.00, $40.00, $40.00, $100.00 (this sheath is for the Australian made Ranger Knuckle Knife). (Wright Collection)

The sheaths on this page are the main focus of attention. They are fine examples of WWII Theater Art. Both sheaths and one knife handle pictured to the right have been covered using colored pieces of bamboo to form the pattern. This was likely done in the Philippines at the end of WWII. Pictured below are hand carved sheaths that show island women "in the buff." Prices given are for sheaths with their respective knives. Collectors value (top, upper) $200.00 (top, lower) $300.00 (bottom, left to right) $200.00, $300.00, $300.00. (Wright Collection)

10

Other Styles & Patterns

This chapter covers other styles and patterns that do not fall into any one category. You will see group photographs of many different knives. Some of these photos will show styles and patterns already pictured, but they have been grouped together to make a very interesting photograph.

This very unusual handmade Theater Knife has a 7" double edge up swept blade. It has a heavy cast aluminum guard and pommel with a handle made from red and black Micarta, Plexiglass, aluminum, and brass spacers. This knife is much above average quality. Collectors value without sheath $250.00. (Wright Collection)

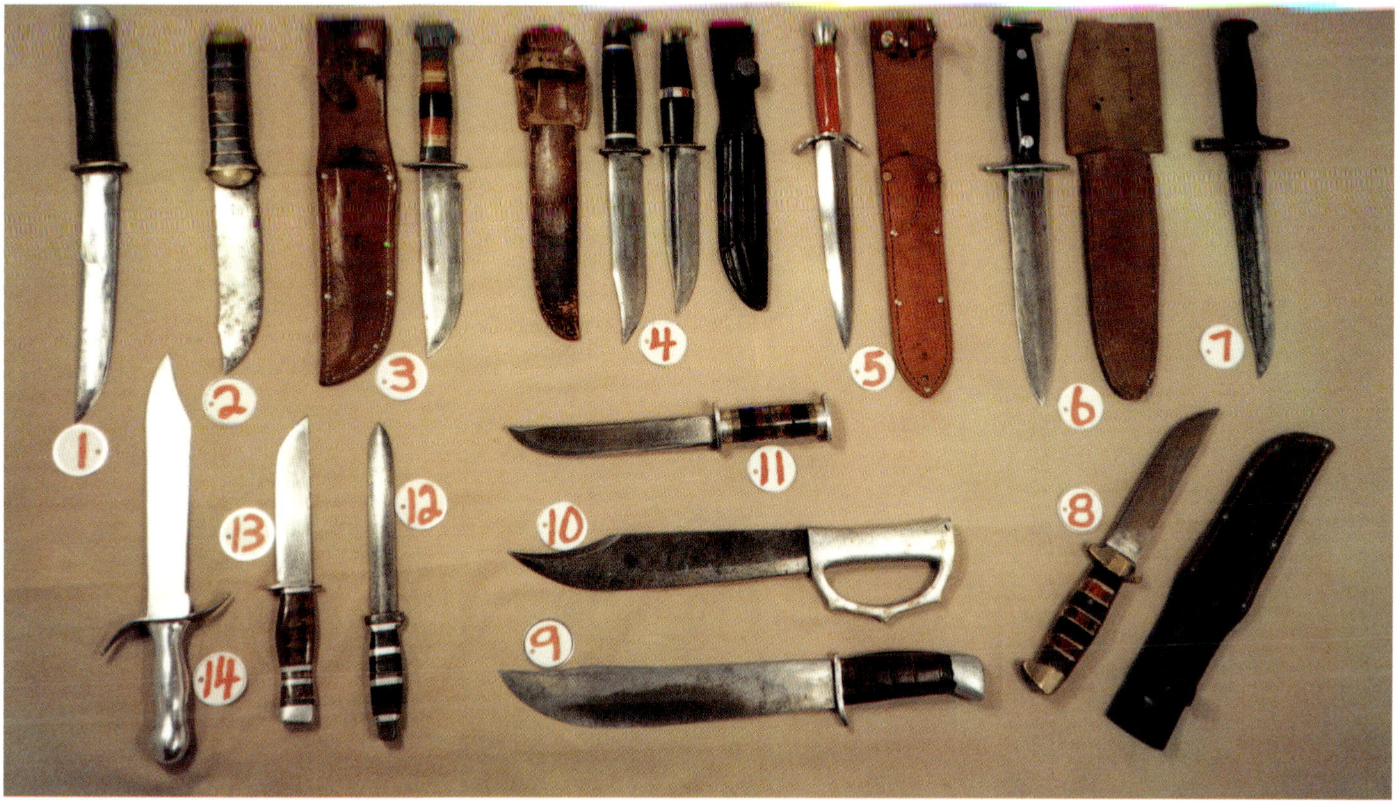

Collectors value for knives on this page: 1. $45. 2. $75. 3. $80. 4. $250. pair, 5. $175. 6. $185. 7. $50. 8. $75. 9. $100. 10. $500. 11. $65. 12. $40. 13. $42. 14. $85. 15. $50. 16. $85. 17. $75. 18. $55. 19. $47. 20. $100. 21. $85. 22. $95. 23. $75. 24. $125. 25. $300. 26. $55. 27. $375. (Wright Collection)

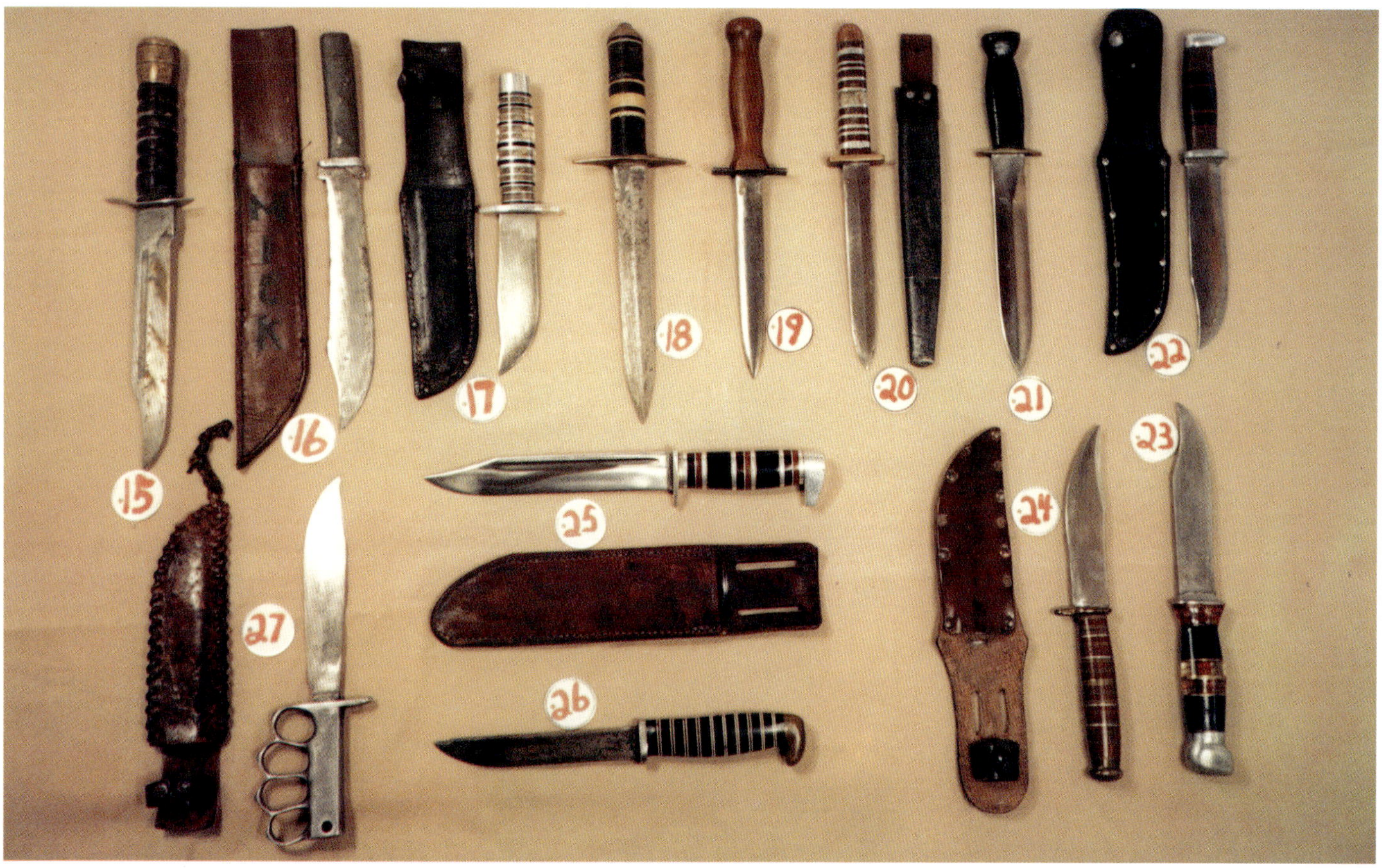

The knife above resembles a Scimitar. This style of knife was popular in areas close to North Africa. It is possible that this style of Theater Knife came from the North African Campaign. This large well made knife has a blade length of 10" and is 2 3/4" at the widest point. The stainless steel cross guard has been brazed to the blade, and the pommel is cast of brass. The handle is made of Plexiglass, red Lucite, black Micarta, and aluminum spacers. The collecrors value reflects that a sheath does not accompany the knife. The proper sheath could add as much as 50% to the price. Collectors value $450.00. (Wright Collection)

This well made Theater Knife resembles the famous Marbles Trailmaker™. The blade is 11 3/8" long and is 1 1/2" wide. Like the Marbles Trailmaker,™ this knife has a brass cross guard and aluminum pommel. Collectors value $350.00. (Wright Collection)

Above, Left: The knives on this page are of different styles and patterns. The blade lengths vary from 6 1/16" to 8 1/2". Collectors value (top to bottom) $200.00, $225.00, $75.00, $150.00 (left, knives under) $200.00, $225.00. (Ballard Collection)

Below, Left: Both knives above have long cross guards. The top knife has a 10 3/4" blade and the total length is 15 5/8". The bottom knife has a sturdy blade that is 8 1/8" long. The long cross guard has large ball quillions. Both knives are of very good quality and have nice leather sheaths. Collectors value (top) $300.00 (bottom) $400.00. (Ballard Collection)

Collectors value for knives on this page: 1. $100. 2. $110. 3. $300. 4. $250. 5. $80. 6. $100. 7. $70. 8. $75. 8. $75. 9. $65. 10. $70. 11. $65. 12. $75. 13. $35. 14. $150. 15. $75. 16. 295. 17. $135. 18. $250. 19. $125. 20. $65. 21. $395. 22. $450. 23. $75. 24. $60. 25. $70. 26. $95.

Collectors value for knives on this page: 1. $65. 2. $58. 3. $85. 4. $85. 5. $75. 6. $65. 7. $100. 8. $75. 9. $90. 10. $185. 11. $125. 12. $185. 13. $125. 14. $95. 15. $60. 16. $55. 17. $110. 18. $68. 19. $40. 20. $85. 21. $65. 22. $50. 23. $250. 24. $125. 25. $225. 26. $425. 27. $135.

The 8" blade of this knife could have been made out of a sword blade, and the overall length is 12 5/8". The steel cross guard is hand forged. The handle is made from a walking cane. The top part is multi-colored Bakelite, and the bottom is part of the wooden shaft of the cane. Collectors value $300.00. (Wright Collection)

These WWII Theater Knives are better than average quality. The blade lengths range from 5 7/8" to 6 7/8". Collectors value (top) $175.00 (lower left to right) $175.00, $150.00, $225.00, $200.00. (Wright Collection)

This set of cook's knives was likely made during WWII. They are hand made and have handles constructed similar to other WWII Theater Knives. It has been said that "the army runs on its stomach," and the cook keeps the stomach full. It only makes sense that the cook would have a set of knives similar to the ones carried by the fighting men he served. Collectors value $275.00. (Wright Collection)

Pictured above is a group of long bladed knives. The lengths vary from 10 1/4" to 11 3/4". These knives could have been made for Army or Navy cooks. Collectors value (top to bottom) $60.00, $75.00, $35.00, $250.00, $50.00. (Wright Collection)

The aluminum pommel of this knife is marked "39099980," which is likely the serial number of the owner. This knife has a 6 3/8" saber ground blade. The sculpted aluminum cross guard was cast onto the blade. The handle materials consist of red and black Micarta and bone. The sheath is unusual, and is made to hang on a web pistol belt. Collectors value $450.00. (Wright Collection)

These two knives were made in Finland during WWII. It was reported to me that this kind of knife was made out of shot down Russian aircraft and sold or traded to German soldiers. The top knife has a 6" blade and is 9 3/4" in overall length. The lower knife has a 3 3/4" blade and is 6 3/4" in overall length. Collector value $150.00 each. (Wright Collection)

This high quality knife has a 6 3/4" blade with a nicely formed blood groove in each side. The heavy-duty hand guard and pommel are cast out of aluminum. The handle materials consist of Plexiglass, colored Lucite, and brass. The sheath is hand tooled and very well made. Collectors value $400.00. (Wright Collection)

A very unusual knife is pictured above. The blade length is 9 1/4" long and 1 5/8" wide at the point. The back edge of the blade has been sharpened almost all the way to the hand guard and is 3/8" thick at the bottom. The hand guard and blade were forged from the same piece of steel. The hand guard is supported by aluminum under it. The handle materials include black Bakelite, colored Lucite, Plexiglass, brass, and aluminum spacers. The sheath is made out of a razor strop. Collectors value $500.00. (Wright Collection)

Pictured here is a group of rare multi-colored Bakelite handle WWII Theater Knives. Bakelite is an early form of plastic (chemically known as phenolformaldehyde) that was invented about 1920. Bakelite was commonly used in the 1920-1950 time period to make many different things. Jewelry, poker chips, radios, kitchen utensil handles, salt and pepper shakers, telephones, gearshift knobs, and toys are just some of the things that were made from Bakelite. It is very hard, will not burn, and is easily shaped with a saw, grinder, or file. The colors are vivid and brilliant, especially when different colors are placed next to one another, making Bakelite an excellent choice for knife handles. The Bakelite used on WWII Theater Knives came from other previously manufactured items. Bakelite was made in many different countries of the world. It has been reported to me by WWII veterans that Bakelite poker chips were used in the handles of many knives they made. Many WWII knives have a piece or two of Bakelite in the handle, however, a complete handle of multi-colored Bakelite greatly increases the value of the knife. Blade lengths vary from 4 1/2" to 8" for the knives pictured above. Collectors value with sheaths (left to right) $400.00, $300.00, $400.00, $350.00, $350.00 (bottom) $300.00. (Wright Collection)

Above, Right: A group of WWII "Sweetheart Jewelry" is shown. Wives, mothers, and sweethearts of WWII servicemen wore this jewelry, which was sometimes given to them by their men in military service. Most of the items pictured above are made from Bakelite. General MacArthur and the jeep are made from another early form of plastic. The anchor and wings with a .30-06 bullet are hand made out of Plexiglass. The airplane and tank are pencil sharpeners made of Bakelite. Sweetheart jewelry is worth from $25.00 to $1,000.00. Collectors value for above items: Bakelite poker chips $3.00 each; Bakelite pencil sharpeners $75.00; large Bakelite dice $75.00; Bakelite Patriotic dress buttons $25.00 each. (Bill and Debbie Wright Collection)

Pictured above is jewelry and other items made from Bakelite in the 1920 to 1950 time period. The carrot, bunch of bananas, and oars with anchor are considered WWII sweetheart jewelry. Collectors value: carrot $700.00; bunch of bananas $500.00; oars and anchor $500.00; pipe $100.00; corkscrew $125.00; salt and pepper shakers $75.00; other Bakelite jewelry $100.00 to $350.00. (Bill and Debbie Wright Collection)

The aluminum handled knife on the left was made at Pearl Harbor. Blade lengths range from 5 3/4" to 9 7/8". Collectors value (top) $300.00, (left to right) $850.00, $150.00, $300.00, $125.00. $125.00. (Wright Collection)

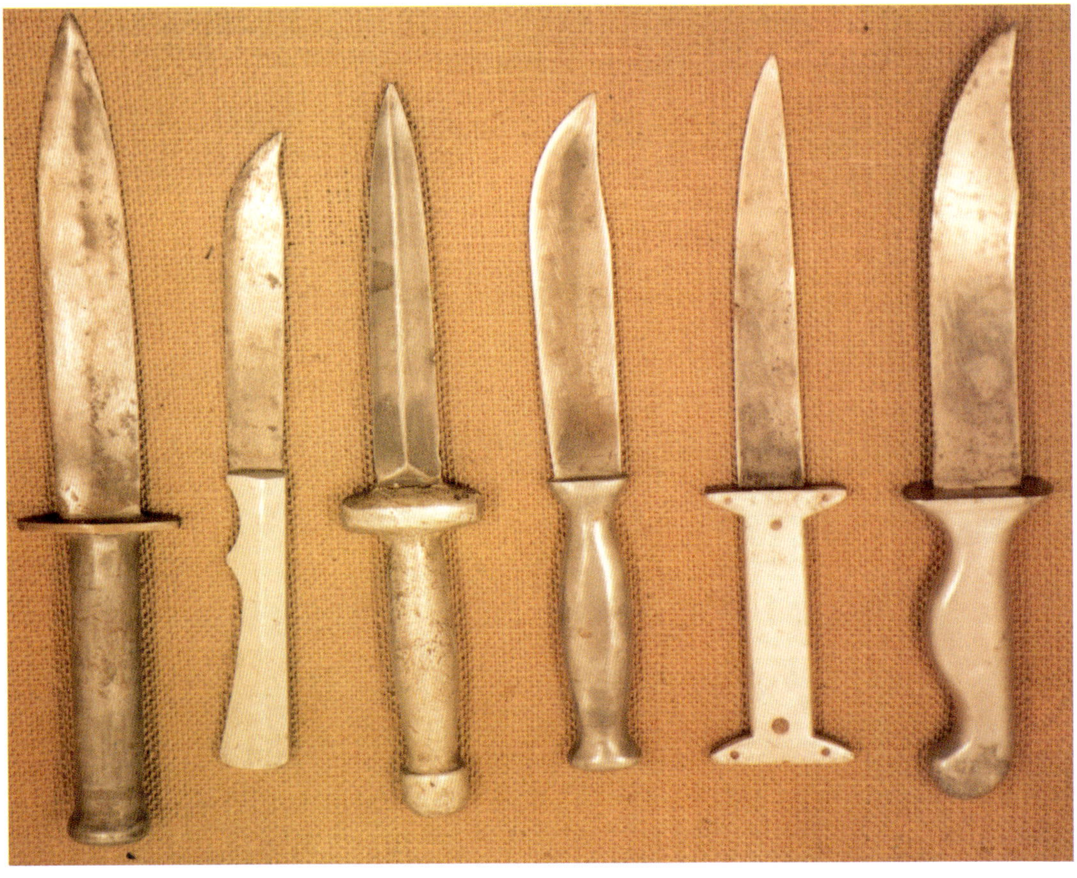

These aluminum handled knives are different shapes and styles. The blade lengths range from 5 1/8" to 7 7/8". Collectors value (left to right) $75.00, $50.00, $75.00, $65.00, $50.00, $125.00. (Wright Collection)

Collectors value for knives on this page: 1. $50. 2. $85. 3. $125. 4. $60. 5. $125. 6. $75. 7. $65. 8. $37. 9. $100. 10. $200. 11. $100. 12. $125. 13. $110. 14. $275. 15. $65. 16. $100. 17. $175. 18. $100. 19. $175. 20. $125. 21. $125. 22. $90. 23. $150. 24. $595. 25. $125

The top knife has a 5 1/4" blade. The hand made sheath has a heavy brass tip. The lower knife is better than average quality and has a 6 3/4" blade that is well finished. The aluminum pommel has the initials "E.S." The sheath was made from a cut down bayonet scabbard. Collectors value (top) $85.00 (lower) $125.00. (Wright Collection)

The top knife is a sturdy knife of average quality. The lower knife could have been made to be used by a paratrooper. Its purpose could have been to cut tangled parachute lines. Collectors value (top) $75.00 (lower) $125.00. (Wright Collection)

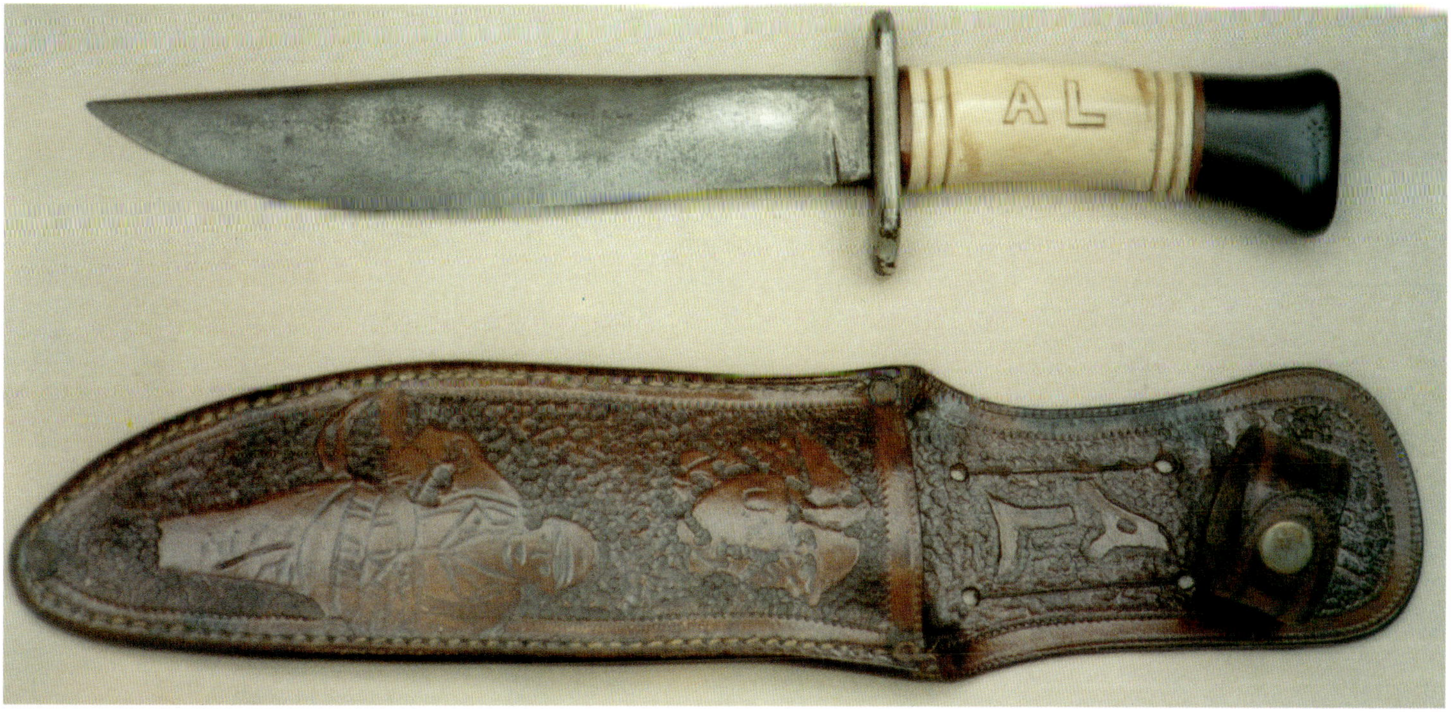

AL owned and or made this fine WWII knife and sheath. The 7 1/2" blade is 1/4" thick. It could have been made out of a leaf spring, because of its thickness and its slight curve. The handle is made from bone, red Micarta, and black Bakelite. The sheath has a hand carved soldier in full battle dress, "AL 1944," and an eagle. Collectors value $750.00. (Wright Collection)

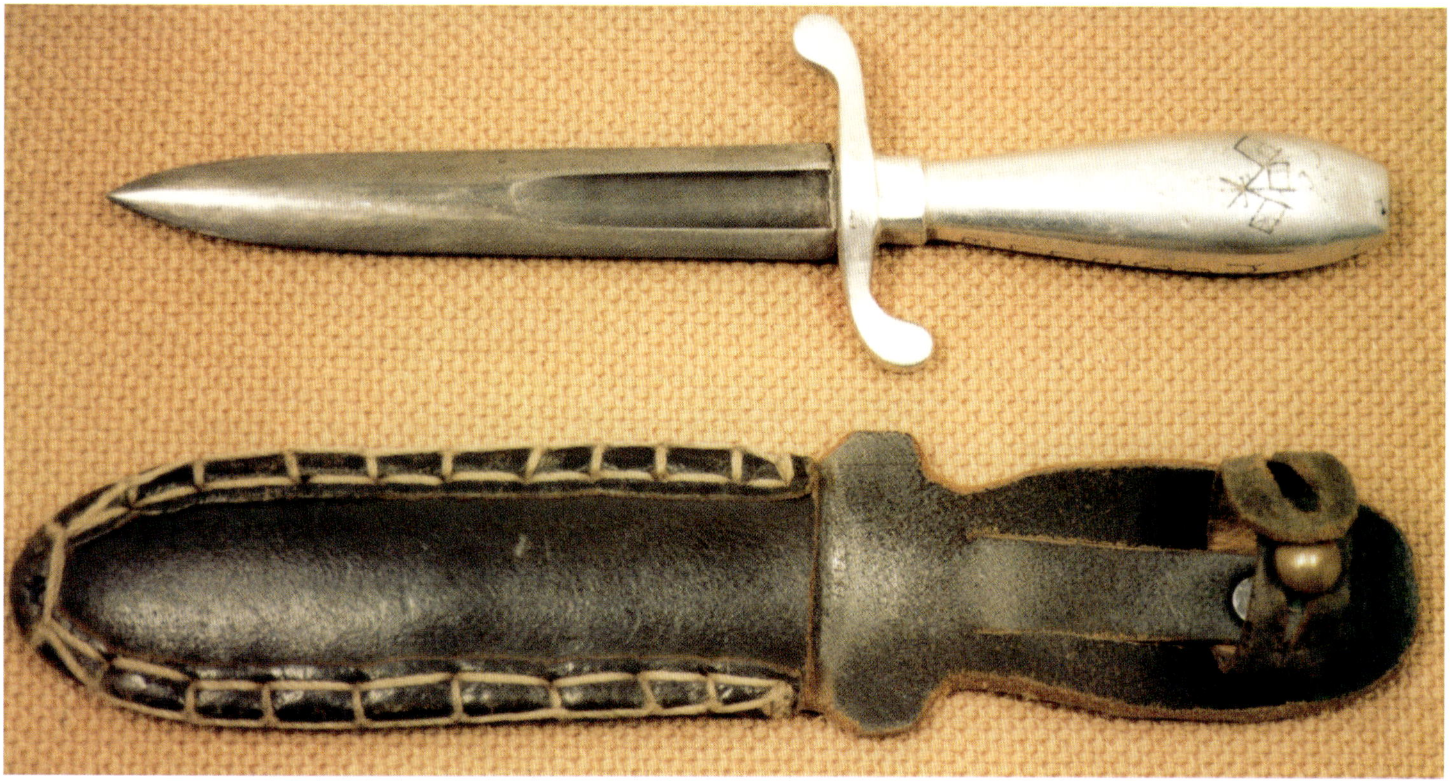

The 4 3/4" blade of this small but hefty knife was made out of a sword or bayonet. The one piece cast aluminum cross guard and handle have several markings. It is marked "BRUNO," with three flags (American, French, and British), a "German Eagle" and "Swastika," and "Moselle" (a river that runs through France and Germany). Collectors value $200.00. (Wright Collection)

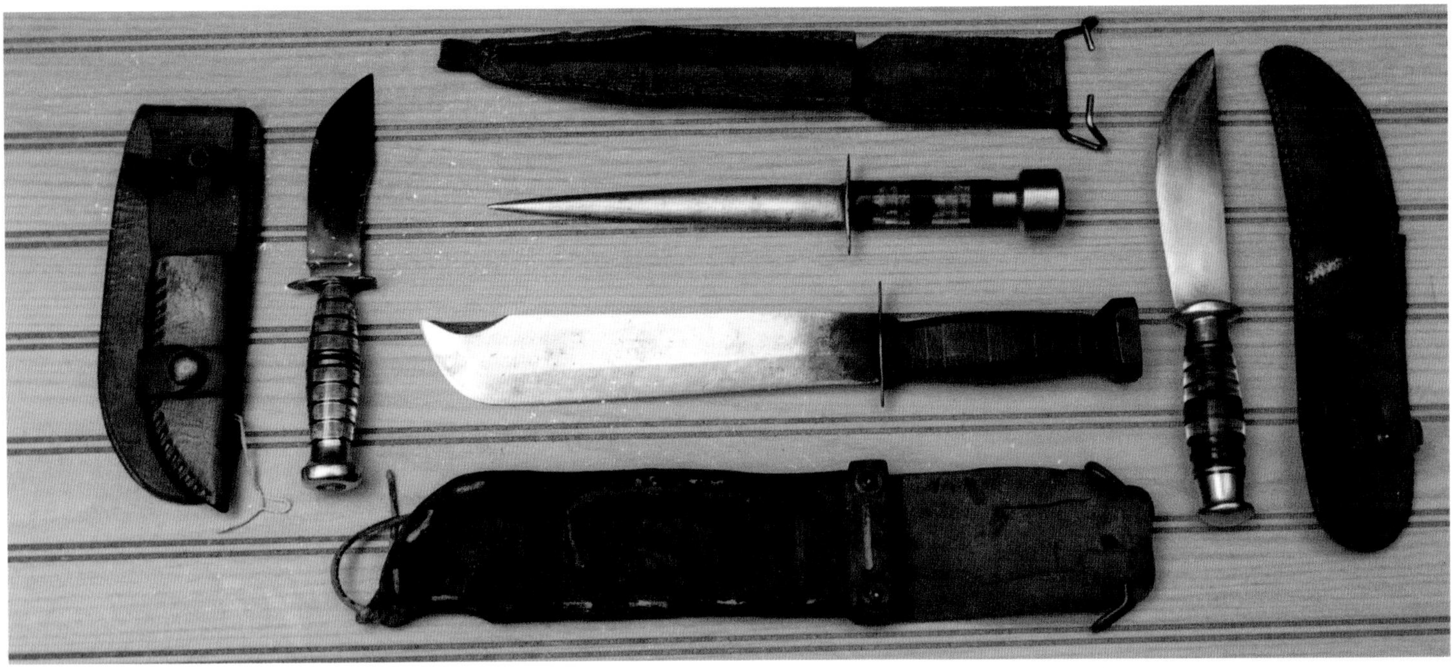

The group of Theater Knives pictured above differs in size, shape, and design. Blade lengths range from 4 1/2" to 9". Collectors value (top picture) (left) $125.00 (right) $100.00 (top) $175.00 (bottom) $150.00 (lower picture top to bottom) $100.00, $40.00, $85.00. (Wright Collection)

The 9 1/2" blade and hand guard of this very unusual WWII knife is made from one piece of steel. The handle tang is brazed on to the guard. The sculptured handle slabs are made of Micarta. There is nice floral engraving on both sides of the blade. The heavy-duty sheath is riveted and sewn, and has canteen pouch snaps to hold the back together. Collectors value $600.00. (Wright Collection)

The 6 3/4" blade of this knife was not made out of a saw blade. The notches on the back of the blade were filed, maybe for decoration, or to help prevent the thumb from slipping when pushing on top of the blade. This knife has an aluminum cross guard, handle spacers, and pommel. Brown Micarta spacers are between the aluminum. The pancake sheath is nicely embossed. Collectors value $275.00. (Wright Collection)

The Theater Knives on this page have long blades ranging from 9 1/8" to 10 1/2". They are well made and have colorful handles. Collectors value (top picture) $200.00 each (bottom picture) $175.00 each. (Wright Collection)

The above Theater Knives vary in style and quality. Collectors value (first row left to right) $225.00, $100.00, $200.00, $175.00, $250.00, $275.00, (second row left to right) $125.00, $65.00, $175.00, $125.00, $125.00, $200.00. The aluminum handled knife is marked "MILPAR," $300.00 (bottom left) $275.00 (bottom right) $350.00. (Wright Collection)

The knife on the right was made from a rare KA–BAR deep-sea diver's knife. Bakelite was a common material from 1920 to 1950. It is rare to see Bakelite used on a knife handle, and knives with complete multi-color Bakelite handles are even rarer. The center knife has a multi-colored Bakelite handle. The knife on the left has the rare Kris blade. Collectors value $350.00 each. (Wright Collection)

The top knife has an 8" blade that is 1/4" thick. The handle is made from clear Plexiglass spacers. The colors were painted onto the tang of the knife. The lower knife was made from a bayonet, possibly Japanese. Both knives pictured here are above average quality. Collectors value (top) $300.00 (lower) $275.00. (Wright Collection)

Right: Collectors value for knives on this page: 1. $85. 2. $40. 3. $225. 4. $65. 5. $40. 6. $125. 7. $50. 8. $65. 9. $70. 10. $50. 11. $75. 12. $65. 13. $75. 14. $125. Pair 15. $45. 16. $275. 17. $75. 18. $85. 19. $275. 20. $50. 21. $100. 22. $140. 23. $395. 24. $495. 25. $85. 26. $100. 27. $60.

1
2
3
4
5
6
7
15
14
13
12
11
10
9
8
16

17
18
19
20
21
22
24
27
23
26
25

Pictured above is an impressive selection of quality WWII Theater Knives. The blade lengths vary from 5 1/4" to 8 5/16". A wide variety of designs and materials were used. Collectors value with sheaths (top to bottom) $125.00, $300.00, $150.00, $125.00, $400.00, $175.00, $225.00. (Wright Collection)

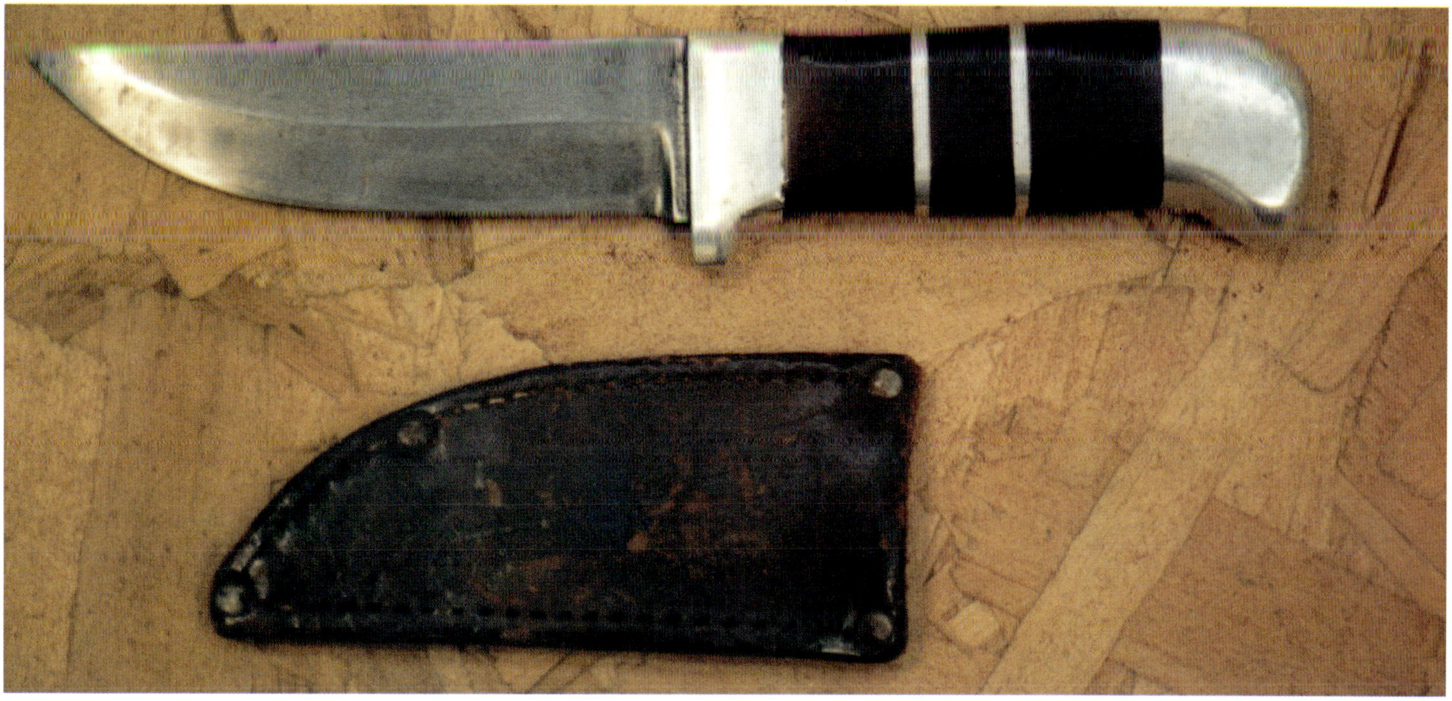

Pictured here are small knives with blade lengths ranging from 3 3/4" to 5 3/8". These knives were quite versatile and could be tucked away in a pocket, boot, concealed inside a shirt, or worn on the belt. Well made small knives are hard to find. They should be added to any WWII Theater Knife collection and not overlooked. Collectors value (top) $125.00 (bottom left to right) $100.00, $125.00, $75.00. (Wright Collection)

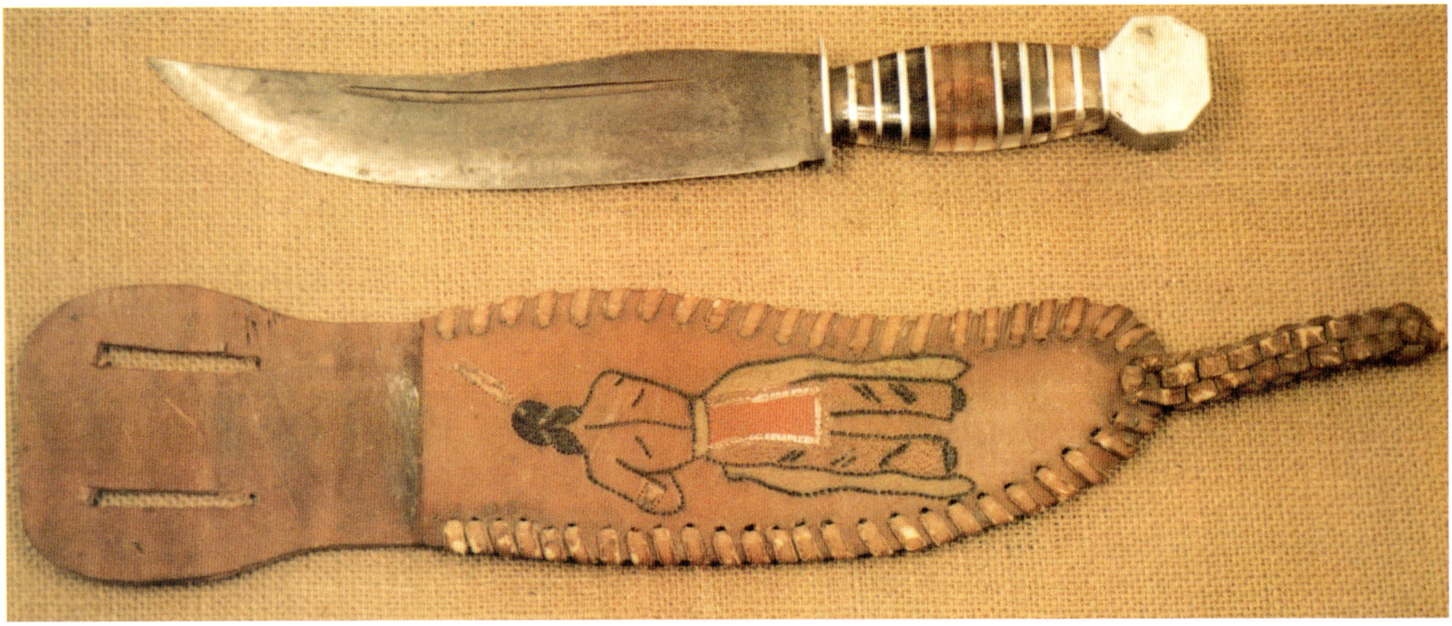

I wish I knew more about the history of this very interesting knife. The blade measures 8 3/8" and has an overall length of 13 1/8". There is a small aluminum cross guard and large pommel. The handle was made from 1/4" Plexiglass and aluminum spacers. The heavy-duty leather sheath is bound with thick leather lacing and has an Indian embossed into it. Collectors value $500.00. (Wright Collection)

The 6 7/8" blade of this knife was forged from 1/2" steel. It has an aluminum cross guard and skull crusher pommel. The materials used in the handle consist of Micarta and Plexiglass. The sheath is very plain and is made of two pieces of leather hand sewn with heavy string. Collectors value $225.00. (Wright Collection)

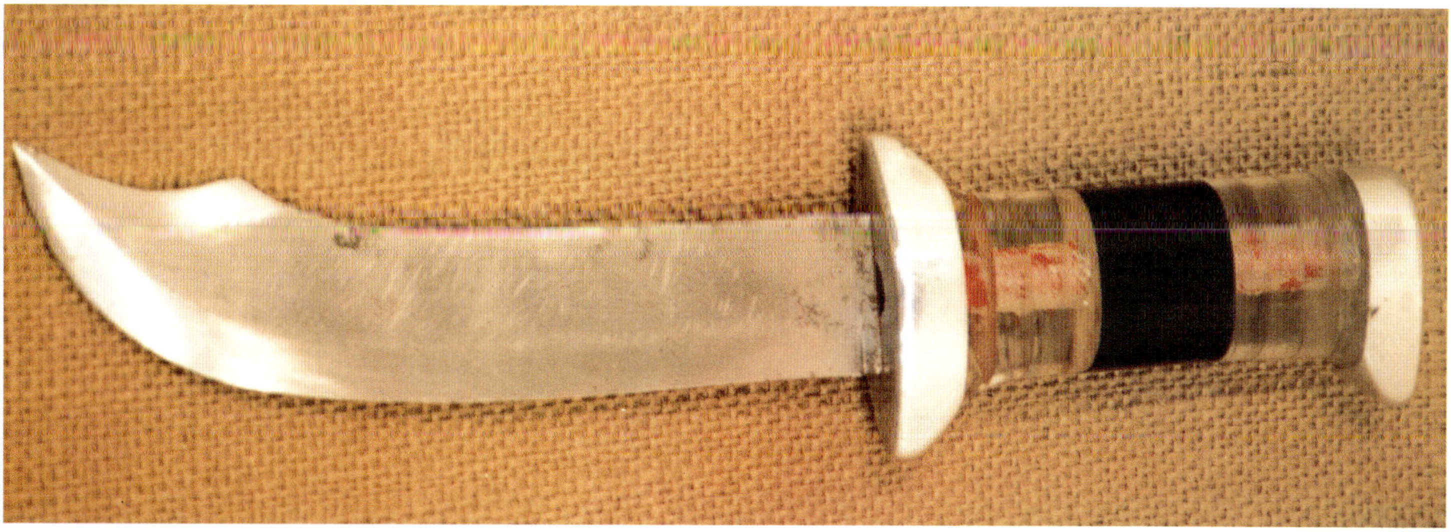

This WWII knife may have been made in the North African Campaign. It has an unusually shaped 6" blade with the clip point sharpened. The handle has 1/4" Plexiglass spacers that could have come from a downed aircraft. Thick aluminum was used to make the cross guard and pommel. Collectors value $200.00. (Wright Collection)

This knife also could have been made in North Africa because of the unusual style of blade, which is 7 1/2" long. The aluminum cross guard is cast onto the blade. This handle also has 1/4" Plexiglass spacers. Red, green, and white stones are mounted into the pommel and cross guard. There is a woman's picture mounted in the pommel. Collectors value $350.00. (Wright Collection)

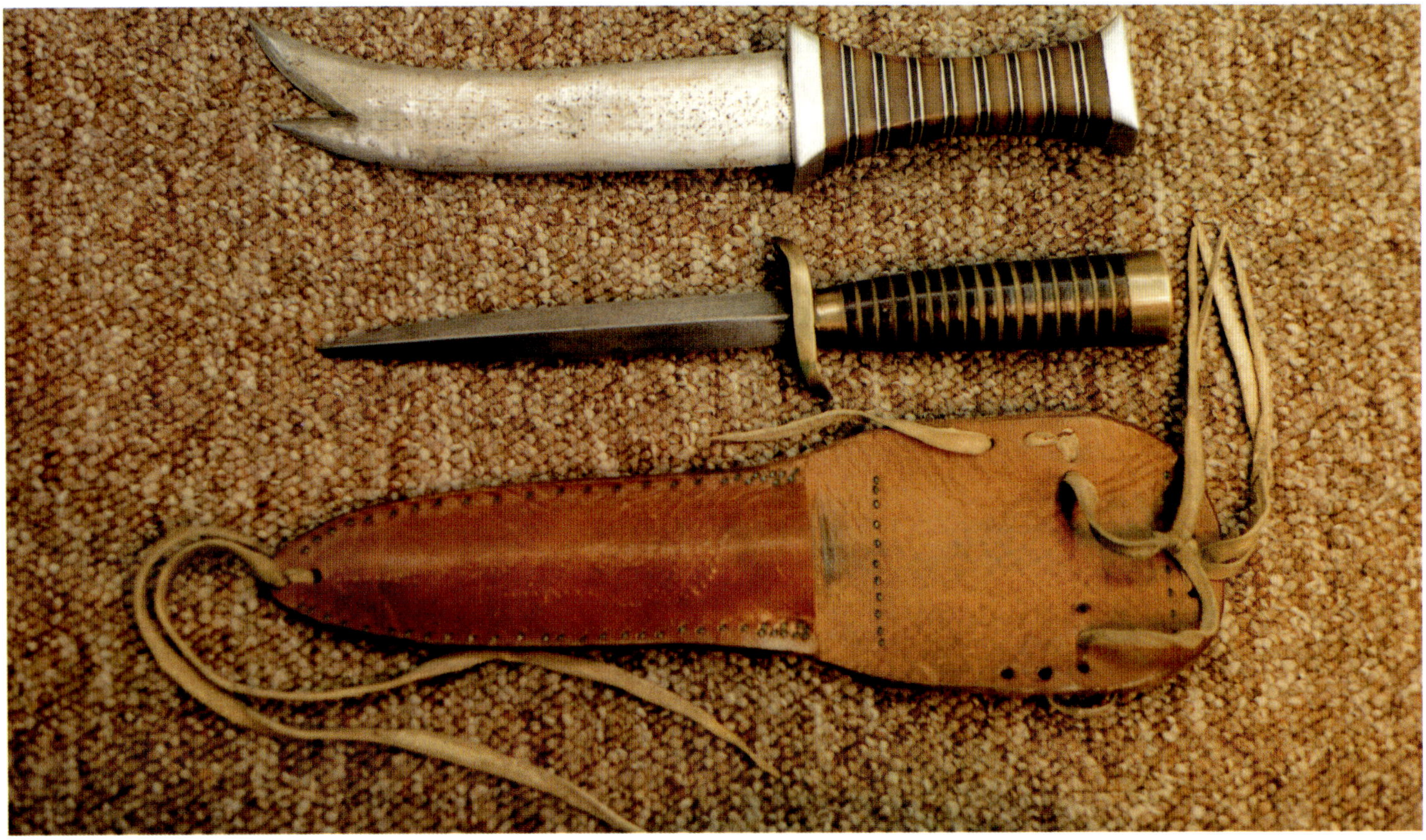

Above: The blade design of the top knife is one of the most unusual I have ever seen. It has a double point sharpened on all sides. The blade length is 6 3/4" and the width is 1 3/8". The lower knife is a double edge dagger. The blade is 7/16" thick and 5 3/4" long. This knife is very heavy and sturdy. Collectors value (top) $175.00 (lower) $200.00. (Wright Collection)

Left: These two hand made knives appear to be of WWII vintage and made by the same maker. These are the only two knives I have seen with this unusual design and style of blade. It is unusual for WWII knives to have deer horn handles. The knife on the left has a 7" blade, while the knife on the right has a 6" blade. Both knives have the original sheaths. Collectors value $150.00 each. (Wright Collection)

Collectors value for knives on this page: 1. $125. 2. $110. 3. $75. 4. $25. 5. $125. 6. $35. 7. $90. 8. $40. 9. $75. 10. $100. 11. $45. 12. $65. 13. $35. 14. $65. 15. $75. 16. $40. 17. $125. 18. $175. 19. $100. 20. $35. 21. $55. 22. $75. 23. $125. 24. $125. 25. $60. 26. $250. 27. $200. (Wright Collection)

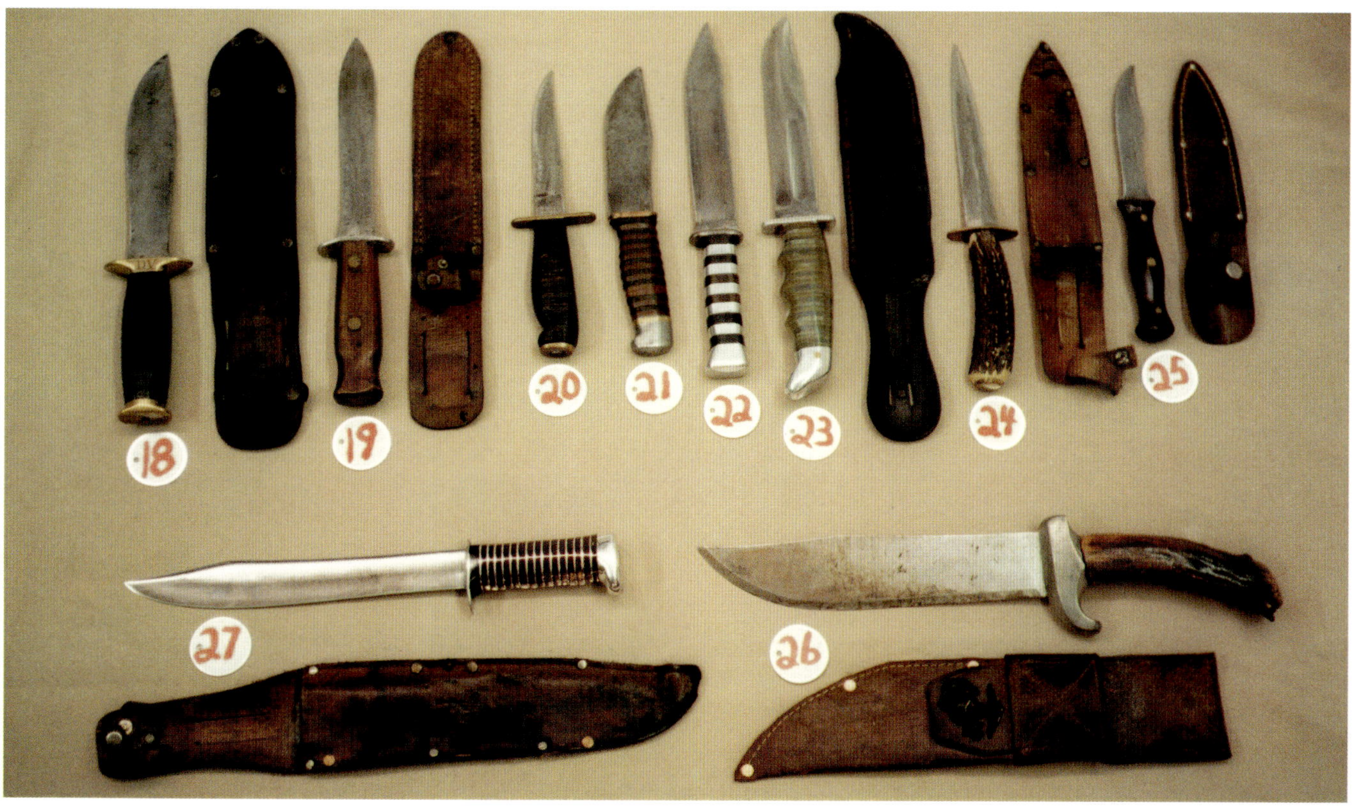

Left: These two WWII fighting knives are of high quality, both in fit and finish. The top knife has a 7 5/8" blade and has an aluminum cross guard and pommel. The colorful handle was made using red, black, and tan Micarta spacers, along with aluminum. The lower knife has a 6" blade and a red Micarta handle with finger grooves to give a better grip. Collectors value $375.00 each. (Wright Collection)

Below: The blade of the center knife was skillfully made from a file and measures 5 3/8". The total length is 9 3/4". The left knife has a blade length of 6 1/2", and the knife on the right has a 6 1/4" blade. Collectors value (left to right) $100.00, $375.00, $150.00. (Wright Collection)

The above dagger was expertly ground from a file. The 7 1/2" blade is 1/4" thick. It has a 1/4" thick copper cross guard and a coffin shaped aluminum pommel. The handle is made of leather, Micarta, and copper spacers. The quality hand made leather sheath is decorated with different patterns and designs. I have seen two other sheaths made in the same style using very similar designs. Collectors value $275.00. (Wright Collection)

This small but useful knuckle knife has a 5" clip point blade with a sharpened false edge. The handle was made using brown Micarta, Plexiglass, and aluminum. The cross guard is made of steel, with the knuckle bow made of stainless steel. The knuckle bow is attached to the pommel with a machine screw. The heavy-duty sheath has a copper band around the top and brass at the end. Collectors value $275.00. (Wright Collection)

11

Philippine Vicotry Knives

Many knives were made in the Philippines following the end of WWII and were sold or given to GIs by local natives. They were made in many different sizes, shapes, and qualities. It has been reported that many of the blades were hand forged from Jeep leaf springs. Many of the sheaths were wooden, and finely hand carved with designs of spread-winged eagles, "U.S.," and "VICTORY." Mother of Pearl was inlaid into some sheaths forming words or elaborate designs.

The smaller knife pictured above has a 7 1/2" blade. The sheath is carved with a star and the raised letters "U.S.," and has four Mother of Pearl inlays. Collectors value $50.00. The bottom knife has a 10 7/8" blade and is 15 1/2" overall. The sheath is highly carved and decorated with designs, an eagle with shield, and the word "VICTORY." Collectors value $75.00. (Wright Collection)

The above knife and sheath are of outstanding quality. This knife was presented from "COL. M. PERALTA JR. C.O. 6 MIL. DIST." as a "SOUVENIER OF WORLD WAR II." The clip point blade is 9" long and the overall length is 13 1/4". The finely engraved brass cross guard has floral design top and bottom. The exceptional quality turned handle has a brass collar. The wooden sheath is flat on the back and rounded on the front, with a brass tip and throat that is highly engraved. I only know of three Philippine knives of this quality. Collectors value $500.00. (Wright Collection)

To my knowledge the blades of all Philippine Victory Knives are hand forged. The 15" blade of this knife is no exception. The sheath has the word "PHILIPPINES" inlaid in pearl. The carving on the sheath is of a spread wing eagle on top of a shield with Stars and Stripes. The handle has a small pearl inlay carved with designs. Collectors value $150.00. (Wright Collection)

The 8 3/4" blade of this knife is stamped "NEGRITO BOLO," and is 1 7/8" wide and 1/4" thick. The handle is made of black water buffalo horn and is hand carved. The sheath is marked "SGT KIDD." Collectors value $100.00. (Wright Collection)

The above Philippine knife has a 20 1/2" blade and is 26" overall length. This sheath is pearl inlaid with the words "CAPT. M.E. HALL PHILIPPINES CELU." There are 112 pearl inlays on the sheath and 21 on the handle, some of which are a dog, sailing ship, freighter, anchor, half moon, and star. Collectors value $250.00. (Wright Collection)

This group of Victory Knives is small in size, ranging from 7" to 10" in total length. The handles and sheaths are made of wood and are individually hand carved. Collectors value $25.00 to $50.00 each. (Wright Collection)

A good quality Philippine knife is shown above. The sheath has 50 pearl inlays and the handle has 10. The blade length is 16", and the overall length is 21 1/4". Collectors value $150.00. (Wright Collection)

The handle and sheath of this Philippine knife are hand carved. The blade length is 7 5/8". Collectors value $65.00. (Wright Collection)

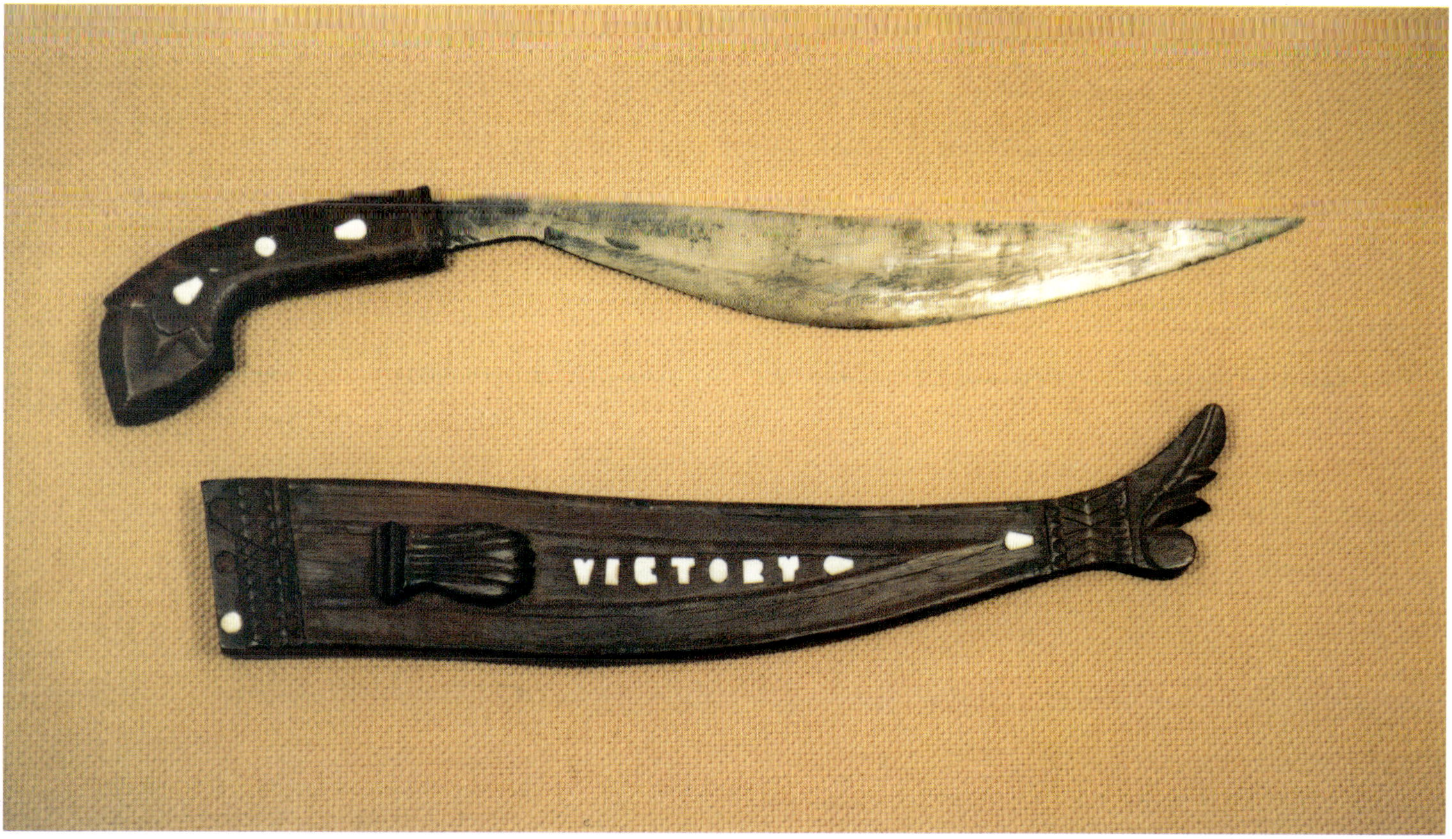

These two are good examples of why this type of knife is called Philippine VICTORY Knives. Pictured above is a knife that has an 11 5/8" blade and is 16" overall. The hand carved wooden sheath has the word "VICTORY" inlayed in pearl. There are three small pearl inlays in the handle. Pictured below is a knife that has an 11 1/4" blade. The wooden sheath has a large "V" (for VICTORY) carved into it. An unusual feature of this knife is the knife and sheath are inlayed with aluminum instead of pearl. Collectors value (top) $135.00 (below) $100.00. (Wright Collection)

Bibliography

Buerlein, Robert A. *Allied Military Fighting Knives and The Men Who Made Them Famous*. Richmond, Virginia: The American Historical Foundation, 1984.

Cole, M.H. *U.S. Military Knives Bayonets & Machetes* Books III & IV. Birmingham, Alabama: M.H. Cole, 1979 & 1990.

Flook, Ron. *British and Commonwealth Military Knives*. Shrewbury, England: Airlife Publishing Ltd., 1999.

Gaddis, Robert L. *Randall Made Knives* .Boulder, Colorado: Paladin Press, 1993.

Huie, William Bradford. *Can Do!* New York, New York: American Book-Stratford Press, 1944

Hutchins, Dan and Sebie. *Old Cowboy Saddles and Spurs 5th Edition*. Santa Fe, New Mexico: Dan & Sebie Hutchins, 1995

Janzen,. Jerry L. *Bayonets From Janzen's Notebook*. Broken Arrow, Oklahoma: Cedar Ridge Publications, 1987.

Levine, Bernard. *Levine's Guide To Knives and Their Values 4th Edition*. Iola, Wisconsin: Krause Publications, Inc., 1997.

Sargent, Jim. *America Premium Guide to Knives and Razors 5th Edition*. Iola, Wisconsin: Krause Publications, Inc., 1999.

Silvey, Michael W. *United States Military Knives 1941 To 1991*. Sacramento, California: Michael W. Silvey, 1992.

Silvey, Michael W. *Knives of the United States Military WORLD WAR II*. Sacramento, California: Michael W. Silvey, 1999

Smith, Towsley and Mandell. *Hear The Hammer*. United States: John Mandell and Frank Towsley: 1995.

Stephens, Frederick J. *Fighting Knives*. New York, New York: Arco Publishing Inc., 1980.

Publications

The National Knife Magazine, The National Knife Collector Association, 7201 Shallowford Road, Chattanooga, Tennessee 37424

Knife World, Knife World Publications, PO Box 3395, Knoxville, Tennessee 37927

The Blade Magazine, Krause Publications, 700 E. State St. Iola, WI 54990-0001